Squirrel

£3 MILLION IN 3 WEEKS

The Squirrel Syndicate – A Gambler's Tale

£3 Million In 3 Weeks - The Squirrel Syndicate - A Gambler's Tale

Published by The Conrad Press Limited in the United Kingdom 2022

Tel: +44(0)1227 472 874
www.theconradpress.com
info@theconradpress.com

ISBN 978-1-915494-08-5

Typesetting and cover design by:
Charlotte Mouncey, www.bookstyle.co.uk
Cover design created with photograph of syndicate by kind permission of Nigel Bennet of NB Press Ltd, other images are the authors own or stock imagery by www.istockphoto.com and pixabay.com

The Conrad Press logo was designed by Maria Priestley.

Printed and bound in Great Britain by Clays Ltd, Elcograf S.p.A.

£3 MILLION IN 3 WEEKS

The Squirrel Syndicate –
A Gambler's Tale

RICHARD BROCKLEBANK
AND CHARLES YATES

Biographies of the authors

RICHARD BROCKLEBANK

Shiny silver sixpences flying out of a one-armed bandit when he was knee-high to aged aunts allowed him to open his first bank account with a deposit of ten shillings and helped push the young Richard towards a lifetime of punting.

With grandparents based in the seaside resort of Rhyl in North Wales, Richard was a regular at the Penny Falls in the many beachfront arcades when still in short pants.

His punting path was further fortified when his first flutter on the Grand National was a winning one on Well To Do ridden by Graham Thorner in 1972.

As time moved on, brainy Richard's mathematical ability shone through at Stockport Grammar School and he was aimed towards Oxbridge, but the teenage Squirrel had other plans.

Signing up for physics at Nottingham University, Richard discovered he preferred pubs to lecture theatres, and soon realised he could boost his modest student allowance by playing quiz machines.

Richard left uni with a very ordinary degree, but a bulging bank roll, thanks to those pub machine prizes. He later embarked on token gainful employment with the local water board, but was making a bigger splash earning tax-free tenners from the likes of DLT's *Give Us a Break* and Barcrest's Tic Tac Trivia machines, often during leisurely lunch breaks away from the water testing laboratory.

Quitting the day job, Richard went quizzing full-time and through that sub-culture he met another old grammar-school boy Ken Burrell, who helped put him on the trail of Tote pool bets on the horses.

The pair started winning them for fun, using a mathematical approach as well as form selections. Between the Tote jackpot punts, they were travelling the UK playing pub quiz machines.

It was during later Scoop6 years that Richard met Charles Yates, the co-founder of The Squirrel Syndicate. They were both chasing a £238,000 bonus fund at Newmarket races on 2000 Guineas Day in 2003.

The pair got on famously and combined forces to land millions in pool betting punts for their pals, as this book will testify.

The Squirrel still does pub quizzes with Ken, and they have been part of a formidable outfit in the Tameside Manchester Quiz League, with former *Mastermind* winner Dr Gary Grant, sadly deceased *Egghead* Dave Rainford, and 'The Governess' Anne Hegerty from ITV's *The Chase* among the brainiac squad.

CHARLES YATES

The antithesis of his posh pal, Charles – despite having an upper-class name –came from a council estate on Merseyside and went to a comprehensive school, where he at one point achieved one O level and a CSE.

He puts his love of gambling down to his dear old dad and some childhood escapades that netted him a small fortune. He was a small boy at the time, so everything was pretty small back then.

His father, a veteran of the North Atlantic convoys in WW2, would have been 100 this February, but having cheated death in his youth, like so many of his generation of ex-servicemen, he had a real love of gambling, mainly on racehorses.

The young Charles would listen to their remarkable war stories and adventures, which were often more akin to the capers of Phil Silvers in *Sergeant Bilko* than the John Mills seriousness of *In Which We Serve*. But the old sailors were all punters and loved a flutter.

While in his teens, Charles skipped school to visit bookmakers collecting their weekend football coupons. This was in the days before Oddschecker and the internet, so he would place them all on a table and circle the away teams that appeared to be over-priced and offering value.

His favourite coupon, it transpired, was the Stanley one, as their odds compilers regularly made ricks with their picks. He could back away teams in trebles, and at the big prices, got great returns. This was to lead to his first incident of being barred from the bookmakers.

Fortunately, Charles in those days had some friends who would slip into the shops with his coupons. But one by one they went off to further their educations at university, or borstal, or HMP Walton. The moment passed at just about the same time as the odds compilers at Stanley's surely got the tin tack.

His initial career plan was to become an apprentice artificer in the Royal Navy, so he did go on to get some more qualifications, another half-dozen O levels along with some A levels. But a fractured lower back while skipping school for a day at the beach turned into a lucky break. His playground pal Dave, who joined up to be an RN apprentice, was badly burnt when an Exocet shot through HMS Sheffield in the Falklands.

That episode and *The Sun* headline 'Gotcha' after the sinking of the *Belgrano*, spurred Charles to become a tabloid journalist as he felt sympathy for the Argentinian conscripts killed, and later his own friend injured in action. Punting remained a weekend pastime and his salary was often supplemented with a bet or two.

Charles was eventually appointed TV editor at *The Sun* and did the first stories on the gameshow *Who Wants to Be a Millionaire?* which the newspaper sponsored. The programme went on to become the most successful British quiz show of all time, and coincidentally was the show where Richard's quizzing pal Dave Rainford won £250k.

It was after a successful spell as TV editor that Charles brought 'The Squirrel' column to life for readers of the Saturday racing section, later penning the 'Scoop6 Spider' column in the *Daily Record*. And the rest, as they say, is history.

CONTENTS

Foreword by Frankie Dettori

They say I'm a legendary jockey, but I am lots of other things as well and love sport of all kinds. I plan to ride plenty more winners and maybe the legend will live on even when I've stopped riding, but the public will ultimately be the judge of that.

Career highlights are plentiful and The Squirrel Syndicate actually tipped my first Derby winner Authorized at Epsom back in 2007. I've been Champion Jockey three times and ridden the winners of more than 500 Group races, including twenty English Classics.

That marvellous British Champions Day at Ascot in 1996 saw me hailed a hero by punters everywhere for riding those Magnificent Seven winners. They're making a movie about that glorious day, but this book actually features a couple of the punters who made a small fortune backing the winners.

While I have my flying dismount after a big win, the boys behind this book do a barmy Squirrel dance. We're just all natural entertainers they say, and I suppose I have to agree with them as they're both a bit older than me.

For decades I've been doing my thing on horseback, but even before I started riding in the UK the authors of this extraordinary book were backing winners. And when you've met them you soon enough know that they are not completely nuts.

For equally legendary in the gambling world is The Squirrel Syndicate and I know both founders as fellow members of the Albatross Club. That they've put pen to paper to share their joy of horseracing is commendable, and potentially profitable for plenty of readers.

As a jockey, I know the fractions and want to get a great position, but as gamblers these guys know the mathematics and use their skills to get a winning position with their permutations and general punts.

Sharing the joy of horseracing is something we all have in common. It's the greatest game in the world, and from landing on British shores as a teenager unable to speak a word of English, I've scaled the heights of global racing.

The Squirrel Syndicate say I'm the best loved jockey on the planet, because I've got charisma – which is charming of them. When asked to write this foreword I was almost lost for words. They helped me though, suggesting I should use the line I previously used about a top sprinter I rode for nine of her wins back in the mid-nineties - so here goes: 'Lochsong – she's like Linford Christie... without the lunchbox.'

It's a fact, and that quote probably highlights that they are both full of fun and their book is hilarious in places, though they are serious about their maths and *Racing Post* form study. The fantastic thing about horseracing is how it brings people from all walks of life together.

The thoroughbred is a wonderful animal, so majestic and noble. The Sport of Kings is equally loved by the working man, and these chaps have humble roots along with a real passion for the racehorse. Luckily for the rest of us they're not able to ride the horses.

It was great though that they wanted to get involved in ownership after their record-breaking wins, and that should be saluted. They're both happy to share the joy of big wins with their syndicates online.

Bringing their love of the game to a wider audience is wonderful, and the fact I'm mentioned more than a dozen times in their book in glowing terms is a real honour. They certainly jogged some happy memories for me and they do pop up in the most unusual places.

At Chantilly on French Derby day, one of them was there wearing his bright yellow Albatross tie, and asked if I'd pose for a picture with his Professor friend's son on his first trip to the races. I am sure the French teenager had no idea who I was, as I'd finished riding and was in a shirt and tie rather than racing silks.

They told me afterwards that the teen had loved his day at the races. They didn't tell me that his dad was an Everton fan, but I wouldn't have held that against him despite my passion for Arsenal. The Squirrel Syndicate's close shaves with soccer punting success in the chapter entitled Brazilian Gone Wrong made me smile, and I am sure other bits of the book will make readers laugh out loud.

Horseracing is tremendous entertainment and we all embrace it from different angles, but at the end of the day all of us... jockeys, trainers, owners, breeders and gamblers just want the best for the horses that give rise to the sport we love.

The love of racing and punting just leaps out from the pages of this book. My latest book with Harper Collins was entitled *Leap Of Faith*, and I have every faith this new Conrad Press book will be enjoyed by readers everywhere.

July 2022

Chapter 1

BONUS JOY

The magnificent grey colt Malt Or Mash was on the rails at the back of the field with half a mile to go. It needed to overtake twenty-two horses to win the race and earn the syndicate a tasty £1,137,972.

You couldn't have scripted a more dramatic finish to a one-mile four-furlong race. It was like having Seabiscuit and Red Rum rolled into one with a large helping of Breeders Cup Juvenile winner Arazi thrown in for good measure.

That fantastic fortune of £1 million-plus was the bonus fund in the Tote's Scoop6 – a bet televised each weekend that we just loved winning. The viewers at home had heard Channel 4 presenter Derek Thompson explain how a portion of our winnings was going to a charity fund for children with cancer, so it was pretty fitting that a horse called Philanthropy had shot to the front in the early stages.

In all the years playing for high stakes, no million meant more to us than this one. It was a special day that would secure The Squirrel Syndicate a spot in gambling folklore and cement a place in the betting history books for a bunch of punting pals.

The next £1 million win is what drives us on now. That Saturday, though, it was jockey Ryan Moore driving on Malt Or Mash that was occupying our every nerve ending. On the outside we remained our usual calm selves in the build-up to the race. We had more than a million reasons to keep cool heads.

You can't beat the adrenalin rush and the brilliant buzz you get out of having a free chance at winning more than £1 million. It beats backing a winner, as this is a bet to nothing – a bonus that is worth a potentially life-changing fortune.

People who don't punt rarely appreciate the amazing generosity of bookmakers like the Tote. You've already played for the big prize, but they want you to have some more and the bonus is great fun. The National Lottery back then was not really in the same league. This was man against bookmaker's machine and tens of thousands of other punters. But the bonus means you can plan a day at the races when the stakes are phenomenally high without any extra outlay on your part.

When Malt Or Mash began his run as expected shortly before 3.15 pm, it was relentless, magical and marvellous with a bit of magnificence thrown in just for good measure.

We were all cheering and whooping as trainer Richard Hannon's silver steed streaked past the entire field before they hit the furlong marker.

All the form, all the variables on the day – the ground, the draw out of box thirteen – pointed to Malt Or Mash winning, ahead of a horse called Sanbuch. It was doubly thrilling to see the blue and yellow of that Luca Cumani-trained colt emerge from the pack as the sole challenger. We all kicked ourselves that we didn't hammer them for the one-two with the Tote Exacta and the forecast, but we'd clearly had a million and one hundred thousand other things on our minds that day.

Malt Or Mash had beaten Sanbuch before and for us he was the main danger, although we had considered the favourite Pippa Greene as a potential improver. The ticks were already in the boxes for Malt Or Mash and as ten of us gathered round a table in the Panoramic restaurant at Doncaster, that one horse was all we had on the menu of selections.

Ryan rode a brilliant race. Malt Or Mash was a magical horse on the day, but never did go on to bigger and better things – though none would ever have been bigger and better for us. The value of victory to the winning connections was £1.1 million less than our bonus fund pot but, as far as we were concerned, for those involved in producing the Black Minnaloushe colt, to win the November Handicap and the first prize money of £36,420, it was job done.

The whooping had started almost as soon as jockey Ryan made his move round that final bend. We were yelling with joy, clapping, hugging and kissing as he stormed across the finish line. Next time we'd like more ladies at the races with us – as there was only one female at the table and the rest of the jubilant crew were all blokes, so there was a bit of stubble rash to contend with.

As he passed the post the lady, Richard's wife, Ruth, turned and said: 'I can't believe it.' But we all knew it was real – the gambling gods were smiling again.

When you win, you've got to enjoy it. And we loved every minute of it. Murf, a barking mad psychiatric nurse, was whirling like a dervish and the group were all giddy; drunk on the moment.

That tremendous success in the November Handicap was the culmination of an incredible three weeks with over £3 million in winnings in the bank.

If you're going to gamble you've got to believe you're going to win, otherwise it's a very expensive pastime. Playing to win is where it's at for The Squirrel Syndicate – it's exciting to take part, but winning is what pays the bills and gives you that great glow of self-satisfaction.

When you've done the hard part and landed six consecutive winners to claim the Scoop6 win fund, those nice people at the Tote always give you a free chance at the bonus fund, which can be a real nail-biter.

Mathematically, we try to back most of the runners in most of the races to win the Scoop6, but with bonus selections, when you're the sole winner, you just get the one pick. Get it right and it's money in the bank, get it wrong and you'll have to get it right another day.

On that sunny November Saturday, Ryan cleverly moved his mount out to the right as he came off the final bend and with four furlongs to run, we were already feeling pretty confident.

Winning is a habit and back then we were all hooked on it. Jockeys like Ryan Moore, Richard Johnson, Ruby Walsh, Frankie Dettori, Kieren Fallon and Graham Lee were great men to have on your side in the battle with the bookies. Sir AP McCoy was probably the greatest of them all - his retirement was a sad day for punters everywhere.

Winners ride winners and on that afternoon at Doncaster it was High Noon in the race for the 2007 Flat Jockeys Championship. Two stars, Seb Sanders and Jamie Spencer, were going at it hammer and tongs on Town Moor. The day turned out to be the best ever tipping Saturday in The Squirrel Syndicate's regular *Sun* racing column with four winners in the paper and the other two picks just beaten in photo finishes.

We were convinced that a horse called Inchnadamph would win the eighth and final race on the Doncaster card to ensure that Spencer got to share the Jockeys' Championship trophy with Sanders. On any other day we'd probably have backed that outcome on the computer with various betting exchanges. We'd even made it the banker in the regular Saturday column in *The Sun's Favourite* racing pull-out.

But we'd spent several days focusing on the seventh race on the card and when we'd got that right with our Malt Or Mash moment, we just ordered more drink. By the end of the night several of the syndicate members were just like Father Jack out of *Father Ted*. For the record, Inchnadamph did win and the Jockeys' Championship was divided between two worthy rivals. By the time they cracked the bubbly though, we were already celebrating with copious amounts of vino.

It's funny how alcohol helps fuel us all at times of heightened emotion. Marriages, christenings, funerals and £1 million-plus Scoop6 wins all go considerably better with the finest red and white wine and, if that's not available, then pints of mild, or even mixed.

On the morning of the win a little bird dropped a message on the back of punting Pete Chapman as we headed to the racecourse. Quick as a flash, the other syndicate members on that fateful day asked him for his pick in the big race. 'Malt Or Mash,' he muttered. Pete didn't want to force home the point as he knew the final decision on the selection in the bonus race lay elsewhere. But nobody else wanted to be too forceful either in their prediction apart from a certain tabloid hack in our midst who was all over Malt Or Mash like a rash. The lads had put in anything from a tenner to a thousand or two, in the previous week's five-figure stake, but all were equally involved in the win.

It really is much better to win with your mates because if you win on your own all you do then is get the drinks in. Funny how nobody buys you a beer when you can't find a winner to save your life, which is inevitable from time to time.

Winning with a syndicate means you've got lots of pals who want to get the drinks in as well. And if it all goes pear-shaped then we've all lost a proportion of the stake we'd rather not have parted with.

Syndicates come in all shapes and sizes, as we shall see as this curious story unfolds, with Bulgarian gangsters, pirates, Yardies and all kinds of undesirables keen to get in on the act.

On that day at Doncaster, there was a space at the table for gambling guru Ken Burrell, a wizard with the permutations and a quiz ace with general knowledge to match his mathematical abilities. He was often the voice of reason when someone else in the syndicate wanted to stake a fortune that could just as easily be lost as end up on a winner. We waited for Ken's call before making the final pick. When he came up with Malt Or Mash, the die was cast – he's a great judge of form.

The night before we'd been down the pub, poring over the form with syndicate stalwarts and then enjoyed a pre-race chomp on a curry from the marvellous Moti Mahal restaurant in Hazel Grove. The flavours were fantastic and the chicken *jahangiri* was truly special, but no matter what taste we had on the palate we couldn't get away from Malt Or Mash.

With the Scoop6 bonus you must make your selection an hour before the race time – by ringing the Tote hotline number. It's on syndicate speed dial as we've called it many times in the first twenty or so years of the bet being run.

The great thing about the Scoop6 is when you win it on your own you get the chance to win another fortune for free, but even better is when you win it with other ticket holders. Then, if you combine forces with some of them, you have more than one pick to land the bonus fund. That makes life much easier and makes the day at the races potentially even more fun as you get to meet a great variety of winning characters. And we've had some fantastic days at the races as you'll find out, including one record-breaking £3.1 million Tote dividend in March 2009.

Anyway, after Malt Or Mash won, The Squirrel mascot suit was taken from cold store and slipped on in the racecourse restaurant. We're sure a lot of people were very puzzled by the sight of a seven-foot squirrel doing a dance by our dining table. But it's part of Squirrel tradition – slipping on the suit and doing a dance.

Psychiatric nurse John Murphy – who knows a thing or two about nuts – had carried The Squirrel suit on an earlier expedition to Doncaster – so it was now his son Andrew's turn to slip into the costume and dance like a demented rodent freed from his drey.

We were dancing and singing all night afterwards. Nick, the mini-bus driver, was one of the luckiest blokes at Doncaster that day. Professional photographer Jon 'Biddy' Baxter ducked out at the last minute and Ken Burrell couldn't make it, so Nick landed a £135 ticket with a five-course meal thrown in on top of his handsome wages for the day of driving. He lived just a stone's throw from Edgeley Park football ground and probably wasn't used to seeing winners like The Squirrel Syndicate, as the Stockport County form back then was far from consistent.

The day had started with champagne, but as was often the case, it ended with Robinsons mild. We might have won three million quid, but the alcohol intake that night in The Three Tunnes probably killed three million brain cells.

One of our number had placed all his money on Malt Or Mash with William Hill before heading off to Doncaster. He reasoned it would win and wanted to ensure that he at least had some beer money in hand if it did and the syndicate bonus pick had been a different horse.

Several hours after the race Tony, the manager at William Hill, had insisted that the winnings weren't being handed out unless our inebriated friend was in more sober company, for fear of him being mugged, or simply dropping the dosh in the street. Well, he wasn't in sober company for several days, but the mention of a few names of less inebriated regulars helped get the grands in his hands.

High comedy ensued back in the pub as tenners were falling from his pocket as he attempted to buy everyone a drink. A small boy called John Shields had been brought along by his parents to join the celebrations. With blond hair and a big angelic grin, he duly wandered round after our intoxicated punter, picking up the notes and saying 'You dropped this.' But the overjoyed syndicate member simply ruffled his hair and informed him 'It must be some drunk's money and they won't miss it.' We were quite lucky that the normally clear-headed and sensible chap hadn't been given the £1,137,972 by the Tote, otherwise that could have been lining that little nine-year-old lad's piggy bank as well. It was like a scene from the film *Whisky Galore,* only with real ale replacing the shorts.

A week prior to this, the syndicate had gathered in that same pub for another Saturday afternoon attempt at the Scoop6, and another winning weekend was on the cards. A couple of pints of mild and a winner or two helped the afternoon pass with a bit of banter and the odd bacon and egg butty. Legend has it the former landlord's father, Jovial John, once charged a customer extra when he discovered a double yolker in the egg box. But, at £2.60 for a bacon and egg barm and half a portion of chips, you can't complain.

The syndicate was thirty-strong, a few more than the week before, but the Scoop6 was worth playing as we'd missed a near £1 million bonus seven days earlier. Patience is a virtue and they do say that good things come to those who wait. Funnily enough, nobody had won the win fund the previous week, so by the time racing got under way, there was a bumper £424,674 in that pot alone.

Yet the real prize was that elusive bonus fund that would take the haul in eight days to another £1.5 million. And, we were very glad to report, it was yet another amazing afternoon that left us all jumping for joy.

It was a slow start as the favourite got beaten in the first race by Classic Legend at 11-2 and there were still 70,000 tickets going on to the second leg; much more than you'd normally expect. And when Lothian Falcon won that at 9-2 there were still thousands left in. But when Very Wise won the third at 7-1 there were only 1,594 tickets left.

At that point it was looking like we had a very good chance and when second favourite Ollie Magern won the fourth leg at Wetherby at 11-4, there were just 202 tickets remaining.

The way we do the Scoop6 is permutations using bankers, but we'll get round to that in a bit more detail later. With Paris Bell winning the 3.40 at Ayr at 7-1, there were just thirty-nine tickets entering the final leg.

The bet used to be pretty straightforward to follow as Channel 4 generally announced how many tickets were left in after each race and, if they didn't, you could always check out the Tote pages on teletext or online.

These days ITV don't promote the bet, but then again, they don't have the viewers they used to either. All the same, exotic bets like the Scoop6 with a big pool are a secret ingredient that can actually boost viewing figures if embraced by a broadcaster – just look at *Who Wants to Be a Millionaire?* if you want evidence of interactive TV shows boosting ratings. The tabloid hack in the syndicate had actually helped to promote that, and earned a mention in the book about the making of *WWtBaM?*

Before that sixth leg, we knew we'd already won as we had a ticket on every horse in that last race. There were just thirty-one other punters still in the pool who could have had a crack at that amazing bonus with us. The eight-runner affair at Newmarket had five of the horses well covered by Scoop6 tickets, but remarkably three of the field had just one ticket on. Those three were all running for The Squirrel Syndicate to take down the full win fund again and give us another single pick for the bonus.

We were expecting at least a couple of tickets on every runner, and were genuinely stunned when Jalmira at 8-1 just got home in front with one ticket on it which was obviously ours. It was yet another Irish winner that had set us on our way to a second £1.5 million fortune in a fortnight.

The atmosphere in that historic coaching house The Three Tunnes was very different from a couple of weeks earlier when our first amazing win had come in. This time the winner was greeted with a mixture of shock and silence. The syndicate members, scattered round the racing room, couldn't quite believe their eyes.

It was almost like lightning striking twice – except this was potentially a couple of lightning bolts worth £3 million. That's a lot of money, if that's not stating the obvious. To say it was really exciting was an understatement. It was astonishing and every few weeks back then we tried our best to land the Scoop6. Nowadays the National Lottery Must Be Won draws offer The Squirrel Syndicate some value. Back then, though, that win was even more incredible as we won it on our own and 8-1 was the longest price of any of the winners.

There is a lovely lady called Agnes Haddock who landed £688,000 for £2 after picking horses with nice names, but for us it was more about the numbers. The Scoop6 was the best value bet in Britain and we were surprised that more people didn't win the pool with us. We knew it would be very difficult the following week, with just one pick for the £1 million-plus bonus fund. But back in November 2004 another Squirrel Syndicate, with a single pick on Blue Americo, had landed one of the biggest ever bonus dividends handed out by the Tote – a whopping £802,040.

On the Sunday, we were still in shock and slightly hungover from the amaretto and champagne cocktails as we'd seriously expected more ticket holders to be coming along to Doncaster to win the bonus with us.

Factory worker Phil Harding, then aged forty, of Stockport, Cheshire, who had a tenner on with the syndicate, praised the group's punting prowess in the local paper, as word of our incredible win spread like wildfire. Phil said: 'He's got to be the luckiest red squirrel in Britain – we all just hope he's not a dying breed and can carry on caning the bookies for years to come.'

Pub landlord Barry Richardson, then aged fifty-two, was woken from his slumbers at the Bowling Green by a journalist inquiring if he'd won £3 million. If Baz had won £3 million, he wouldn't be telling anyone, so the reporter had no chance of running his headline 'Bowled Over at The Bowler by £3 Million Win.' As Barry told us later, 'Every bugger keeps coming in expecting me to buy all the beers as they think I'm a millionaire.'

Well, one day we're sure Barry will be, but getting used to winning with The Squirrel Syndicate was particularly hard for him back then as he's a lifelong Manchester City fan and it's only in recent seasons that they've started winning stuff. Before the oil-rich Arabs purchased City, Barry was more used to having the blues than most people. The £3 million wins did coincide with the arrival of Sven Goran Eriksson at the City of Manchester Stadium, so Baz's winning streak had been prolonged by a good run from his favourite team.

Another syndicate member, nutty nurse Murf, aged fifty-four, told the press: 'Lightning striking twice is amazing – I put a small bet on the other week in memory of my mum, Aggie, who had passed away suddenly a few days before. I reckon she's riding the winners for us up in heaven – nobody can believe that we've won the Scoop6 twice in the space of three weeks with just one ticket on the Irish winner in the last leg each time. It's certainly a case of Irish eyes smiling on us.'

Well, Irish eyes were smiling, but not as much as some of the lads in the pub. Punting Pete's dad, John, had a faraway look in his eyes... he was already dreaming of a foreign holiday with his share of the winnings. Within days he'd booked a villa as big as the Panoramic restaurant at Doncaster racecourse for a family holiday in Majorca.

And he knew a thing or two about incredible coincidences as his father, Jack, had served in Egypt in the 1920s with the Royal Horse Artillery. About seventy-five years later, as Jack was in his nineties, John took him along to the hospital in Manchester for an appointment.

Now, his dad had been kicked in the side by a horse during active service and had been operated on in a field hospital. He still bore the scar. When the surgeon contemplating carrying out the latest operation on Jack saw his scar, he inquired after the injury. When he heard the where and when of the accident the medic was stunned as it transpired his own grandfather was surgeon general with the Royal Horse Artillery and here he was staring at his dear departed relative's handiwork. So lightning striking twice was always a possibility with players like John in the syndicate – just a shame his horse-loving dad, Jack, missed out on the history-making win.

But several syndicate members imagined close relatives, gone but not forgotten, would be riding out the winners every step of the way during the remarkable run of thirteen racing triumphs that yielded that bumper £3 million-plus payday.

Up in the North East, one little lad was oblivious to all our delight – it was tiny Thomas Russell whose name had been put to a cancer charity by his loving family after bravely battling the disease – in the shape of an aggressive neuroblastoma which he'd been diagnosed with as an eleven-week-old baby.

No matter how much you win or even lose, it's always good to remember that health is wealth. Whatever you've got in the bank, at the end of the day, it's only money. If you've got your health, then you're truly lucky.

Thomas endured an eighteen-month battle with cancer before he was given the all-clear in December 2006. He was a lovely little smiling miracle and his mum and dad, Dave and Joanne, as well as big brother, Harry, were very happy to have him home and healthy again, up in Sunderland.

The syndicate got involved with Thomas as one member of the group, sprightly Steve Schofield, used to play football with his West Ham-supporting dad, Dave, and the www.ThomasRussell cancertrustfund.co.uk was the obvious place for a charity donation after our sensational wins.

It was a no-brainer for every single syndicate member to donate a portion of each winning stake to the charity, which aimed to buy equipment for children's wards at hospitals in Thomas's native North East. Sadly, the ground-breaking treatment that went on to save the lives of hundreds, if not thousands, of other babies worldwide, left Thomas with a condition meaning he needed a double-lung transplant.

Surviving cancer, surviving a global pandemic, and then surviving the double-lung transplant, Thomas was truly a battler. Tragically, an infection struck and just as he was about to get back on his feet last autumn and aged sixteen and a half, his life was claimed by the bug, coupled with sepsis. His funeral was a tribute to a battling lad who loved WWE, but those in attendance knew he had more fight in him than any of those telly wrestlers he adored.

Every big winner can suffer with 'the dread' – the thought that everything is going so well that surely something terrible is just around the corner. Squirrel Syndicate members have suffered since the win, but they're mostly all still in one piece and so are their families. Some things are much more precious than winning Scoop6 tickets.

Big wins are brilliant, but they do throw into sharp focus lots of other things. At the end of the day, we're doing it for the excitement, and all agree that winning a fortune on top is great fun.

As jockey Mick Fitzgerald famously said after winning the Grand National in 1996 on Rough Quest: 'That was better than sex.' Well, we'd be betting he didn't get his leg over with Mrs Fitzgerald for a day or two after that comment, but having had some big wins, we think we know where he was coming from, if you'll pardon the expression.

Chapter 2

THE JOY OF SIX

Some days you just have to put your betting boots on. The odds may be stacked against you, but the reward can be so big that you've got to give it a go.

Saturday October 20th 2007 was most definitely one of those days. There were 107 runners declared overnight in the Scoop6 – a number that would normally ensure most people's betting boots never saw the light of day. But the second biggest combined rollover pot in the history of the Scoop6 meant that something had to be ventured.

There was a whopping £1,674,472 in both funds – with a bumper £958,743 in the win pot and a further £715,729 in the bonus bin before racing had even started. The Tote were tipping a £2.5 million pot if a single winner could collect the bonus bonanza the following week on top of the win fund. And they were offering 33-1 that a £2 winner would land the windfall on their own. We reckoned that was more a 100-1 shot, so we were not tempted to have a bet as insurance.

It was Cesarewitch Day at Newmarket – a fantastic staying race over two miles and two furlongs and you really needed a horse with stamina to land the pot. The weather all week had been wet and the mudlarks were all at the top of the betting. Among them were Macorville, Dr Sharp and the Philip Hobbs-trained favourite Fair Along. One of the syndicate's leading maths maestros Richard Brocklebank had a fancy for Irish trainer Tony Martin's 14-1 shot Leg Spinner, but the consensus of opinion was that the turf would never be dry enough for this confirmed good ground lover.

When we assessed the races, we realised that, even if we had a million to stake, we could put it all on and still not find six winners. We were usually keen to get involved when there were about thirty per cent fewer runners than this 100-plus extravaganza, but we felt the win fund could reach a record-breaking £1.5 million and wanted to have a shot at it. The best approach was to have a speculative punt. Not just a £2 line though. If you can afford it, why not give it a go? We meant a considered perm that would cost into four or five figures. We'd wheel out The Squirrel Syndicate and we'd all be in it to win it.

Well, a permutation costing just over £16,000 that Richard came up with, gave us only a six per cent chance of winning. Ken urged caution as he suspected The Squirrel Syndicate really had gone nuts on this occasion. In his considered opinion it was worth keeping the powder dry for the week after, as nobody was likely to win it with such a difficult card. Ken would have been very right as nobody would have won it if we'd not put OUR bet on.

But other syndicate members could see the massive purse and were eager to give it a go. That six per cent chance of a winning dividend, which the bet had at the beginning, was worked out by Ken and that wasn't just a win as a single ticket. The most likely outcome if we did win was that we'd share the dividend with other ticket holders and the pot would be split. Incredibly, the pool reached a Tote record level of £1,519,301 as the first race at Newmarket got underway.

In The Sun racing column, which the tabloid hack did with Richard on a Friday afternoon after reading race ratings and studying the form, The Squirrel Syndicate's scribe was sure that either impressive Longchamp winner Toylsome, or French raider Literato, should be the banker. We'd recommended a bigger than usual perm to the readers – a single selection in leg one, three in legs three, five and six – and two in the other two legs. The 1×3×2×2×3×3 perm worked out at 108 £2 lines costing £216 and would have cost £21.60 per person for a ten-strong syndicate.

Toylsome failed in the first leg, but Literato went in at 7-2 in the 3.15 at Newmarket in the fourth leg. We'd tipped Fonthill Road at 13-2 to land the banker Nap in the paper the week before and were kicking ourselves that we'd not followed it up with Literato. We'd also tipped From Dawn To Dusk at 11-4 which won the 2.20 at Cheltenham, so thirty-three per cent success out of the six races in the column wasn't a bad tipping strike rate.

We always wanted to give the readers a good winner, happily splitting Scoop6 pots with *Sun* readers in the past, and were set to divide up more with them in the future. During those Squirrel Syndicate days at *The Sun* more than £10 million was won by readers who loved the weekly column.

The Tote were really keen to ensure that this massive pot got as much publicity as possible and Paul Petrie, their highly respected PR manager, rang The Squirrel Syndicate hotline requesting the furry fellow's top tips for punters playing the Scoop6.

We were big fans of the Tote as they'd handed over millions to us down the years, clearly we were more than happy to help. Unbeknown to us they'd also contacted some of our super punting pals and asked them for their tips on landing the Scoop6 as well.

Sadly, not a single organ published the words of wisdom from some of the best bettors in the business. But for the sake of sharing those gems with our readers, below is the press release that Mr Petrie issued ahead of that fateful day. It included several top tips and a fascinating fact sheet that is also worth reproducing:

Some of the biggest Scoop6 players give their tips on what it takes to win the toteScoop6

Richard Brocklebank, aka The Squirrel

- Join up with your mates – winning the Scoop6 is so much easier for a syndicate – as a group of people can stake more on the bet and the extra permutations improve punters' chances of landing the big pot.

- Try and find a longshot to land a top prize – as any outsider above 10-1 can help to knock 95 per cent of the other ticket holders out of the bet.

- Place the bet as late as possible – that way punters avoid non-runners and can include any last-minute steamers in their selections.

Chris Broom

- Go with your own judgement – you can't blame anyone else
- Try to be different from the crowd – that will offer you the greatest value and the chance to win large dividends

Dave Nevison

- Forget about trying to win the place part of the bet – go for winners
- Don't be afraid to have one banker – and not in the last leg
- Be ruthless – the two quids multiply quickly so take out those nearly horses

Harry Findlay

- Never do a 2×2×2×2×2×2 perm – you will never win with that sort of bet
- Find the banker in one of the early legs

ToteScoop6 Fact Sheet

- Combined rollover of £1,674,472 is the second biggest in its betting history – record pools, £1,909,472, was achieved in May 2007
- Win fund rollover of £958,743 is the second biggest in its betting history – record win fund, £1,054,523, was achieved in May 2007
- Bonus fund rollover of £715,729 is the seventh biggest in its betting history – record bonus fund, £1,537,626, was achieved in February 2000
- Largest win dividend – £1,132,657 – achieved by Stuart Bolland in November 2004
- Largest place dividend – £39,240 – September 2006

- Largest bonus dividend – £1,339,148 – Haydock 2004
- £116 million – turnover generated since the bet began in 1999
- £80 million – the amount paid out in winnings since the bet began in 1999
- 32% – the amount of turnover expected to be contributed to the toteScoop6 by major syndicates – the same as £2 punters
- £2,472,015 – the amount won by £2 punters this year on the Tote Scoop6

Talk about helping to set the scene for a history-making win. We'll explain more about those super punters later. But The Squirrel Syndicate's advice to *Sun* readers that Saturday was sound. It was 'Get together with your mates' and we practised what we preached by forming a sixteen-strong syndicate to land the big win and we were to have a free chance to add a further £955,968 to our haul in the shape of the bonus fund.

It was a truly sensational afternoon, but that six per cent chance of a win when the bet started was immediately reduced to just a two per cent chance of glory when Miss Lucifer won the first race at 20-1. Larger than life Channel 4 personality of the time John McCririck had tipped the Barry Hills' longshot in *The Sun* pull-out, and we'd included it in our selections as the Lambourn trainer had a good record in the race with big-priced fillies.

But there were only 21,340 tickets left in the Scoop6 after that 20-1 shot had sluiced in from over 800,000 tickets at the beginning. The perm was hanging by a thread, but we had told punters that a longshot was essential for a big win, so we weren't totally desolate. We do prefer the big-priced winner to come in the last leg as that is less wearing on the nerves.

When From Dawn to Dusk won the second leg, as tipped by us in *The Favourite's* racing pull-out, there were 4,708 tickets left in. The third leg was already up with King Orchisios sprinting in at 9-2 at Catterick and the ticket numbers had been whittled down to 594. When our other winning tip Literato won at 7-2 in the fourth leg, there were still 228 tickets remaining. In the fifth leg at Cheltenham a horse called

Knowhere came from nowhere to win and at that stage there were only fifty-two tickets left in the pot for the final race. And of those fifty-two, we owned eight.

The Squirrel Syndicate gathered in the pub, and we watched the Cesarewitch with bated breath. We decided we'd all be bowled over if Leg Spinner won as we held the only ticket on that. But our in-house hack had three winners already up in two Lucky 15s and he'd got two of the syndicate's other picks, the mudlarks Macorville and Dr Sharp, running for him to win a small fortune –£100,000 on each bet. On the other hand, Leg Spinner would win all of us a large fortune, so he selflessly decided that that was the horse to cheer home after doing some basic mental arithmetic.

The race unfolded in one county and finished in another, as the Cesarewitch is the only race in the calendar that starts in Cambridgeshire and finishes in Suffolk. The consensus was still that Leg Spinner couldn't win on the soft ground but Richard, who'd insisted on putting him in, pointed out that as it was one of the later races the course had chance to dry out as the meeting progressed.

Newmarket drains very well and when it stops raining dries out relatively quickly as there is a chalk base beneath the turf. Leg Spinner, as a result, had a great chance, and that 14-1 wasn't a bad price for a class horse. That culinary giant and one-time leading Liberal Sir Clement Freud – who'd tipped Pipedreamer to win the Cambridgeshire just like The Squirrel Syndicate had a week or so earlier – also advised Leg Spinner in his column in *The Sun*.

During the race we focussed on a horse called Inchnadamph with bright yellow silks and a vivid red cap. He was a consistent stayer and loved top of the ground having won six races from one mile and five furlongs to two miles on good to firm and good going. The seven-year-old Inchnadamph was racing prominently as they came into the final four furlongs and was weaving forwards, which indicated to us that the ground was not good to soft as described in the official going report. It had clearly been drying out, so we scanned the pack for the green and red colours of Leg Spinner, and there he was – running on strongly.

Now as he was pointed out in the boozer, we all started clapping and cheering, and when he hit the front, we were jumping for joy. The favourite Fair Along was running on for a place and Carraciola an old hand of Nicky Henderson was the nearest danger. And Ken would have been right; if we'd not placed the bet, the Scoop6 would not have been won as Leg Spinner would have ended up like Carraciola – a horse without a single ticket on it.

For the record, Inchnadamph finished about twelve lengths behind Leg Spinner in fifth and went into the notebook as a next time out winner. Three weeks later he was to pass the post first as predicted at Doncaster on another astonishing afternoon for The Squirrel Syndicate of Saturday chums. After Leg Spinner stormed home – we all got the drinks in and a few extra trays of Robinsons mild were served in The Three Tunnes that day. We were all in party mood and were sure that England would win the Rugby World Cup afterwards.

The celebrations were bittersweet for joker John Murphy who had called in to the boozer to inform friends that his mum, Aggie Murphy, had died suddenly at the age of eighty-four, and on the spur of the moment he'd decided to place a small bet in her memory with The Squirrel Syndicate. Cricket club stalwart John, who found it very fitting that Leg Spinner had landed the loot, told us: 'She loved a flutter on the big races and I'm sure she'll have been smiling down from heaven on The Squirrel Syndicate. Since the Second World War she'd lived in Cumbria and loved the red squirrels up there. It was very fitting that I put a few quid on in her memory. I just wish the England cricket team had a winning leg-spinner as well.'

Another chap, Dave Crosby, forty-two, had fitted a headlight bulb for a cack-handed syndicate member without taking payment – the punter promised to put a tenner in the syndicate pot for him. Dave was delighted when later a large wad of more than £900 in notes was handed over in exchange for his favour on the light front.

Stockport Rugby Club second row Nick Blashill, forty, a property developer with Bulgarian connections, was also among the winning syndicate and went on to watch the Rugby World Cup after missing all the races as he played in a tough 17-17 draw away at Buxton in Derbyshire. Nick was gutted by the England defeat, but he had well over a hundred thousand good reasons to be happy with the Scoop6. He was jubilant afterwards and said: 'I only wish I'd been able to watch them romp home. The Squirrel Syndicate is a sensation and it's an honour to be part of the furry fellow's club. For years he's been urging us *Sun* readers to get together with our mates to win the Scoop6 and it's just great when it comes off. I went to celebrate at my local rugby club and to watch the final with all the lads.' And just like the rest of us, he didn't see anything wrong with that try. Nick said: 'After our amazing victory on the punting front I was sure England were on a winner as well. That would have been the perfect end to the perfect day.'

We'd not had a bet on the rugby although we'd noted for months and years that Harry Findlay had been urging everyone to get on the All Blacks – he was in deep to the tune of over £2 million, but there's a man never afraid to pull his betting boots on.

Two other syndicate members, pub landlord Barry Richardson and office boss Steve Schofield, were on a five-a-side tour of Hamburg with their Aged Dribblers soccer squad. Barry phoned base back in Blighty and said: 'We scored in Hamburg, but we struggled to find anywhere to watch the race. It was a top trip though with a share of £1.5 million waiting on our return – I might even buy a round of drinks when I get home, but then they don't call me 'Mr Meanie' for nothing. I might wait to see if The Squirrel Syndicate gets the bonus winner at Doncaster next Saturday before splashing out.'

The Irish-trained Leg Spinner had literally bowled every other punter out of the Saturday TV bet that had started with a bumper 800,797 ticket holders playing for the massive pool. But there are still people nearly dying of thirst in The Bowling Green, and a fair few other pubs for that matter, as they wait patiently for Baz to get a round in.

The brilliant win set us off on a bonus hunt that was to take syndicate members to Doncaster on two very contrasting days. A couple of days after Leg Spinner's win, Richard was on the plane to Majorca with his young family as the cheque for £1.51 million was landing in The Squirrel Syndicate bank account back home in his name.

One newer member of the syndicate, was a bit concerned when he heard he'd hopped on a jet out of the country. His share of the win ran into a substantial six-figure sum and he'd feared Richard was doing a runner.

But far from being in the Bahamas, or even Brazil, Richard was being eaten alive by mosquitoes in Alcudia – a Majorcan resort apparently built on a swamp, if the plague of nipping flies he had to contest with was anything to go by. By all accounts, the accommodation was middle-of-the-road and nothing like the sumptuous Sandy Lane Hotel in Barbados, or any other lap of luxury destination in the Caribbean, that he could now easily afford.

Richard was on the hotel balcony enjoying a pre-lunch gin and tonic when his mobile rang. A great booming voice he knew well was on the other end. 'Congratulations, Squirrel! Good luck with the bonus race,' boomed Harry Findlay – legendary gambler and owner of rising superstar Denman, a horse that had all the hallmarks of a Gold Cup winner. And he went on to do just that.

Anyway, Harry was obviously planning a large perm to try and win the bonus the following week if we left it behind. Now Betfair had offered us a £100,000 line of credit to ensure we could lay off some of the other horses and emerge a winner whatever happened in the bonus race. But The Squirrel Syndicate was on the attack and we reckoned winning the Scoop6 again was the best insurance of getting the bonus fund if we missed out this Saturday.

We'd collaborated with Harry in the past and knew that telling him the name of our bonus selection would save him thousands, probably a five-figure sum on his perm, so we did the decent thing and gave him the name. Harry has always been a real punting pal and we've never once had a situation where either of us has broken our word on a Scoop6 agreement. You take as you find and if people are as good as their word, then you've got to trust them.

A small contingent of The Squirrel Syndicate made the pilgrimage across the Pennines to the newly opened Doncaster racecourse. That man Murphy was clutching The Squirrel suit, shaking his head and saying, 'Never again will I get lumbered with this bushy-tailed burden.'

The purpose of the trip was to try and land the bonus, but also to introduce members to tiny Thomas Russell who was raising funds for cancer research and hospitals in the North East. Four of the syndicate members planned to journey up to Sunderland for a fundraising dinner that would see the charity set up by his mum and dad reach its initial target of raising £50,000. We'd hoped a chunk of the bonus fund would push it even further on, but some days things aren't just meant to be.

The bonus race at Doncaster was the 2.30 sprint, and we'd gone for How's She Cuttin', a speedy mare with a rail draw – though it was soon apparent that it didn't help being drawn on the stands rail at Donny that day, as all the winners were running up the centre of the track.

The bonus race was worth around £10,000 to connections, but the favourite King Orschisios, although looking first class in the paddock, never got in the race. The second favourite, which was our choice, drifted like a barge on course, and the third favourite Kay Two had the jockey unseated as the starting stalls opened.

A horse called Safari Sunset won and at least one of our number John Chapman had a few quid on it. Not really the result we wanted – the stewards even inquired into the running of the favourite.

But we do remember another Scoop6 race at Bath when Darryl Holland was riding a warm favourite with just our ticket on to win a substantial six-figure sum. The horse was going very nicely until it disappeared out of view behind a hillock on the course, only to reappear at the back of the pack. The horse then stayed on to the home turn when, all of a sudden, he veered to the right out of camera shot and once again was right at the back. He stayed on like a good 'un up the home straight but couldn't peg back the gelding that had got first run on him. And subsequently a substantial Scoop6 win fund went into Harry Findlay's back pocket. So, very well done against the odds!

But The Squirrel Syndicate, although losing, wanted to ensure that charity emerged a winner. With that in mind, tiny Thomas turned up at the course with his dad, Dave, and The Squirrel suit was duly donned. A collection of pictures was hurriedly taken on the grass in the family enclosure – smiles were broad, but it was really gutting that we never got a run for the money from the horse.

The lads and ladies had gone goat class – the poor pensioners and regular racegoers who'd once been members of Doncaster's popular Diamond Club were now relegated to the family enclosure as well. And the thirsty punters that day at the renovated course had a forty-five-minute queue for a pint of over-priced beer at a bar where two barmaids were running the entire length of the forty-foot plus facility to serve their customers. Even young Thomas Russell wasn't terribly impressed by the racecourse, but his smiling face was testimony to the fact that he enjoyed his first ever meeting with a giant squirrel.

Thomas's consultant Quentin Hewson Campbell put all the winning and losing into perspective when he told the miraculous story of the toddler's survival against all the odds after being diagnosed with a neuro-blastoma at just eleven weeks old. Thomas had been the first baby to be bombarded by high-dosage chemotherapy and survive. His treatment was to be used as a blueprint to help others unfortunate enough to find themselves in the same difficult situation. Now that's what you call being very lucky, for the other children and their parents would have the treatment knowing it was possible for them to survive.

Chapter 3

THE START OF A SYNDICATE

Life's a gamble... or so they say. After all you don't go to the Olympics thinking you're going to finish second... so don't go to the bookies, log on to the internet, or do battle with Betfair, believing you won't win.

July 20th 1969 is a highly memorable date as that was when Neil Armstrong became the first man to walk on the moon. There aren't many people on the planet who don't remember that name. Yet it can't have been quite as brilliant being his mate Buzz Aldrin – as very few people remember you for finishing second. There is a lot to be said for being number one – another valuable early lesson for many of The Squirrel Syndicate being of a certain age. Decades later we were all to do a bit of moonwalking ourselves in celebration of some really big wins, but we'll leave the Michael Jackson dancing until later.

We remember the Scoop6 launching in July 1999. It was a slow burn and the stake of £2 with no fractional option was prohibitive. At the time the jackpot could be played for 5p a line, though that went up to 10p then 50p. But more recently the minimum stake has been dropped to 1p-a-line for perms. The early Scoop6 pots were slow to build, but shrewd punters felt they were worth monitoring. The jackpot with the lesser minimum stake was generally a lot more attractive.

With the Scoop6 scorching along towards that first Christmas reaching six figures, it was becoming very interesting. From memory, January 2000 started with £917,000 in the win fund and it went to a seven-strong German syndicate, christened The Munchen Gladbackers. Among their number was a chap called Simon Springer, a Munich-based bookmaker with four betting shops, who later ran the online betting firm Bet3000. They had a crack at a bonus to take their win past the £1 million mark, but they failed to find the winner of the Warwick National. The race was rebranded The Tote Scoop6 Warwickshire Gold Cup and later renamed the Warwick Classic Chase. Years later we went along to Warwick for another night out after chasing a £750,000 bonus and just like The Munchen Gladbackers we left it behind, but more of that later.

Of course, nobody would ever have heard of the Munchen Gladbackers if Ken hadn't halved the perm The Squirrel came up with the previous Saturday... but that falls into 'the one that got away' category.

At the end of April 2003, Ken and Richard landed yet another Scoop6 and once again lots of others won it with them. They had two tickets once more and were invited down for some hospitality by the Tote as they chased the bonus the week after on May 3rd. It was this fateful 2,000 Guineas Day that Richard was to meet his future punting pal Spider, though at this time he was just a humble hack for *The Sun* on a jolly with his wife, Anne. He had done a story in the racing pages that day about his Scoop6 win and desire to team up with others to take down the £239,000 bonus fund.

Anne was wearing high heels, so their progress to the hospitality tent wasn't the fastest. En route they stopped to place a Lucky 15 in the course betting shop – not something he usually did with Anne on his elbow. Anyhow, his good lady wife decided that the stake of £1 each way was a bit steep, being the good husband, he halved that to 50p each way.

As he dashed toward the Tote hospitality with a fresh Scoop6 bid in his mind, he was asked to slow down, which he dutifully did. Arriving in the Tote tent in the centre of the course, Spider, as he was to later become, valiantly attempted to get his Scoop6 on. Alas, by the time the ticket went through, the opening leg at Uttoxeter was off and a void receipt was churned out instead of a live bet. His selection was 20-1 winner Hayden's Field, which put almost everyone out of the bet, but it was going to get a lot more painful as the day wore on.

He was wandering round the tables talking to people, when he happened upon Richard, who was there with his wife, Ruth, and their friends Baz and Helen Peak. Immediately, Richard agreed to join his winners' alliance, as long as the hack went for a horse drawn low. He had picked three in the race and of those drawn low liked Marsad. He tried to argue against the rail draw suggesting congestion could be an issue and he preferred Fire Up The Band drawn on the other side, or the Irish raider Perfect Touch drawn alongside that one. He had backed Marsad to win the race the year before at 20-1, so agreed to row in with Richard and Ken, making it his bonus selection, and they would make their two picks. He also signed up a red-haired lady we nicknamed the 'gambling granny,' to join us in the bonus chase, so we had four running for us.

Just before the thirty-runner sprint at 2.55 pm, a group of the Tote's guests were escorted across to the winners' enclosure for a pre-race chat with Channel 4's anchorman Derek Thompson. Taking a shine to brunette Anne, Tommo asked her what she was selecting, but she responded pointing behind her: 'I leave the horses to him, so I can go shopping afterwards.' Apparently, lots of ladies liked that reply.

Telly interview done, Spider was then planning to slip off with £800 in his pocket to bang it on his other fancy, Fire Up The Band, which was in his Lucky 15 at 8-1. He also aimed to have a tenner on the exactas with Fire Up The Band, Perfect Touch and Marsad. At this point Anne suggested he should stay and not leave her with all the strangers. So, the planned £800 single and the tenner exactas never came to pass.

Dandy Nicholl's sprinter Fire Up The Band now 4-1 favourite absolutely hosed up from Perfect Touch at 11-1 in second for a 46-1 exacta. Suffice to say, Spider's first thoughts were not on getting the first three in his Lucky 15 up. It was to get a lot worse when his final selection Dermot Weld's Refuse To Bend at 9-2 won the Guineas, so instead of collecting over £5,000 on the Lucky 15, he bagged just over £2,500 for his 50p stake each way. He hadn't had his £800 on Fire Up The Band, which was available at 5-1 and bigger, so another £4,000 missed, not to mention the £460 off the exacta.

But the coup de grâce was that nobody landed the Scoop6 that day, so around £67,000 went begging on that, though if they'd walked just that bit faster it would have gone to one winning ticket and he'd have had it in his pocket. It's only money and as they say 'Money can't buy you love.'

Anne was actually a midwife, but she kept that quiet as she chatted to Ruth, who was eight months pregnant at that point. Thomas Brocklebank duly arrived a few weeks later. For The Squirrel and his missus, that was like hitting the jackpot, blackjack and the Scoop6 all in one.

A few months later on August 2nd, Ken and Richard had landed another Scoop6 with the biggest priced winner of the six races at just 10-1. They ended up splitting a £500,000 pot with a few others including a chap called Chris Broom who had placed his perm via Bill Bailey at RaceBets. It was on the morning of the bonus race on August 9th that Richard got a phone call from Spider wishing him well and suggesting he shouldn't leave the £600,000 bonus behind this time, which was a nice touch.

The Tote would normally have laid on a splendid lunch in a box for groups of up to about a dozen bonus chasers, but this time they offered a buffet in a draughty marquee and Chris Broom decided it wasn't worth making the trip to Newmarket for it, so Richard never met him in person.

The Tote had selected the fifteen-runner Swynford Paddocks Hotel 'Silks In Silks' Handicap over a mile and two furlongs, with a penalty value of £4,299 for the low-grade Class E event. Ken and Richard had collaborated with Chris and the other bonus hunters to select a horse each. One of them was Ian Wood's four-year-old Debbie, carrying 8st 4lbs under Willie Supple, which got the job done at 8-1. Ken and Richard had landed more than £168,000 with their share of the win and bonus funds. It certainly made the trip back to Manchester go so much faster, with that bumper comedy cheque from the Tote in the boot of the Mondeo. That year they had also landed a £156,238 jackpot at Lingfield, so the harvest from Tote bets was brilliant.

To celebrate, they decided to lay on a treat for all their pals in the shape of a coach trip from Manchester to Beverley Racecourse. They invited Spider with Mrs Spider and enjoyed filling their glasses with champagne as they jumped on the bus in Stockport, before picking Ken and the rest of the crew up at the Stretford Arndale. They had booked a pub on the outskirts of Beverley for lunch ahead of racing, and we had a jolly decent day out. Spider's good lady now being unmasked as a midwife meant she got on well with Ruth, who was also a nurse with the NHS.

Little did any of us know then just how well we would all get on and then go on to celebrate some sensational wins, way beyond all our wildest dreams.

Meanwhile, 2004 was upon us and our Scoop6 success was to continue. Though probably the highlight of the year came around the same time as the birth of The Squirrel Syndicate, but more of that later. Ken and Richard did actually land three bumper jackpots in four weeks and The Spider was invited in for a few shekels. They started with a Sandown payday of £59,000 for a 50p line. A week or so after that, we got £134,000 for another 50p perm at Haydock and then – all in a matter of days – we were off to Chester for £135,000. It was a magical spell and Richard and Ken were both still emptying quiz machines for fun with their encyclopaedic general knowledge. Life couldn't get any better, or could it?

Being mainly based in the North West, the Welsh seaside resorts of Llandudno and Rhyl were known to many members of the syndicate – along with Abersoch, which many referred to as Bramhall-on-Sea as most of that affluent Stockport suburb's residents washed up there in the summer months. Value was to be had all over Wales, but once a syndicate member on a race trip headed off to the races at Bangor. He ended up in the Welsh cathedral city in Gwynedd instead of Bangor-on-Dee, which is literally on the other side of Wales, not far from Chester. His coastal route to the wrong venue took him through Rhyl and much leg-pulling was done upon his return to The Three Tunnes after the lad's non-racing day out.

The Squirrel Syndicate's online incarnation was born in that very pub, as The Spider once got accosted for a payout by a chap who hadn't paid in towards the bet one week when we won. The character concerned was a bit down on his luck and balding to boot, so Spider took pity on him, popping to the cashpoint to get £900 as that's what a tenner in the syndicate was worth that weekend. Spider fell for the line, 'You know I am good for a tenner' – as the chancer had lobbed the occasional tenner in previously. Spider resolved to catch up with the chap on the next occasion we took a punt. It was about four weeks later when we played and lost, but the pub trip to collect the tenner owed didn't quite go to plan as the joker explained that he wasn't in the syndicate that particular weekend. The jungle drums from pub to pub were all you needed on a Saturday to know if The Squirrel Syndicate had won. Richard explained that the same thing kept happening to him. The pair resolved to put the syndicate online. The computer could say 'no.' If you were not in, then you were not in. A bit like a Welsh sheep farmer on Valentine's Day – they have an uncanny knack of knowing if they are in, or not. And that's how The Squirrel Syndicate was reborn online.

Back in the 60s in Rhyl, a chap called Albert Gubay ran a rock stall in the resort before hitting pay dirt. Mr Gubay went to a relative's wedding in the USA and enjoyed the discount shopping on offer. He saw a gap in the market and spotted the potential for discount stores in the UK. He sacked the rock stall in Rhyl and set up the first Kwik Save discount store in Prestatyn.

Like many Squirrel Syndicate members, Mr Gubay believed the banks rip you off and he managed to set up his own bank, Anglo-International, in later years on the Isle of Man. He made millions with the Kwik Save empire then sold it and set up another 3 Guys empire in New Zealand and then the USA and later sold Tesco their first super-stores in Ireland. Mr Gubay was to become the first entrepreneur to make millions on three continents in retailing.

Shrewd Mr Gubay made fortune upon fortune along the way. Not so long ago he owned the Total Fitness chain of gyms as his flair for founding a fortune continued. His was a remarkable success story rising out of sunny Rhyl. The syndicate's tabloid hack once interviewed him and learnt a very valuable lesson that offering value can make you a mint. In punting terms taking the value is everything – if you can back the same horse at 25-1 with one bookmaker and 16-1 at the rest... there's only one place to put the bet on.

Every true Squirrel Syndicate member has a love affair with the Grand National and they all have different tales to tell. Richard Brocklebank's love of the big race began at a very early age when Well To Do won the marathon at Aintree in 1972. The headline in the *Daily Mirror* on National Day was 'Well To Do Will Do For Me!' and the young Richard took Newsboy's advice. His first ever selection in the Grand

National bolted up at 14-1 carrying 10-13 – for years we all reckoned it best to back horses carrying under eleven stone in the race and it's a maxim that still holds true to this day.

Talk about being born lucky though as not many people pick the National winner anyway, let alone at such a healthy price. The horse was by French-bred Phebus out of Princess Puzzlement, and jockey Graham Thorner got him home ahead of Terry Biddlecombe on Gay Trip – the winner of the 1970 Grand National at odds of 15-1. That previous winner was the first selection and bet of the tabloid reporter, who later became The Spider with his weekly 'Scoop6' column in the *Daily Record*. The Squirrel Syndicate is like a stick of rock with members each having their own special Grand Nationals and those race winners were the names running through the syndicate's very core. It's a race that they've all always loved due to their roots in the North West.

Captain Tim Forster, the trainer of Well To Do, became no stranger to the winners' enclosure at Liverpool. He also trained Ben Nevis to win the race in 1980, and Last Suspect to succeed in 1985. The latter two won at enormous prices, 40-1 and 50-1 respectively, and each was backed by The Spider's dad, Charlie, a great fan of the horses and a Royal Navy sailor on the North Atlantic convoys in World War Two. Captain Forster was another military man and a renowned pessimist, but syndicate members en masse find it's always better to look on the bright side. A study has shown that optimists suffer less heart disease – it's a natural way of avoiding stress. We reckon the good Captain did well to train two more National winners after Well To Do with such a negative outlook – he might have trained another couple if he'd only expected more to win!

Thanks to their ages and love of racing, every original Squirrel Syndicate member was a Red Rum fan as well, so that provided lots of them with Grand National wins in 1973, 1974 and again in 1977. That massive battle with top weight Crisp will be re-run for generations as Rummy managed to get his head in front. That was one of the great examples of just how hard it is to carry top weight to victory in gruelling staying handicaps.

The old rule was well worth following in the mud at Chepstow over three decades later when Halcon Genelardais carrying 11-12 was just beaten a head by Miko De Beauchene off a perch of just 10-5 in the Welsh Grand National. The Alners who looked after Miko were always great trainers of staying chasers, just like the McCains. The sands of Southport worked wonders for Rummy and gave us all a lifelong love of McCain horses in the National. It was to pay off big time decades later when a fair few of us lumped on Amberleigh House to win the big race at 25-1 and 20-1. Still the winnings went on fine ale and good fun in, of all places, The Three Tunnes.

McCain's Cloudy Lane was quoted at 25-1 to win the Grand National in 2008 as the weights came out. A fair few had a decent bet for old time's sake. The horse was backed all the way in to 5-1 favourite and the big prices marked on our slips were looking good. Nobody laid off their bets on the Betfair exchange to get stakes back. On race day, a good few were kicking themselves for not doing so, as proven stayer Comply Or Die won, beating Cloudy Lane thirty lengths into sixth. The pair had met at Haydock a few months before, and over the shorter trip Cloudy Lane had come out on top.

It wasn't as if Eider Chase winner Comply Or Die wasn't well in, but the perceived value of Cloudy Lane at such big odds put a fair few off wading in again on a horse that started the day at 10-1 as it was forties and fifties when the weights came out. A winner is a winner, no matter what and, when the David Pipe-trained bay gelding under Timmy Murphy entered the winners' enclosure at 7-1 joint favourite, a good number of the guys realised they should have taken the 10-1 as it was value after all.

Some decades earlier, Foinavon's 100-1 Grand National triumph in 1967 had cost an acquaintance of Richard Brocklebank a fortune. Well-respected punter Tony Fairburn, who ran the highly successful Pot-Hunters Syndicate, missed out on a bumper payday because of it.

He told Richard and Ken one day how he had a very good tip for one of the races in the daily double on that Saturday in 1967. He crossed the tip with every runner except one in the other race, which he thought had no chance. The horse he left out was of course the fluke winner, Foinavon, and when his tip duly flew home first in the other race, he realised he'd missed out on a massive payday as there had been a very good rollover on the old Tote daily double. Years later when covering big fields in perms, that story stood The Squirrel Syndicate in good stead as Richard and Ken often slipped in an extra perm taking into account some of the enormous outsiders. You generally have a much better chance of picking up a big dividend if you cover all the horses in a race, but exactly how much you collect on pool bets depends how many other punters follow your picks. As The Squirrel Syndicate found out years later on more than one occasion, swimming against the tide was worthwhile a few times, as coming up with that all-important winning single ticket could be the result.

In 2009 the Venetia Williams-trained Mon Mome won the Grand National at 100-1 and The Squirrel Syndicate was toasting the triumph with champagne and other bubbly beverages. The horse was backed at 40-1 when the weights came out along with Butlers Cabin at 25-1. When the flag went up the latter was favourite at about 7-1 and Mon Mome was 100-1. It was an absolutely amazing winner to have and several syndicate members have paintings of the horse hanging in their homes. Let's say they all won a few quid and were more than happy to splash out on commissioned paintings by Ian Fennelly of the 100-1 winner for their hallways. To back a favourite at 25-1 is a result, but to have the winner at 100s was a much better one.

It wasn't a freak result like Foinavon, as only four months before, Mon Mome had been sent off the 7-2 favourite for the Welsh Grand National, so how it was 100-1 on the day at Aintree was amazing. It even paid around 156-1 on the Tote, but sadly The Spider reporting trackside on the big race never spotted that before the starter set them off. The internet, betting exchanges and modern betting is all very high speed and as a result it is hard work to keep on top of it all 24/7. Punters can get fantastic rewards, but they must always remember there are lots of other very precious things in life. Just don't tell them that when they're cheering home the winner of the Grand National at 100-1. After the race, a photographer friend of The Spider called to say, 'That was better than sex'... he had backed the horse to win a fair few quid. When later quizzed about the comment, the snapper pointed out that, at that particular point in his life he wasn't getting any, so no significant other was being slighted.

Chapter 4

VIVA LAS VEGAS

It's the gambling capital of the world and most members of The Squirrel Syndicate have a tale to tell of the bright lights of the Strip. Both Richard and the hack had been to Las Vegas on countless occasions. One for card counting and the other mainly for scribbling stuff down for publication round the planet.

As a result, one found himself in the legendary Griffin Black Book, while the other had his endeavours in the public interest splashed all over that other inimitable publication *The Sun*. Bizarrely, years later, like two star-struck meteorites both those worlds collided when a soap scriptwriter called John Stevenson turned up at Richard's car showroom to flog a green Mercedes. For it turned out jovial John had penned the *Coronation Street* Las Vegas spin-off that had seen the hack and a handful of his showbiz writing colleagues, including the effervescent John Mahoney from the *Daily Star*, transported to the Nevada Desert by the Granada TV press office for more than a week.

Scriptwriter John was a very amusing chap and did a lot of the comedy in the programme back in the day. With Jack and Vera Duckworth in the cast, John's genius was evident in their spin-off DVD *Viva Las Vegas!* as that feature-length production saw the TV cast and crew rocking up at the Rio in the mid-1990s.

Layabout couple Jack and Vera were played by Bill Tarmey and Liz Dawn. Liz at this point owned The Grapes in Manchester centre, where Richard many moons before had met Dave Rainford, a *Who Wants to Be a Millionaire?* £250k winner and later, a TV *Egghead*. The phrase 'small world' springs to mind. Also in the show was an actor called Neville Buswell, who starred as Ray Langton twenty-one years earlier but then quit to become a casino dealer in Las Vegas. As well as the

Duckworths in Vegas to renew their wedding vows, hairdressers Maxine Heavey and Fiona Middleton, played by babes Tracy Shaw and Angela Griffin, were also in the gambling capital of the world for comical antics that often backfired.

The hack had some fun in *The Sun* with pictures of both actresses Angela and Tracy. Even more entertainment for the masses followed when the latter's then boyfriend Darren Day turned up to help turn Las Vegas into Sin City. Spider tells a rather curious story of Darren in a Las Vegas sex shop before going for the ride of his life on the rollercoaster at New York, New York. But as they say 'What happens in Vegas, stays in Vegas.' But to be sure it made *The Hangover* Las Vegas movie look tame as some of Her Majesty's merriest tabloid hacks tripped the light fandango.

Mark Billings' book, *The Ultimate Edge*, tells the terrifying tale of Alexander Taylor being battered by six casino security guards in a bizarre case of mistaken identity at Lake Tahoe. He'd won over $1.5 million playing blackjack and ended up being beaten to a pulp by mistake. The casino never even found the computer strapped to his leg when they realised he wasn't their target, Rick Sandler, as they and their boss busily made up assault charges against him for allegedly thumping a couple of his security guard assailants. It's a funny old world and the hack was all too aware that a good hiding could be round the corner if the Granada press team decided to take out a Mafia-style hit on him for going one exclusive too far.

The potential downside for a punter of getting a thump for being too lucky is always in the back of your mind; except in Vegas, we all know the Mafia stories and a quick slap might be the least of your troubles. One-way helicopter rides to the centre of the Grand Canyon are part of the folklore, where they drop you off mid-air and you're told to make your own way back minus the chopper. Or a limo ride into the desert and the chance to dig your own grave. It's best not to dwell on them though, as you might never gamble again. As our tellies these days keep telling us, 'When the fun stops, stop!'

Meanwhile, Richard was also enjoying some fancy footwork on the Strip with Mr Magic Shoes himself, Gene Paoli, a card counting pal from Chicago, who had already ended up blood-soaked in Peaches nightclub in Stockport on an earlier expedition across the pond.

Gene was an Italian-American, tall with short, black curly hair and a receding hairline. Weirdly, when he first called Richard, there was a play on the telly about some American bloke with an English mum and they sounded so similar. His family had a bar and restaurant back in Chicago and Gene had what he called his 'magic shoes', which were ordinary shoes fitted with a toe-operated computer button to assist him with his card count.

While in Vegas he decided to have a new pair of playing shoes made. He took his ordinary shoes to be modified at a repair store on Paradise Road, near Tropicana. He explained to the cobbler how he needed them done so he could use the buttons with his toes. While he was in the shop, a rather attractive young lady entered. Not wanting to miss an opportunity with the fairer sex, Gene decided to exhibit the footwear and explain how his magic shoes could waltz her away to places she could only imagine. She appeared very impressed, by all accounts. It turned out she was also massively attentive; not because Gene was a babe magnet, but because she was a dealer at The Aladdin.

The blonde reported the incident to her bosses and they in turn called the Griffin Detective Agency and the Gambling Commission. When Gene returned to collect his new pair of shoes, there was a posse of agents in attendance. Turning swiftly round after entering the doorway, he was on his toes before anyone noticed. Unfortunately, the Griffin guys were so impressed with those magic shoes that they put out a 'special' sheet on them. A Griffin sheet is a bulletin containing interesting information that cannot wait for the regular bi-monthly publication. The bulletin is then delivered to Griffin subscribers all over the world, so Gene had, in a manner of speaking, shot himself in the foot.

Talking of backfiring, Richard's last trip of the '90s to Las Vegas with Gene occurred around the same time and, having enjoyed the Rio, where oddly enough Granada TV had hosted the British tabloid press, previously it was on the itinerary for the jaunt. Both the hack and Richard had enjoyed the Brazilian-themed atmosphere with the stage show featuring dancing girls, writhing on colourful carnival floats hanging from the ceiling and circulating the casino floor.

On this 1990s expedition, Gene, his wife, Malene, and Richard had gone into the Rio, which incidentally has a fantastic view across towards the Strip from the Voodoo Lounge on the rooftop. Anyway, as they were counting cards and it was going to be a long day at the office, Malene left them. Having forgotten the golden rule of never outstaying your welcome, they both got stuck into a heavy-duty card-counting session. Gene wasn't the most cautious customer, as the hilarious magic shoe episode possibly highlighted.

As it so happened, they enjoyed a spell of moderate success and secured complimentary tickets with $50 of free drinks in the lounge bar. Looking back, that might have been a ruse to get them off the tables. Yet, somewhat naively, they thanked the staff and decided to take up the offer. The lady at the bank desk asked Richard to stand a bit nearer the window as he was cashing their chips. He was suspicious, so asked 'Why?' and she replied, 'So that I can see your t-shirt?' Gene had left a little ahead and they planned to meet before hitting the bar.

After pocketing the folding, Richard headed to the meeting place and explained to Gene what had gone on and thought leaving might be a good idea. Gene suggested they carry on with the plan for free drinks, but as Richard had his suitcase in the hire car, they could both nip out and get changed. They headed out to the car park, popped the boot and changed into completely different shirts. Rather pleased with themselves they returned to claim their free drinks.

They began with a nice bottle of Californian sparkling wine from the bar and went and sat down at a good table overlooking the dance-floor. Yet before they managed to have even a couple of sips of their freebie, they were surrounded by a mean-looking bunch of smart-suited characters.

A big, fat, bald bloke, looking not unlike Boss Hogg from *The Dukes of Hazzard*, was their leader wearing a white suit. A couple of other massive guys, wearing earpieces, who wouldn't look out of place stepping off *Airforce One* in their black suits were the backup. Another two younger, wiry types, dressed just in grey shirts and slacks were backing them up. This pair looked like a couple of martial arts experts straight out of a Chuck Norris movie. Lumbering to the front was black suit number one, who demanded to see their ID. He displayed a lapel badge saying Detective Robert Zimmerman, which was no doubt designed to make them suspect he was some sort of police officer. Richard realised later that he was nothing of the sort, just a casino heavy using Bob Dylan's real name on his badge to misdirect the audience.

This pretty fierce group of characters announced they both had to leave and NOW. Rick and Gene were in no position to argue and stood up from the table. The enforcers removed the bottle of bubbles from Rick's hand and placed it back down. It wasn't the moment to ask if they could take it with them, as they were quite aggressive.

Instead of the casino exit, they got ushered towards a nondescript-looking wall and in it was a concealed door. They had visions of a Lake Tahoe-type thrashing coming their way as they were guided into this service area corridor, full of air conditioning ducts and boiler pipes. The intrepid pair feared the worse, as the sweat of pure fear started dripping on to their shirts, and they were led another hundred yards or so along the corridor. It seemed like they were being swallowed up into the bowels of the casino. The front of Richard's mind was filled with the potential horror of what was going to happen. Both had heard the Lake Tahoe story and were perspiring like a prince in a pizza parlour.

The bogus Zimmerman character halted them and then read out a warning from a card he produced from his pocket, which was apparently a Section 86 Notice under the US Criminal Trespass Law. This meant they could never go back to the Rio without permission. They were then photographed and that gave them each hope that their boyish good looks might well be saved. After the photography session was over, one of the karate kids kicked opened a fire door, which led directly out into the desert sun.

Outside were two far more friendly guys on mountain bikes. They greeted Rick and Gene and explained they had been briefed to escort them back to the car and off the premises. Feeling a little less fearful now, Richard asked them: 'Do you treat all your customers this way?' One replied: 'No Sir, you are in select company.'

They got back to the hire car and headed off away from the premises, which was a good result as they still had a bulging bankroll of dollars which they had liberated from the blackjack tables. It stopped the trips to Vegas for more than a couple of decades. They were told they would be put in the Griffin Black Book, which isn't the most helpful place to be featured if you are an advantage blackjack player. Almost an end to the new career before it had got fully going, but there was always the horseracing and lots more of that later.

The hack just kept right on visiting, mainly on expenses, and even got to a world title fight at the MGM Grand with his legendary photographic friend Arthur Edwards covering the event ringside. After that '£3 million in three weeks' episode, he later went back with the family for a week visiting all the shows from *Mamma Mia!* to Cirque du Soleil's fantastic Beatles extravaganza *LOVE*.

Richard's next trip to Las Vegas came in June 2019 for Halim Khan's stag do. Halim was one of our lawyer chum Mike Green's mates who Rick had met on Mike's 50th birthday trip to Cape Town, which was a golfing, wine tasting and fine dining treat. On the return to the casinos, Richard didn't do much gambling. The journey was all about enjoying the bars, the shows, the food and a few rounds for the golfers.

While in Vegas, Richard took the opportunity to pop along to the Flamingo and say hello to sports book manager Pete Saxton. He had moved there from Poynton, Cheshire, after winning very nearly £250,000 backing Frankie Dettori's Magnificent Seven on that fateful day at Ascot in September 1996. A bit more about Pete and his tale follows much later, as he was friendly with the hack even before his big win.

Suffice to say, Frankie made a lot of people very happy that day. One in particular was a joiner called Darren Yates, who put his last few quid on the seven and landed £550,000. Darren used the money to good effect and set up a building company, eventually selling one of his businesses for around £20 million. Darren then spent £1.8 million on four horses, including purchasing the most expensive National Hunt horse ever in the shape of Interconnected, for £620,000.

At the time of those horse purchases, Darren told a friend: 'After the win in 1996, I bought a couple of horses at £10,000 each with Jack Berry – Seventh Heaven and Toriana – but I also bought three-bed semis for around £20,000 each and they were much better buys. I used to buy a lot of cheap horses and have been doing that for around twenty years. I didn't have the money to buy nice horses, so I made it pay by gambling. I'd love to have paid a lot less for Interconnected.

'I'd really rather not hold the record for purchasing the most expensive National Hunt horse ever! The best one we had in the earlier gambling days was Kingscroft. We bought him at the sales for £25,000, an ex-Mark Johnston horse, and he had suffered an injury – a problem with a suspensory ligament that wasn't totally gone. We took our time getting him back with trainer Michael Herrington and his handicap rating came down to around sixty-eight from eighty-four. When he was ready, we ran him at Haydock and had apprentice Jacob Butterfield taking 5lbs off, so we were 20lbs in hand. We backed him from 25-1 down to 12-1 and won £350,000 that day, but he only just got up and won by a short head.

'We had another coup with Dazeen at 33-1 at Wolverhampton after eighteen months off with Robert Winston riding and I have a room at home with pictures from these great days at the races. The trainer was Paul Midgley and we backed him at 33-1 into 16-1 to win £250,000. We also won a couple more hundred thousands with Dazaki at big odds.'

We just love the audacity of gamblers like Darren who, as a carpenter by trade, knows a thing or two about hard graft, and you have to work hard to land gambles like that. On that fateful *Magnificent Seven* day in September 1996 when the Italian jockey rode all the winners on the card at Ascot, Darren had staked £60 on a Super Heinz and £1 each way on the accumulator.

He revealed: 'I'd paid the betting tax on top of 5p in the £1 and that saved me £27,000 as the win with William Hill was for £550,823.54. That's the most I've ever won, but the other year at Ascot I had backed Frankie to win a £1 million on that day when he got the first four winners – I still managed to land more than £250,000 at the meeting. Ladbrokes once offered me a VIP account on a Friday and on the Monday, they closed me down as I'd won £150,000 that weekend. I'd love Frankie to ride a Classic winner for us.'

His wife, Annaley, isn't complaining as Darren has been lucky in love as well as business and racing. The dad-of-two even named one of his horses after his adoring wife, though Annaley My Darling wasn't the winning machine they were hoping for. The pair live in a sprawling home in the seaside resort of Lytham St Annes, Lancashire. They have been together decades and their youngest, Bradley, now aged twenty-three, wasn't even born when Frankie rode those seven stunning winners, though his big sister Natalie, now twenty-seven, was a toddler.

Darren once said: 'I like naming the horses. Annaley My Darling was probably the only way I could have justified buying another horse at that time. Carlos Felix was the favourite son of the famous Spanish playwright and poet Lope de Vega, which is the name of the sire of my latest yearling, hence his name. I've given myself a two-year plan, we have the jumpers with Dan Skelton and I'll be taking stock and seeing what happens.'

The Squirrel Syndicate really hope for Darren's sake and that of racing that he gets Frankie to land a Classic for him, but like all successful punters he's giving himself thinking time. His 2019 spending spree started with the purchase of a horse called Blaklion for £350,000 to run in the Grand National, but the horse picked up an injury. Unperturbed, Darren went to the sales at Aintree almost on the eve of the big race and purchased Don Poli to run in the Grand National for £170,000.

Darren added: 'It was always my dream to have a runner in the Grand National and that was a fantastic day at the races that we both enjoyed, but next year with a little luck we'll be back with a proper chance of winning the big one.' He had no idea that Covid-19 would mean that the only Grand National any of us got to watch last year in 2021 was the virtual race on ITV.

Frankie firmly helped Darren get on the ladder, and funnily enough, the other year The Squirrel Syndicate was at an Open Day at Warren Greatrex's yard in Lambourn. There they met Mike Grech and Stuart Parkin, who actually owned Interconnected at that time. It was at their dispersal sale of 28 NH horses where Darren picked up Interconnected.

Mike and Stuart were on our table in a vast marquee at Warren's Uplands Stables Open Day. They had popped down from Greater Manchester in a helicopter; well, we guessed it was their chopper that was pitched up next to Richard's Range Rover during the day. The first person we bumped into on arrival was fellow Albatross Club member Ken Rhatigan, a well-respected local council leader. Many people believe Ken would make a first-rate prime minister, so if Boris gets on his bike, we know where our vote is going. His horseracing tips alone could cut the National Debt.

We also encountered Samantha Hills doing her Albatross Club photography session with a couple of rising stars in the shape of Miss Honey Ryder and Western Ryder, but sadly the latter is no longer with us. We mention Sam as we bumped into her Uncle Charlie Hills, the trainer, having a glass or two with Frankie's agent Peter Burrell in the Pheasant Inn and Hotel, a few miles away after stopping for a livener after lunch. They were both in good spirits and introduced us to the hotel owner, Mr Greenall, who offered us a discounted stay on our next expedition to the Lambourn Valley. It was another place with initials LV, so echoes of Las Vegas, but the room wouldn't be a freebie, although you never know. On the plus side, we won't be getting barred, or battered, visiting the Pheasant Inn.

Chapter 5

THE SQUIRREL IS BORN

It was a sunny morning July 27th 2004, when Spider made the phone call... it was strange, but it sounded fun as it was a sort of treasure hunt for a very expensive engagement ring lost in the woods which are in the red squirrel reserve in Formby, Merseyside.

Well, lost may not be the correct word, as apparently England soccer star Wayne Rooney's then fiancée Coleen McLoughlin had allegedly thrown the £25,000 sparkler into the trees after a row at their nearby £900,000 Formby mansion.

Now normally Richard wouldn't be contemplating looking for a needle in a haystack, but just a few days earlier he'd bagged £125,000 along with six other players with a wonderful Scoop6 win, so the thought of uncovering a diamond ring that wasn't buried treasure appealed. It had apparently got there when the then eighteen-year-old Coleen had reportedly flung away the expensive token of Wayne's affections. She was in a rage after confronting the Everton player about his supposed fling with twenty-one-year-old hooker Charlotte Glover, or so the newspapers claimed. It was clearly all just a storm in a teacup, or even D Cup, as Wayne and Coleen went on to marry in a multi-million-pound ceremony on the Italian Riviera in June 2008.

Anyhow, back in July 2004 Richard's new Bentley needed a spin and Spider reasoned that a trip to the seaside would take his mind off the free shot he had at landing the £375,000 Scoop6 bonus fund that coming Saturday. It had after all been preoccupying Richard and Ken's thoughts since the previous Saturday's win.

Richard rolled up at the squirrel woods expecting to see scenes like those from the California gold rush, but fortunately it wasn't that busy. In fact, it was pretty quiet, though a team from *The Sun* newspaper were on the spot with a metal detector and scouring every inch of the near hundred-acre wood.

They hadn't had much luck it transpired, yet inside a few minutes of stepping along the spectacular squirrel walk, Richard had spotted a sparkler about fifteen feet from the edge of the path. *The Sun* investigators were stunned, which was just what Richard had expected when he'd called into a couple of charity shops en route to purchase a few specimens just in case his luck ran out and he didn't find the real thing!

The nice chaps from *The Sun*, including The Spider, then offered to buy him lunch on their lavish expense accounts if he would chat to them alone about his sensational discovery. A free lunch would go some way to paying off the fuel bill, but what nobody was banking on was the birth of the Scoop6 Squirrel and quite possibly the most sensational syndicate of all time.

Now a few other mums we know, often say that giving birth is one of the most agonising experiences imaginable, but The Squirrel Syndicate literally popped out after a pain-free pint of bitter and a spot of chicken in a basket. The boozer *The Sun* team had taken Richard to was certainly no fine dining experience and Rupert Murdoch's billions were certainly safe in their careful hands.

As they chatted about his 'amazing' find, Richard swung the conversation round to his main intended subject, the Scoop6 bonus that coming Saturday at Glorious Goodwood. He lobbed into the conversation the possibility of wearing a gorilla suit to go to the races that coming weekend on the Suffolk Downs to try and unearth the other Scoop6 winners. And that idea only came up as the pub was near to a fancy dress shop and he'd seen a gorilla suit in the window. But at the table Spider, quick as a flash, made another suggestion… 'Why not go dressed as a giant squirrel?'

The Spider was spot on and that idea did pique Richard's interest, especially when it was suggested it would make the back page of the newspaper if he would pose for a picture whilst sitting on a tree stump reading a copy of their Saturday racing pull-out *The Favourite*. He loved the idea and reasoned it would make him odds-on to find the other Scoop6 winners and perhaps be able to team up with them for a combined attack on that £375,000 bonus. They shook hands and even included Richard's name in their story, which went something like this: 'Among the gold diggers was lucky punter Richard Brocklebank, 39, of Hyde, Cheshire, who won £125,000 on a winning Scoop6 racing bet on Saturday.

He said: 'My luck is really in – I reckon if anyone can find the ring today, it will be me.' Within minutes of stepping into the spectacular squirrel walk, sharp-eyed Richard had spotted a sparkler. He said: 'I'm going to get it valued and if it's Coleen's, I'll let her have it back. I'm hoping to be able to buy one myself this Saturday – as I'm also looking for six other ticket holders who won the Tote's £874,000 Scoop6 jackpot on Saturday. We're all getting a free shot at a £375,000 bonus this weekend – if we get together that'll be £53,571 each, so enough to buy a couple of identical rings to Coleen's. I saw the story on the front page of *The Sun* and thought it was worth a hundred-mile round trip as a bit of a long shot. I'm really surprised that there are only a handful of people prospecting here – I thought it would be like the California gold rush.'

' *The Sun* investigators used an enormous magnifying glass to check the sparklers on Richard's ring – the stones glittered, but we recommended a trip to the jewellers to get the gems valued.' Some of that little lot actually appeared in a newspaper with millions of readers nationwide, so a few of those might have known the other Scoop6 winners. It did not surprise anyone, and it should not surprise those of you reading this book, to learn that the ring 'found' was worth a paltry sum, compared to the one which Coleen had tossed into the woods. But Richard's donation to the charity shop, where he had in fact picked it up, proved money well spent.

On the way out of town, they called into the fancy dress shop by the car park to inquire after a red squirrel suit. The staff looked at the pair of them as though they were slightly deranged and tried to encourage them to hire the gorilla suit, but they told them very firmly that they weren't into any monkey business and it was a squirrel suit, or nothing. And so they left the shop empty-handed.

At that particular moment, they hadn't realised just how hard it was going to be to track down a fancy-dress squirrel outfit. They got the distinct impression by the time they'd rung two dozen fancy dress shops each that there was a collective opinion that these two particular callers were nuts. And that's when a little Squirrel logic entered the equation, as Richard thought to himself, nobody wears a squirrel suit as fancy dress, but what if a red squirrel sanctuary had one as a mascot?

It was like the Penny Falls at Rhyl from all those years ago, as the pair eventually unlocked the very squirrel suit that would lead them to another small fortune or two. It was somehow fate that The Squirrel suit Richard set out to hire was actually in the county of his birth, Cumbria. It came to pass The Squirrel was conceived and The Squirrel Syndicate was about to be born and unleashed on an unsuspecting world.

Richard made the long journey to collect the costume and was set to meet *The Sun* photographer Matt Pover in a nice wooded area, as they wanted the Scoop6 Squirrel to look authentic. The picture Matt took that sunny afternoon appeared in *The Sun* newspaper every Saturday for almost five years, but we're getting ahead of ourselves here.

Firstly, slipping into that rather dated costume, Richard suddenly felt like Clark Kent, Peter Parker and Bruce Wayne all rolled into one. For the uninitiated, they are the alter egos of Superman, Spiderman and Batman in that order. And as he placed that squirrel head on his shoulders, nobody had any real idea that Richard Brocklebank was about to be reborn as the Scoop6 Squirrel and The Squirrel Syndicate would become a stunning success. Now Harry Findlay was already known as Harry the Dog, but he'd have reckoned you were barking if you'd imagine people in the years ahead addressing Richard as The Squirrel!

That Saturday morning, as Richard set off for Goodwood at the crack of dawn, his picture was on the back page of *The Sun*, and the front page of *The Favourite* pull-out was filled with The Squirrel-suited image and the headline: 'Squirrel Ain't Nuts'. It was absolutely bonkers; from that trip to the squirrel woods at Formby, a monster may very well have been born. By the time he got to the track, Richard was already in touch with a couple of other Scoop6 winners. He slipped The Squirrel suit on again by the parade ring, where we recall a certain Clare Balding trying to concentrate on the horses as a seven-foot-tall squirrel attempted to invade the background of her TV crew's shots.

The nice people at the Tote had selected the day's big sprint, the Stewards' Cup, as the bonus race and Ken and Richard had selected

Pivotal Point as their bonus pick. They had teamed up with four other winners from the week before, so if they managed the winner then their £125,000 from the week before was suddenly £200,000. Being a sprint, it was very sudden indeed and the Peter Makin-trained Pivotal Point gambled into 7-1 co-favourite got the job done from stall thirty. Spider, that nice chap from *The Sun,* rang to congratulate them and suggested they might like to do a racing column for his esteemed newspaper, as having a flutter was his Saturday pastime, like most of the nation.

Happy to help as ever, the Scoop6 Squirrel was just about to get the legs to carry him forward for more than a decade. That Sunday they worked on a follow-up article under the headline: 'Squirrel Nut-Win'. Basically, *The Sun* loved the fact that The Squirrel wasn't nuts and that Spider would be providing a weekly column with a low-cost perm for their readers, in cahoots with Richard.

During *The Sun* years The Squirrel Syndicate literally won millions, but more importantly for them was the fact that *Sun* readers who followed the column won in the region of £10 million in those halcyon years. It was astonishing the way that such a small column in a mass market newspaper helped change so many readers' lives. At this point we have to give some credit to *The Sun's* then racing editor Trevor Clements.

Unbeknown to them at the time, Trevor was also a native of Cumbria, so he held red squirrels dear to his heart. Trev also enjoyed red wine and fine ale, so other things he had in common with The Squirrel Syndicate. Sadly, former stand-up comedian Trevor is no longer with us, but he lives on in many memories as a fantastically warm and funny man, who gave the Scoop6 Squirrel the coverage that only a genius could conjure up. With hilarious headlines and great joy, Trevor, with his roots in Whitehaven, made sure The Squirrel Syndicate was poised to go down in gambling folklore.

When The Squirrel's ghostwriter was made redundant by *The Sun,* Trevor turned up at his leaving do and asked, 'What does this mean for 'The Squirrel' column as we love it and want to keep it?' Quick as a flash, Spider, as we dubbed him, chipped up that things would have to change and Trev interjected: 'Like what?' The unemployed scribe then said simply: 'You're going to have to pay me as well as The Squirrel to do the column, as you've had it as a freebie for these past two years!' Big

Trev, he was a pretty tall guy, immediately broke into a broad smile and clapped the freshly unemployed hack on the back and said, 'That won't be a problem.' The sensible scribbler then put in invoice after invoice for his Friday efforts, but sadly Trevor was unable to eke out Richard's wages over the years in the region of £25,000 when he did eventually invoice. But he lives in hope.

His new *Sun* job was a serious venture and he and Spider spent hours doing their best to get the right picks for their readers. They had phenomenal success with their banker selections, but they always told the readers that the key to unlocking a fortune was to find the longshot. Now we did manage a fair few of them along the way, but one of our form choices tipped at a big price in *The Favourite* was Cockney Rebel in May 2007 when he landed the 2000 Guineas at Newmarket under Olivier Peslier. That 25-1 win was no shock to us, or to *The Sun* readers who followed the column. It was indeed happy days when he beat the high-class Vital Equine, his Champagne Stakes conqueror, by a length and a half at racing HQ. The Squirrel Syndicate simply loved longshots as they unlocked the single ticket wins.

Just to prove that result was no fluke, Cockney Rebel followed up by landing the Irish 2,000 Guineas at the Curragh three weeks later in equally impressive style. That made him only the sixth horse in racing history to pull off that particular double and the last racehorse to achieve that feat was Rock Of Gibraltar – who actually ran a slower time than Cockney Rebel in both races. Unfortunately, Cockney Rebel incurred a pelvic injury in the St James's Palace Stakes at Ascot when favourite at evens. This became Rebel's last race as he then suffered another injury to a tendon on the gallops and when connections heard it would take three months to heal, they retired him. He stood at the National Stud in Newmarket from 2008 until moving to stand at the Haras de Saint Arnoult stud in Normandy, France, in 2013. To date the most successful of his progeny has been the hurdler Cockney Sparrow.

Those early days of *The Sun's Favourite* racing column were great fun and they'd often go for a pint, or two, or even three, at what was then a fantastic old-style boozer on the A6 in Hazel Grove, Stockport, The Three Tunnes, when the column was put to bed. This being the old printing term for sending the hard copy off to the presses.

In June 2005, we had tipped up another longshot when we fancied six-year-old Sergeant Cecil, trained in the West Country by Rod Millman and ridden by Alan Munro to land the Pitman's Derby at Newcastle. We were on at 33-1, but the Sergeant only ever had one run in him and he came hard and late to land the race at 14-1 from Tungsten Strike and Far Pavilions. It was a wonderful bit of tipping and on the same day another *Sun* favourite tipster Sir Clement Freud also gave the nod to longshot Sergeant Cecil to win the twenty-runner Northumberland Plate – to give the race its proper name.

At Trevor's funeral we later learned that Sir Clement was apparently on £5,000 a week for his column and we were getting a fraction of that. Back in the day, Trevor would apparently pop along to Sir Clement's club and hand over the readies in cash. We can only imagine what fine cigars and brandy were taken on those particular paydays.

Jockey Alan Munro forged a fantastic relationship with the six-year-old stayer and he did us plenty of favours that season landing the Ebor at York at odds of 11-1 and then the Cesarewitch at Newmarket at 10-1. In pulling off that remarkable hat trick, Sergeant Cecil, who had been purchased for £1,000 as a foal, became the first horse in history to land the tremendous treble of all three top staying handicaps in the British racing calendar.

His owner was a chap called Terry Cooper who named the horse after his father, Sergeant Cecil Edward Cooper. What a way to remember your dear old dad! And Terry had to chip in an extra £400 to the breeder Don Hazzard in Dorset when his horse won two races. The Squirrel Syndicate reckons Terry won a fair bit more than that, backing his horse to do that unique treble, so won't have been crying into his champagne for too long having kicked in the extra payment clause.

The following season, as a seven-year-old, Sergeant Cecil transitioned successfully into weight for age races and landed another decent treble of the Lonsdale Cup, Doncaster Cup and Prix Du Cadran at Longchamp on Arc Day. And for those three superb victories none other than The Squirrel's all-time favourite flat jockey was on board; yes, the legendary Frankie Dettori.

After the Doncaster win on September 8th 2006, Frankie said: 'This horse hasn't stopped surprising people and he's become a household name. He doesn't know how to run a bad race and he's always there for you.' Gushing with pride in the Town Moor winners' enclosure after his length victory from Alcazar, trainer Rod Millman said: 'The horse is a privilege to be involved with. He's just a great credit to the team. I'm just the front man.' The final win of his phenomenal career, particularly when you consider the initial purchase price of £1,000, was the Yorkshire Cup in 2007 under Jimmy Fortune. The old warrior never won another race, but was retired to do a spot of dressage and ended up living out the rest of his retirement with his owner Mr Cooper.

The Squirrel Syndicate has no immediate plans to put themselves out to grass, but will be looking out more winners from our collection of slightly musty copies of *The Favourite* from the super soaraway *The Sun* years. We do recall not long after the column started getting an invite from The Tote's then supremo in charge of business development Ed Comins for a memorable day at their box at York. Ed was gushing in his praise for *The Favourite* column revealing that before we launched it, the Scoop6 featured syndicates placing major bets and lots and lots of £2 players, but after The Squirrel spread the word, they started to see lots of perms put on by pals down the pub of £50, £100, or even £200, or more. It was very nice that Ed had noted the difference we'd made to the bet in just a few short months of weekly publicity. The Squirrel Syndicate was born in The Three Tunnes and it was fitting that we met many other pub syndicates with decent wins back in the day.

Chapter 6

SYNDICATE EARLY YEARS

Those nice people at the Tote really relished the new 'Scoop6 Squirrel' column and readers of *The Sun's Favourite* pull-out were swiftly warming to their new furry friend. It was wonderful as far as we were concerned, as we were suddenly breathing new life into what for us was the best bet on the planet.

In October 2004 we got the Tote to hand over some £1,000 perms to *Sun* readers. The win and bonus pools were building and the Scoop6 was being rejuvenated by a rather large Scoop6 Squirrel spreading his permutations on a weekly basis in *The Favourite* pull-out. The Tote were quick to ride the crest of this new wave with their generous offer via the column's ghostwriter Spider.

On October 16th we revealed how joiner Anthony Ion, aged forty-five, from Newcastle-Upon-Tyne, had landed the free £1,000 perm and that week we made Quedex, at 66-1 in the Cesarewitch, the 'Scoop6 Squirrel' column's single banker. It was a longshot, but we felt it was a value bet to nothing and would be paying more than 16-1 for the place if things didn't quite go to plan.

The eight-year-old had no luck in running and was beaten by just over a length after being backed into 33-1. If only Mr Ion had slipped The Squirrel Syndicate's single banker in his £1,000 perm, he would have collected four place lines of £2,306 each, so a bumper £9,224 for taking a chance on our recommendation. We did do well with those single bankers, but we probably never tipped that many at 16-1 that won, so we took the 66-1 at those place odds all day long.

It was that same month October in 2004 that one of the most tragic episodes in Scoop6 history unfolded. It was the penultimate leg in the bet on October 30th when the drama began to take shape. In the 3.10 at Newmarket, The Squirrel's selection, the Mark Tompkins-trained

Babodana under Darryll Holland at 9-2 favourite, passed the post a short head in front of John Gosden's 5-1 joint second favourite Sleeping Indian under Jimmy Fortune.

Following a lengthy stewards' inquiry Sleeping Indian was awarded the race with Babodana placed second, but the pain of that decision only became evident when David Barron's Zero Tolerance under Paul Hanagan at 9-1 won the 3.45, the final leg of that week's Scoop6. And it wasn't evident to everyone at first glance how heartbreaking it was for one particular pensioner. Yet in a living room in Walkergate, Newcastle, Jack Lee, aged seventy-five, was cursing those stewards at HQ for reversing the placings had cost him a single ticket Scoop6 win and a tax-free pension top-up of £859,000 – not to mention a crack at the bonus.

When news came out about just how hard the stewards at Newmarket had caned Jack, punters everywhere shared his turmoil after his £2 bet so narrowly missed landing him a proper fortune. Even cold-hearted bookies, like Totesport and Ladbrokes, wanted to help and offered Jack a £500 free bet the following week. Jack was an absolute gentleman who loved his Saturday afternoon racing, and The Squirrel Syndicate challenged him to a head-to-head tipping contest in *The Sun* that coming Saturday. We spoke to Jack on the Friday ahead of publication and that's why we know he was a true gent. Jack gave us the benefit of his wisdom and was going to the races at Doncaster the next day with some pals for a great day out. We wished him well and Jack was also due on Channel 4's *Morning Line* and we promised to tune in.

The head-to-head with your furry friend started that Saturday at Wincanton and both the syndicate and Jack tipped up Comply or Die to land the 2.05 for a certain Martin Pipe and a chap, called in those days simply AP McCoy. AP duly romped home on the future Grand National winner in the ToteScoop6 Rising Stars Novices' Chase. In the next leg at Doncaster Jack managed another winner with Quito at 7-2 favourite that beat our selection of Millennium Force 13-2 into second place. The next leg was the November Handicap at Doncaster and Jack plumped for 20-1 shot Distant Prospect who came a gallant second when our selection failed to make the frame.

In the next leg, the 3.10 at Wincanton, it was Jack's turn to finish out of the frame with our selection Gunther McBride landing the place money in second at 7-2. Then in the 3.25 at Doncaster Paul Hanagan did us a favour getting the Richard Fahey-trained Breaking Shadow home in front at 16-1 with Jack's pick out of the frame. We managed a place in the final leg, the 3.40 at Wincanton, with Howle Hill at 7-2 while Jack's selection finished down the field.

That very Saturday a punter from Cadishead, Greater Manchester, called Stuart Bolland included The Squirrel's 16-1 winner Breaking Shadow in his perm and became the first millionaire in a British bookmaker's shop, collecting his share of the Tote riches from his local Betfred.

Meanwhile, *Sun* reader Russell Smith, a forty-four-year-old bricklayer, from Canvey Island, Essex, found the first four winners, but left The Squirrel Syndicate's 16-1 winning pick Breaking Shadow out of his perm which left the loot to Stuart. Big-hearted Stuart, aged forty-two, who won a bumper £1.1 million, did a deal with Betfred to present Jack with a cheque for £15,000 as a gesture of goodwill, but on the eve of the handover ahead of Stu's attempt at the bonus race, the unlucky pensioner passed away.

The bonus race that coming weekend was the Paddy Power Gold Cup at Cheltenham. Course and distance winner Monkerhostin off bottom weight looked to have a great chance for trainer Philip Hobbs. As well as a £115,658 Scoop6 win fund that Saturday, there was also a massive jackpot rollover that reached £365,824 at Cheltenham. Now four of the Scoop6 races were at the Cotswolds track and The Squirrel Syndicate decided to try and land either the Scoop6, or the jackpot, as the final leg in both would be the 3.55 at Cheltenham.

Ahead of racing, Spider had taken a call from a regular column reader who had won the Scoop6 previously, and he was quizzing the correspondent on why we had tipped Monkerhostin to land the Paddy Power Gold Cup. Spider explained that, pure and simple, Monkerhostin looked to have a great chance and probably had Paul Nicholls' Thisthatandtother under Ruby Walsh to beat, with Martin Pipe's Celestial Gold under Timmy Murphy a longshot well worth considering.

Now Spider had invested a tenner on the three of them in combination exactas and, when Celestial Gold at 12-1 beat Thisthatandtother at 13-2 with Stuart Bolland's bonus pick Monkerhostin at 3-1 favourite back in third, he was particularly happy. The exacta paid £171.30 to a quid stake, so he had a nice tickle to a tenner though had failed to place a £1 on the trifecta, which paid a bumper £1,021 to a quid.

Our main aim was the bigger prize of the Scoop6 though and that bonus had now rolled. We had another four legs to get through the Scoop6 and our hands on that £115,000 prize with just two legs left in the jackpot and two races remaining at Cheltenham. The Scoop6 winners at Wetherby and Uttoxeter went in and the penultimate race at Cheltenham went to Pipey and Timmy again with Stormez at 7-1.

That took us into that final leg with a few shorter-priced runners for a single ticket Scoop6 win and the longshots at Cheltenham for a possible £365,824 jackpot win or rather half of that as we were playing to 50p. When the 3.55 went to 10-11 favourite Cerium for Paul Nicholls with Ruby Walsh on board we'd landed a single ticket Scoop6 win, so happy days. Though the second was Phar Bleu at 20-1 for trainer Georgina Nicholls with a certain Barry Geraghty on board and if he'd been a few lengths faster then we'd have settled for the single ticket jackpot win. With hindsight, it was highly likely for an additional outlay that we could have landed both, but eighteen tickets collected £14,429 each from the jackpot, so leaving it behind wasn't the end of the world.

Richard had been watching the races with Ken in Stretford and when that 3.55 was won, it was time to slip out for some celebratory pints just like the lads down The Three Tunnes. A little knees-up after putting yourself in pole position for a crack at the £800,000 bonus fund never goes amiss.

Before heading out for a few well-earned ales Richard safely tucked the winning slip in that Saturday's *Favourite* racing pull-out and hid it under a cushion on the sofa at Ken's house for safety purposes. Well, one pint led to another and we all had a fair few, but retrieval of the winning ticket wasn't an issue until after the weekend. Unbeknown to us, Ken's dear old mum, Irene, decided to do a tidy-up and a bit of recycling. The newspapers were collected from everywhere, including a paper with a winning slip for £115,658 placed in it, and dropped off in the nearby paper recycling bin.

It was a weekday before the hunt for the missing ticket got underway. Both Richard and Ken could have sworn they knew precisely where they had left it, but it wasn't there. They turned the house upside down and were puzzled. They thought perhaps coming in slightly inebriated, they had decided to place it somewhere even safer, so the search went on; never for one minute expecting the six-figure ticket to have been spring-cleaned into a skip on the street.

It was only after the panic had truly set in that Ken's dear mother, Irene, asked what all the excitement was about. When they explained they were looking for a particular newspaper, their dilemma looked even darker as she explained she'd popped them all in the recycling skip. At this, the pair set off at full pace for the skip. Thank the Lord the recycling wagon hadn't been and after scrabbling through copies of all the daily and Sunday newspapers, plus a couple of rather interesting Playboy magazines with a few pages stuck together, they finally got their paws on the one the syndicate wanted. It may well have been a sign that the upcoming bonus that turned out to be £804,000 was coming home.

Spider, before we'd realised we were planning a major Scoop6 bonus adventure, had arranged to meet a couple of his pals from schooldays on Merseyside in The Three Tunnes while watching the afternoon racing from Huntingdon and Lingfield that coming weekend. He had clearly had a couple of celebratory scoops the weekend before, and most people in the pub having witnessed this knew we were going for a bumper bonus that Saturday. As he turned up to meet his pals Denis and Yozza, the drummer and bassist from a new wave band called Always Caught In Disney, they were stunned with how many people were clapping him on the back and wishing him well.

One of the wags said, 'Christ, it's like going for a pint with Don Corleone.' When it was explained that his furry friends in The Squirrel Syndicate were aiming for an £804,000 bonus win with third favourite Blue Americo in the fourteen-runner 2.25 at Huntingdon, the guys were pretty stunned.

The day before, we'd narrowed the possible picks down to three or four; with Paul Nicholls and Ruby Walsh, the winning combination from the last leg the week before teamed up on Blue Americo, Mylo the eventual second favourite and well-backed favourite Kelly all in the mix with the longshot Fard Du Moulin Mas a late non-runner. Huntingdon passed an inspection that morning and, with Blue Americo having form on soft ground, that was the choice and he won well enough at 5-1.

With old schoolfriends in tow we were heading into Manchester for extra celebrations. But, when one of Richard's old Stockport Grammar School pals turned up with about four people from his local Max Spielmann's shop, we had no idea how embarrassing it would become.

While Spider's friends stood their corner, buying round after round and revelling in the good fortune, Richard's Cambridge-educated old SGS chum carefully dodged putting his hand in his pocket at every opportunity. By the time we'd reached the later drinks and the fantastic music in the Fab Cafe it was clear he'd not purchased a single drink, which was spectacularly poor form. Yet The Squirrel Syndicate had landed the best part of £920,000 in the past week or so, and we all carried on getting them in until it became a blur.

Thinking back, the band of that name was probably on the playlist at some point. It was a spontaneous knees-up and great fun; even the kids from Max Spielmann enjoyed it and we'd not had a photo finish all day at the races that we could remember. Though after the way the beer was flowing, none of us recall much past Blue Americo winning on the good to soft going at Huntingdon. It turned out that Spider's friends' band was one of the few from Merseyside that failed to make the big time at a point when Radio One DJ John Peel was promoting anything from Liverpool with a pulse.

The week after, we gave Francois Doumen's Baracouda as a single banker in the opening leg of the Scoop6 and he scooted in under that man AP McCoy again, but the pools were pretty drained and it would be a good while before we'd really be pulling on our betting boots again. But the job of assisting regular readers of our *Sun* column continued, despite the abundance of champagne in our bloodstream.

The first weekend in December a month or two later, we tipped up three nice winners in the column at Sandown. In the William Hill Handicap Hurdle, we gave Monte Cinto at 8-1 yet another big race winner for Paul Nicholls and Ruby Walsh; and before the Tingle Creek Chase at Sandown, we gave Contraband at 10-3 with the third winner coming in the last race at Wetherby, Fashions Monty. Those three proved the bedrock of a bet for 'Squirrel' column fan and grand-father-of-two, Jim Spence, aged fifty-seven, from Helen's Bay, County Down, Northern Ireland, who found three winners of his own to land

£13,000 plus for a fifth share of that weekend's Scoop6. Lucky Jim tried to trace the other Scoop6 winners. We published his mobile number in the column, as his fear was that all five would pick the same horse and the bonus of £29,000 would roll without them getting a further tickle.

Funnily enough, when Spider had done the column, we had once again tipped Monkerhostin as our banker to land the bonus race, the aptly named bonusprint.com Gold Cup Handicap Chase at Cheltenham, and in the same race we gave Europa as a longshot. On the Saturday morning Jim rang to suggest we had tipped up Monkerhostin as we didn't fancy it and asked what we really liked; almost a carbon copy of the telephone call that was taken a couple of months earlier.

Well, as it happens we really liked Philip Hobbs' Monkerhostin, who was reunited with jockey Richard Johnson. Spider had backed him to turn the Paddy Power Gold Cup form round with Thisthatandtother for Messrs Nicholls and Walsh. Jim seemed to be suggesting we were steering the readers on a 'wrong 'un', but when he asked what would win, we explained we really, really liked Monkerhostin to beat Thisthatandtother, which it transpired was his bonus selection, with Europa back in third. And so it came to pass, not-so-lucky Jim did ring up after the race and say, 'I hope you had the trifecta.'

Strangely enough, though missing out on the last trifecta with Monkerhostin in, Spider still hadn't learnt his lesson and missed this one at £301.18 for a quid, though did once again have a tenner on the exacta – although on this occasion that only paid about 21-1. Incidentally, none of the other bonus chasers dialled Jim's winners' alliance mobile number, so one of the others joined him on Thisthatandtother while the other three were all on faller Our Vic – nobody went with The Squirrel's winning banker Monkerhostin, but at least Jim had a saver on our wonderful 4-1 shot.

The week before Christmas we gave single banker Rambling Minister which won at Newcastle at 11-10 favourite and our longshot One Nation got backed into 10-1 for a fine six-length victory at Warwick. But the Scoop6 pool had been drained the week before with another five winners and it was time to have the festive season off. With Christmas Day falling on a Saturday, it was a case of a Boxing Day Scoop6, but that day in the Indian Ocean a terrible tsunami struck that claimed

227,898 lives and cost the economy billions.

In Thailand at the time was a TV journalist called Gavin Hill, who was alerted to the disaster by his pal Spider. Gavin polished off his camera and went along to capture some images of the carnage caused by the tsunami. Years later we met up in Blighty with Gavin, who at that point had created and filmed a TV series that was to be called something like *Big Trouble in a Country* that specialised in mail order brides, a title he had not wanted. Richard ended up helping him, via his debt recovery business with Ron Piddington, to successfully win a payout from a UK-based TV company. They had sold Gavin's TV programme to broadcasters in Australia, and he was soon to be big down under, if you'll pardon the phrase.

The next Scoop6 was New Year's Day 2005, but the main aim of our column on January 1st was to bring up the hat trick of single banker winners for readers and thanks to jockey Joe Tizzard and his trainer dad, Colin, we pulled it off. Having plumped for their Brave Spirit in the Betfred 'The Bonus King' Southern National Chase over three miles and three furlongs at Fontwell – it was pretty nail-biting as it turned into one heck of a battle in the closing stages with our 2-1 favourite just holding on by a neck from Peter Winkworth's 16-1 shot Levallois, with that great horseman now turned trainer Philip Hide in the saddle.

With Haydock abandoned the next week, our run of winning bankers came to an end, but normal business was resumed at Wincanton on January 22nd when we gave Christopher the 3-1 winner of the 2.35 as a banker. It was a tasty five-length winner for the combination of Philip Hobbs and Richard Johnson, a formidable pairing.

Our bid for a fifth winning banker from the last six given in *The Favourite* pull-out went pear-shaped in the Sky Bet Chase at Doncaster on January 29th when we tipped trainer Ferdy Murphy's Your A Gassman, only for this fella to spring a gas leak and finish out of the frame in sixth under Brian Harding. An end to the Scoop6 Squirrel banker winning spree was inevitable.

In gambling as in life, the tide goes out, yet you need to still be around for when it next comes in. Little did we know at this point that a tsunami of winnings was still to come during our *Sun* Scoop6 Squirrel Syndicate years. We are very glad we kept dipping our paws in the water.

Chapter 7

MORE SCOOP6 SUCCESS

It was February 2005 when your furry friends were feeling very flattered to have helped a young office worker land more than £230,000 in a Scoop6 win and bonus funds in the same month. The thirty-year-old novice Scoop6 player from Sheffield linked up with us at the start of the month as one of twenty-eight winners of a £300,000 win fund after just fifty runners were declared overnight in the six races in the bet from Sandown and Wetherby.

That week we had confidently predicted the Scoop6 would be won. We recommended a perm with four selections in the final leg at Sandown, which French raider Innox at 9-2 under Robert 'Choc' Thornton turned into a procession with a nine-length victory. That last leg, the three-mile Class 2 Agfa Diamond Chase, only had twelve runners after one of the leading fancies, Bathwick Annie, was withdrawn due to unsuitable ground, and you probably only needed three picks rather than four in the end. The Yorkshire chappie had used a £64 Squirrel Syndicate perm to plunder a small fortune.

This guy from Sheffield called The Squirrel hotline that following week asking if he could link up with us in an alliance of winning ticket holders for a share of a £200,000 bonus fund, and we let him do just that. We also had a kitchen fitter, Gary Foxall, aged thirty-three, who was cooking with gas after his syndicate won £10,547 using our perm. We put him in with us and twenty-three other ticket holders to land a share of the bumper bonus. The Tote selected the twenty-seven-runner Totesport Trophy Handicap Hurdle, and when the Irish raider Essex at 4-1 favourite under Barry Geraghty duly obliged, our new-found Yorkshire friend was thrilled as his internet account was looking even healthier.

For some strange reason, this fella didn't want us to use his name in print, so we had a guessing game on the reasons behind that. Most likely he'd been involved in a messy divorce and didn't want his new gains to get taken into account. Whatever it was, it wasn't our business and he was so complimentary about The Squirrel Syndicate and *The Sun's* Templegate's tips that we were very happy to help him.

Roll on a week or so, and our chums at the Tote told us an internet player from Yorkshire was behind the most recent single ticket £150,000 Scoop6 win. It wasn't rocket science for us to work out it was highly unlikely that two people in Yorkshire at that time could actually use a computer, so we called up the skittish Sheffield resident.

Initially, he was reluctant to confirm his success, but when we explained the clear Squirrel Syndicate logic, the office worker confessed it was in fact him. Once again we could tell the story, but not use his name as he went for a £61,000 bonus in the *Racing Post* Handicap Chase at Kempton.

We were able to use the following quotes from him in that Saturday's column as he said: 'Thank you my *Sun*! I only started doing the Scoop6 after reading The Squirrel and seeing how well he has done. I have been doing the bet on and off but have played about five times in the last two months and this is my third win. For me, Templegate's tips and The Squirrel's perms are a winning combination. The perm landed me £7,000 in place money on top of the win fund of £143,000. It was brilliant.'

As well as The Squirrel's winning single banker Inglis Drever the week before, he'd had a clutch of Templegate winners and Tom Pepper's Nap Whereareyounow – what a sensational advert for *The Sun's* racing pages. Due to his desire for anonymity, the chap turned down an appearance on Channel 4's *Morning Line* ahead of tackling the nineteen-runner *Racing Post* Handicap Chase at Kempton, which had to pass an inspection to race.

Ahead of the opening contest he actually called us to ask what we liked in the race. We had tipped up the top weight Farmer Jack off 11st 12lbs with Richard Johnson getting the leg up for Philip Hobbs in the column, and told him we'd no intention of changing our mind. When his bonus pick later appeared on the Channel 4 screen just ahead of the 3.45, we noted he was on Farmer Jack.

After Jack jumped the last and forged clear for a six-length win as we were watching the Saturday action unfold in The Three Tunnes. The mobile phone went, and it was our chum from Sheffield thanking us for the tip. He didn't have to do that, so it was nice. It was also wonderful to hear that he planned to buy us a pint. Needless to say, he was a genuine Yorkshireman and we've still not had that beer off him.

It wasn't until mid-April that another syndicate of *Sun* readers had a Scoop6 tickle when carpenter Aidie Vearncombe was one of three winners to land a share of the £165,000 win fund. We had tipped up three winners in our column the week before, including single bankers Penkenna Princess at 7-2 and Indesatchel at 11-10 favourite at Newbury, with Genghis up at Ayr, so the other winners could well have been *Sun* readers too. Aidie had a six-strong syndicate including his joiner son Spencer, a chippie off the old block, in his group operating from The Old Inn at Allington in Wiltshire. From memory they never got the £70,816 bonus as we seem to recall it was the nineteen-runner Betfred Gold Cup Handicap Chase at Sandown with the prize money going back to the Emerald Isle thanks to Ted Walsh's 16-1 raider Jack High.

The last week of the month was 2000 Guineas Day at Newmarket, and it was a very tricky Scoop6 indeed with ninety-nine runners and not a massive amount in the win fund thanks to Aidie and the boys. Still, for the sake of *Sun* readers, we were studying hard. Although we kicked off the day with a winning single banker in the shape of Notable Guest at 15-8 favourite with Mick Kinane on for Sir Michael Stoute in a Newmarket race with seventeen declared overnight, as predicted, nobody landed the win fund.

Our run of winning single bankers was going strong into May with Philharmonic storming in at Beverley from stall one in the five-furlong Coachman Caravans Conditions Stakes for Richard Fahey. It was Paul Hanagan, the man again on board, as Philharmonic came with a well-timed run in the final furlong to win, going away by three lengths from trainer Dandy Nicholls' Ayr Gold Cup winning sprinter Funfair Wayne. Beverley has a distinct bias for low drawn horses on the sprint course, so Mr Hanagan was ideally drawn to get a tune out of Philharmonic. He delivered his triumphant run up the rail to make it four winning bankers from the last five weeks for the column.

Just as our winning banker run came to an end, another door opened with a Scoop6 win and once again some *Sun* readers got lucky with us and we reckon fans of the column netted a large slice of the £340,000 win fund. On top of that, we got a share as well, so all was hunky-dory at home in our various dreys. The bonus attempt for the £216,000 in the rollover pool was joyous as we'd got ourselves and nine *Sun* readers in pole position for an extra tickle from a free shot at the winner of the Totesport Silver Bowl Heritage Handicap over a mile at Haydock.

A couple of *Sun* readers though decided against joining us and factory worker Ron McCue, aged fifty-three, of Carterton, Oxfordshire, who won the week before with a £4 bet, went on his own only to then have his selection Notability 3-1 favourite beaten by a short head by 'The Squirrel's' column tip Home Affairs at 7-2. Ron was on a £9.50 *Sun* holiday in a chalet in Cornwall and had just dashed through the door to watch the bonus race and saw The Squirrel Syndicate's pick beat his fancy, but the dad-of-three had even more bad luck on the return from his holiday as he got made redundant.

We had two of our ten combined tickets on Home Affairs with Richard Hughes in the plate for Sir Michael Stoute and a further three on the second and we even had the third Enforcer at 8-1 covered.

The other go-it-alone *Sun* reader was retired club steward Dennis Page, aged sixty, of Whittlesey, near Peterborough, who had been persuaded to have his first £2 on the Scoop6 the week before and turned that into grands with a brilliant bit of beginner's luck. Dennis, who quit work after a heart op, went with his lucky number seven Beaver Patrol and if that eventual fifth had actually won he'd have landed the £216,000 all on his own. That said, Dennis wasn't too disappointed though and told us the Scoop6 was so much better than the National Lottery and he'd be following The Squirrel and forming a syndicate with his brothers moving forward. These days the Must Be Won National Lottery draws are often much better value than the Scoop6 - it's funny how things change.

With the pools drained at the end of May, June was always going to start quietly. A highlight later in the month was the Tote rescuing *Channel 4 Racing* with a £3 million sponsorship deal to keep our Scoop6 Saturdays on terrestrial TV. Only the week before, we'd gone nuts to discover that locals at the Hadley Bowling Green Inn at Droitwich in Worcestershire were actually dining on squirrel terrine. The very thought of them swallowing our common grey cousins left a bad taste in the mouth, but the chef very sensibly took the dish off the menu before the month was out.

June ended with that marvellous 'Squirrel' column tip for Sergeant Cecil in the Northumberland Plate, but we won't go into that again; suffice to say, we were chuffed with the victory. Sadly, for one *Sun* reader from Gwent, they just missed out on the £443,828 win fund after backing the Sergeant and our winning banker Wrighty Almighty with three other good winners, only to stumble in the one other leg; so close, but no cigar, as they say in that particular part of South Wales.

With June ending joyfully, it was only fit and proper that July started with another stunning Squirrel success on the Scoop6 and a bumper £400,000 fell into our syndicate's paws. In the paper that morning, July 2nd, we had tipped 9-1 winner Ace Of Hearts in the ToteScoop6 Heritage Handicap at Sandown on Coral Eclipse Day and chipped in another five nice winners with it in a bumper perm as the win fund had reached almost £680,000. We split that pool with another ticket holder, netting £339,442 from the win portion with a further twelve place tickets worth a whopping £5,166 each - taking the total for the tickle to over £400,000.

That following Saturday morning we focussed the column on syndicate member Steve Schofield, from Stockport, who credited the excitement of the win for putting his glamorous and very pregnant wife, Rachel, into labour forty-eight hours later and delivering a delightful daughter, Olivia. Needless to say, office manager Steve wasn't short of shekels to wet the baby's head and was renowned for his generosity.

But we, and around a dozen others, all wanted a chance at a further celebration in the shape of landing a share of a £290,000 bonus fund having teamed up with the other winner from the week before. It was the forty-sixth running of the John Smith's Cup at York, an ultra-competitive handicap, and it will go down as another wonderful winning day. Aidan O'Brien had sent over the lightly raced and progressive Mullins Bay with Kieren Fallon booked to ride, but the stall nineteen draw was slightly off-putting. Yet, a sustained gamble saw Mullins Bay go off 4-1 favourite. We had him plus the second favourite both covered in the bet. Everyone was clapping and cheering in the Tunnes when Kieren kicked on to draw clear inside the final furlong, scoring by three lengths.

A fortnight later on July 23rd, it was a week before the sixth birthday of the Scoop6. To mark the occasion, the Tote gave us £600 to give away as a free bet with 'The Squirrel' column to be played on the anniversary of that first bet on July 30th. It coincided with the first birthday of the Scoop6 Squirrel and after Steve's daughter Olivia was born, we were on a roll with a birthday boom. For just days after that first anniversary in the Scoop6 Squirrel role, Richard's wife Ruth delivered a new bundle of fluff in the shape of their second son Robert. Now, no matter how much joy we got out of the Scoop6 wins and we did get a lot, nothing compares to the elation of becoming a dad again. So, win or lose, we were all planning to go out celebrating and wet the baby's head.

Incidentally, *Sun* reader Doug Glover, aged sixty-four, won our £600 perm prize. Yet like so many others in that anniversary week, Doug went out in the opening leg after Dancing Rose romped in at 14-1. At Squirrel Towers Richard's house was ringing with the sound of a new-born. Elder son Thomas had taken very kindly to his new role as a big brother. A great result all round.

August 2005 was memorable for many things, one of them being the fantastic Ashes win for England with Freddie Flintoff hitting the Aussies for six at Old Trafford and pretty much everywhere else. Earlier that year we'd bumped into a nice, young Aussie chap, if that's not a contradiction in terms. We met him on our annual pilgrimage to Aintree, and one of his pals was playing at Old Trafford against Freddie and our boys. The initial meeting was on the bus back to Lime Street, as Merseyrail had decided to go on strike for the Aintree meeting, meaning the trains were not running. Scouse shop stewards know how to cause some chaos.

Early evening, we ended up going for a few beers with him in Liverpool and later took him for a curry in Stockport. He loved his sport and wanted to see as much as possible when in Blighty. We told him that York was a great track with some great races. It had the cheapest champagne on any course in the UK, and we invited him along next time we were going.

The Spider's friend and sporting colleague Liam Chronnell was recruited as driver for our Knavesmire Day, and off to York we went, having had the Aussie collected ahead of departure. We had hospitality tickets, but our Aussie chum turned up without a jacket or tie. The dress code meant we needed to loan him some fine Armani threads and a splendid kipper tie - job done. As often happens we did a bit of box-hopping at the track, and bumped into some of our Tote friends entertaining clients in the stand overlooking the finish line.

We reckoned that Liam and the Aussie might enjoy a nibble and a drop of bubbly, so asked if the boys could be invited up. That's when we got chatting sport, and our youthful Aussie mate and Liam could hold their own on almost any sporting topic, so all was going rather swimmingly. Or so we thought, until the Tote's eagle-eyed press officer Paul Petrie mentioned to us that our Aussie chum had no laces in his shoes, or even socks on, which was against the rules in the posh sections. Quick as a flash, Spider suggested it was Bondi Beach fashion and next year we'd all be on the Knavesmire in similar attire sipping our courtesy champers. It was a classic Spider bluff, but true enough you won't catch any fashion-conscious young chap wearing socks anywhere on a racecourse these days. The moral of the story is, never let an Aussie dress themselves ahead of the races, as they may well forget some simple items of clothing; and certainly, their socks.

After the Old Trafford triumph, we couldn't resist a line in the column pointing out to readers that former England cricket captain Mike Atherton, a regular on Channel 4's racing programmes, might be having a crack at the Scoop6 after the Test victory. In the article, we reminded Athers, as if we needed too, that there's only one thing they like less down under than whingeing Poms, and that is winning Poms. That very week, a punter using a £64 Squirrel perm, landed a bumper £536,475 win fund but as ever the bonus rolled over and we lived to play another day.

The year was about to get even more interesting with a surprise appearance on Sky News just around the corner for our bushy-tailed bounder. Talk about life in the fast lane, our many winning bets were very soon to be overtaken by a seven-foot-tall squirrel making some mind-blowing headlines. You really couldn't make it up; or so you might think.

Chapter 8

THE SUN WOT WON IT

Backed from 100-1 to 1-2 favourite, the Scoop6 Squirrel wearing a red *Sun* sash, galloped to glory in the 2005 Mascot Grand National at Huntingdon racecourse.

It was a stunningly sensational betting coup and we left the track with our pockets bulging with cash and the wallets fully wadded up.

From memory, the maximum stake was a tenner and every time we managed to get on, the price changed. While our Scoop6 Squirrel mascot was limbering up in the car park, having signed in to compete in the event on race day. We were going along a row of on course bookmakers taking the fancy prices. Starting at 100-1, it went 80-1, 66-1, 50-1, 40-1, 33-1, 25-1, 20-1, 16-1, 14-1, 12-1, 10-1, you get the gist... all the way down to odds-on in places.

When we arrived at post time ahead of the first hurdle race of the day, incidentally won by AP McCoy on Fire Dragon at 8-1 for trainer Jonjo O'Neill, our furry friend was as low as 1-2 favourite. At that point, we asked an expert on the mascot race if we should keep backing him and the answer was simply: 'Do they give you a return of fifty per cent on your money in the bank?'

Yet why do grown men throw every penny in their pockets, literally hundreds and hundreds of pounds, on another human being dressed as a seven-foot-tall squirrel, we hear you say? Well, the answer was pure and simple – we knew it was great value as Spider was someone who knew more about the mascot race than any other human being on the planet.

A few years before, Ladbrokes had sponsored the event and our punting pal had pocketed a cool five figures after tipping up the Oldham Athletic mascot Chaddy the Owl at 40-1. Very generously, he told all his mates to get on with a maximum stake of a tenner each way.

The Mascot Grand National itself had launched rather inauspiciously in 1999 with just seventeen runners and a victory for the Birmingham City mascot Beau Brummie Bulldog, but the event was the brainchild of racecourse manager Jim Allen and was very soon going to get legs. The next year they got a field of forty-six as Harry the Hornet from Watford FC hit the post in front. But the following year, the event was broadcast live on the BBC with a mysterious mascot called Freddie the Fox winning by a country mile. The winner was later revealed as Olympic athlete Matt Douglas, who had competed in the semi-finals of the 400 metre hurdles at the Sydney Olympics.

Matt, now a solicitor, was unveiled after being run down by *The Sun* bus mascot from that year's race. Spider's photographer colleague Paul Edwards had spotted the winner wearing spikes. When that was pointed out, The Spider remembered seeing The Fox with a rather tall gent dressed in brogues and full racing attire at the start and just then he spotted the same chap with a clutch of accomplices and arms full of £20 notes heading off the course.

Snapper Paul swiftly took a picture and The Spider then dashed after the mystery man he later grew to know and fondly remembers as Harry the Horse – and offered him a deal. It was either The Fox on the front page or find his own face in the paper, clutching thousands, as mastermind of the betting coup. Now no proper punter wants that kind of notoriety. The Fox was now on the run, but this little ruse soon had him uncovered. By all accounts, internet bookies refused to pay out in the region of £20,000 to Harry, but he still got a nice little trackside tickle.

That same year, Cyril the Swan from Swansea City, almost found himself up before the beak after a forty-six-year-old woman from Yorkshire, dressed as a bloodhound, injured her wrist in some boisterous pre-race parade ring pranks. It all proved too much for the Beeb and they never transmitted the event live again.

Spider had been the back end of *The Sun* bus back then, but despite Dazzler the Lion from Rushden and Diamonds being given the trophy, it was noted that the Oldham Athletic mascot looked lively, and the next year he recommended everyone back Chaddy the Owl at 40-1. Weaving an incredible web of intrigue, The Spider uncovered that Chaddy was actually Kevin Williams, aged thirty, a lifelong Latics fan and an extra from *Coronation Street*, who had appeared in scores of famous scenes in the ITV soap's Rovers Return. Once more, you literally couldn't have made it up.

As Ladbrokes – in those days known as The Magic Sign – were sponsoring the event, Spider decided to conjure up five horses at Chester in a 5p each way Lucky 63. A £6.30 bet to go with Chaddy the Owl at 40-1 and that little lot landed him a near £10,000 profit. He also had a scramble round all the Ladbrokes shops to get a batch of single bets on the Owl.

In September 2002, *The Sun* entered a Page 3 girl in the event. Spider ran alongside her as a minder shouting 'Fly Chaddy, Fly' as his feathered find flew in to first place beating around sixty-six other mascots to the prize. The Page 3 girl was puzzled by his bizarre antics, but with his encouragement she managed to clear the hurdles and complete the 220 yards course, an eighth of a mile, or one furlong, to those in racing. The following year Chaddy returned to do the double, but sponsors Totesport had him at 7-4 favourite. There was no chance of winning a small fortune at those short odds but he romped in again.

The following year, Graham the Gorilla from Finedon Volta FC, was triumphant. Chaddy the Owl was nowhere to be seen and a little bit off the radar, but his non-appearance had followed an incident at Blackpool at the start of the football season when feathers flew as he got in a tangle with Bloomfield Bear and threw one of the opposing mascot's boots into the crowd. Oldham Athletic suspended Chaddy for his Bloomfield Road antics, but with Kevin out of the costume, the seed of an idea for a stunning betting coup had been sown. Spider had suffered as the front end of *The Sun's* Donkey in the 2004 renewal and the back end of a bus the year after. At that point, he hatched a plot to win the prize himself as every year *The Sun* comedy entry always opened up at odds of 100-1.

The initial plan was to take the week off ahead of the Mascot Grand National and travel round every bookmaker in the land having a fiver each way on in every shop and in so doing win at least £1 million. It was a pretty cool plan and as we thought, not unreasonably, we could probably manage £1 million at least on this marathon road trip, but it came unstuck as the race this year had a new sponsor an online outfit called 121s.com. Now one of the biggest, if not *the* biggest and most successful bookmakers on the planet, Bet365, were the only bookies taking off-course bets on the day. Back then they only had a few shops round Stoke-on-Trent and Staffordshire, so no chance of the money-making road trip that we hoped for. To add to the heartbreak, the shrewdies from 'The Potteries' were only pricing up the race on the Sunday morning, so not even a chance to stop off en route. Though Richard did suggest his old fruit machine-playing pal Bernard McDonald take a Staffordshire trip to fill his boots in their shops.

Thus, that glorious Sunday afternoon at Huntingdon the only readies we were really going to get were off the trackside pitches, so we steamed in. Though we did have a major distraction as the jackpot that afternoon at Newmarket eventually hit £427,703 and we wanted to land that as much as the Mascot Grand National. Funnily enough, after Johnny Murtagh got Baron's Pit at 20-1 to win the Totepool Diadem Stakes at HQ, we were in line for a decent dividend and, as well as the folding in our pockets, The Squirrel Syndicate had another £33,742 in the Tote account to cheer the boys up on the long car journey north after getting all six up in the Newmarket perm.

That evening when we got in, they had a clip of the Scoop6 Squirrel striding to victory on Sky News – it was almost surreal and pretty much sublime at the same time. The following morning, we had a great mention in the leader column of *The Sun*. And the headline on the story in the newspaper was something like: 'It was *The Sun* wot won it' mimicking their famous headline on the day after the 1992 election when John Major scraped a twenty-one-seat majority for the Tories. On election day, *The Sun*, under then editor Kelvin MacKenzie, had put Labour leader Neil Kinnock's head in a lightbulb on the front page with the headline: 'If Kinnock wins today, will the last person to leave Britain turn out the lights?'

Fast forward a dozen or so years, and that *Sun* article about the Mascot Grand National triumph read: 'IT WAS *The Sun* wot won it... the seventh Mascot Grand National was won in sensational style yesterday by our Scoop6 Squirrel. Thousands of readers were in on the monster gamble at Huntingdon racecourse that saw *The Sun's* Scoop6 Squirrel win the race after plunging in price from 100-1 to evens favourite. And *The Sun's* flying, furry, red Squirrel emulated triple Grand National winner Red Rum as inside was double Mascot Grand National winner Kevin Williams, aged thirty-one, who had won the race twice before as Chaddy the Owl.

Kevin, who stopped flapping about as Oldham Athletic's cuddly owl after last year's second place in the big race, said: 'It's great to get the treble – *The Sun* has done me proud. It's pretty fitting being a red Squirrel and following in the footsteps of Red Rum. I only hope the readers had lots of nuts on as I know the Scoop6 Squirrel tipped me to win in Saturday's paper. All my family and friends have had a few quid on, but not many got the 40-1 that they got at Ladbrokes when I first won in 2002.

'I'm hoping to be back next year to run my heart out again for *The Sun*. I aim to be just like the newspaper – number one again.' Super punter Richard Brocklebank, aged forty, who writes an exclusive column as the Scoop6 Squirrel in our *Favourite* racing pull-out told readers on Saturday that he was hoping for a winning weekend with his runner in the Mascot Grand National. Richard, who collected a bundle of dosh from on course bookmakers, said: 'I am glad that readers lumped on – it's a fun bet. But all is fur in the Scoop6 Squirrel's constant battle with the bookie – *The Sun* simply keeps punters one step ahead of the field.' But last night some bookies were crying foul and calling for fur to fly after *The Sun's* sensational coup in the Mascot Grand National.

Racecourse manager Amy Starkey volunteered to take The Squirrel in to the weighing room to inspect his nuts after the big race and ahead of a threatened stewards' inquiry. Amy said: 'I am satisfied that it's all above board – but we've still got some pretty upset mascots knocking about. They just don't like getting beaten and take it very seriously.'

Sixty-three mascots lined up for the annual event over the 220 yards (one furlong) course, but the Scoop6 Squirrel showed a bushy-tailed behind to second place Sammy Saint, Southampton Football Club's mascot and the Peterborough Sue Ryder mascot Sonny, who finished third at odds of 33-1. Iain Turner, of sponsors 121s.com, said: 'When we heard *The Sun* was going to have a runner in our race, we always knew it was going to be a major contender, but in the end, *The Sun* Scoop6 Squirrel slaughtered the opposition. There was more carnage out there than the year Foinavon won the Grand National at 100-1, but *The Sun* Scoop6 Squirrel showed the courage and agility of fellow National winner Red Rum to avoid the danger. *The Sun* Scoop6 Squirrel was a truly worthy winner of the greatest event in the Mascot racing calendar.'

Bitter bookies Bet365 moaned about more mascot skulduggery and accused late entrant *The Sun* Squirrel of making a mockery of the famous race. Bet365 spokesman Steve Freeth said: 'I'm surprised there wasn't a rat in the race – because we certainly smell one! We received notification of the Scoop6 Squirrel's late entry this morning and the original 8-1 soon became 6-4 after a flurry of interest. We're waiting for a stewards' inquiry – The Squirrel won that far, there had to be an Olympic hurdler in the suit.' *Sun* reader John Murphy, aged fifty, of Stockport, Greater Manchester, said: 'The Scoop6 Squirrel won me £520 last week when I put his longshot Presto Shinko in my bet at 22-1 and now, I've had another touch. The column tipped the Scoop6 Squirrel fur and square, so I've had another winning weekend – you can't go wrong reading *The Sun*.'

We had won more than £2 million as a syndicate since starting the column just over twelve months before and the Scoop6 was going from strength to strength with regular influxes of punters' hard-earned cash to make the pots grow. *Sun* readers were catching on as well and grabbing around a million themselves in that first year thanks to the column and the tips. The Scoop6 Squirrel had certainly started something and wasn't just scratching his nuts.

At the end of October four *Sun* readers enjoyed another Scoop6 bonanza with us as our syndicate, along with them, landed a share of a £590,000 win fund. And *The Favourite* pull-out featured three winners in our 'Scoop6 Squirrel' column, with Templegate and Tom Pepper contributing a winning favourite each at Wetherby and Newmarket.

Since the inception of the column, we had always told readers to find a longshot and this particular week trainer Clive Brittain provided just that on the soft ground at Newmarket with Rajeem at 25-1 under Jamie Spencer, knocking more than ninety per cent of the players out of the pool in the second leg. Each winning ticket picked up £118,000 and among *The Sun* readers in the money was Bryan Coghlin, aged fifty-seven, of Littlehampton, West Sussex, who less than twelve months before had won £2.3 million on the lottery. With the win fund expected to pass the half-a-million mark and just sixty-one runners declared in the bet overnight, we had suggested a lumpy perm for readers of 2×2×2×2×2×4. That equates to 128 lines at £2 each, an overall cost of £256 working out at just over £21 per man for a twelve-strong syndicate. It was probably the biggest perm we had proposed for readers up until that point and it certainly paid off.

The rolling bonus the Saturday after was £381,424 with the total set to smash the £400,000 mark that coming weekend and the likely bonus race would be the twenty-one-runner November Handicap on heavy ground at Doncaster. We had teamed up with some of the others, so at least had a few picks with Ebtikaar and the other 13-2 joint favourite Group Captain both on our side. But on a grey day with showers, to put an extra dampener on things, it was always going to be tough. It was talented trainer Ralph Beckett who spoiled our party, legging up Nelson De Souza on the lightly weighted three-year-old Come On Jonny that sluiced in by seven lengths. A couple of weeks later the bonus had hit £448,097, but that little lot was squirrelled away by another syndicate.

December started with a winning £40,297 November Scoop6 winner from Middlesbrough following up with another Scoop6 win fund after slipping The Squirrel's longshot Verasi at 12-1 into his bet along with our other triumphant tips, Racing Demon and Kauto Star, which landed him £54,000. Unfortunately for him, his second crack at the bonus which now stood at £76,617 in as many weeks, went begging. The week before he had been one of a trio of winners who also missed out on the bonus when they all went alone and each picked the same horse, the losing favourite, as their free punt.

Boxing Day provided a festive windfall for six *Sun* readers among the dozen winners who shared the win fund, each netting a tasty haul of £3,997 - more than enough to clear the Christmas bills. Some of those readers even got a share of the New Year's Eve bonus fund of £124,381 when trainer Alan King's even money favourite, The Hairy Lemon under 'Choc' Thornton, landed the Betfred Handicap Hurdle at Warwick. The Squirrel column even tipped the winner of the opening leg that weekend He's The Guvnor in the 2.10 at Uttoxeter, but having those *Sun* readers add to their spoils was a fairy-tale ending to the festive season for the furry fellow and his friends.

A lady from Liverpool using a £16 Squirrel-style perm had landed a share of the win fund and followed up the week after by taking the whole £21,384 bonus pot when Desert Air at 25-1 won the Ladbroke Hurdle, making it a super start to 2006 for her.

For the city of Liverpool, the lucky streak continued when it emerged that England and Anfield soccer ace Stevie Gerrard's dad, Paul, was among a twenty-strong syndicate from The Swan boozer in the city, who collected £39,504 from the near £120,000 win fund.

Scouser Frank Leonard, aged fifty-nine, got all six winners on his £2 ticket after picking Be My Better Half in honour of his wife of 35 years. Tommy McLean, aged fifty, from Stenhousemuir, and an anonymous punter from Berwick, Northumberland, also shared the win fund with them. Yet the week after, it was back of the net yet again for Liverpool as the Swan Syndicate picked top weight Nippy Des Mottes 2-1 favourite to land the fourteen-runner Connaught Handicap Hurdle at Wincanton, and in doing so collected the £50,792 bonus on top.

That very weekend *Sun* reader Alan Milson, a fifty-five-year-old fan of The Squirrel column used our banker Dom D'Orgeval 5-2 favourite to land £28,922 from the win fund. On his winning Saturday we had recommended a 2×2×1×2×1×2 perm of 16 lines at £2 each costing £32. Van driver Alan had placed his bet in the Coral shop in Romsey, Hants, and had shared the win fund with Alan Ringland, aged forty-nine, from Birmingham, but the pair failed to follow up with the bonus when trainer Ben Pollock's A Glass In Thyne, under Andrew Thornton, landed the sixteen-runner Great Yorkshire Handicap Chase at Southwell on an icy day when Cheltenham was abandoned.

The Squirrel Syndicate slipped into hibernation in February with the following week's Scoop6 scrapped after a big freeze led to the meetings at Newbury and Warwick being abandoned. Though on Saturday February18th, we took a trip out to Haydock Park on Red Square Vodka Gold Cup Day and met a legend of the game while wearing The Squirrel suit. Yes, our red Squirrel ran into Ginger McCain and couldn't help but grab a photo of him patting the furry fellow in the winners' enclosure.

The April before, Red Rum's legendary trainer had landed his fourth Grand National with Amberleigh House that we had been backing at all odds down from 33-1 and was 16-1 when Graham Lee steered the twelve-year-old past the post in first place. On that day at Haydock, Ginger actually landed the last race with a six-year-old called Cloudy Lane. The bay gelding went on to compete unsuccessfully in three Aintree Grand Nationals, but did land a John Smith's Foxhunter Chase over the big obstacles as a twelve-year-old trained by his son Donald.

At Haydock, Cloudy Lane beat trainer Robert Alner's Miko De Beauchene. As a seven-year-old the next year under Andrew Thornton off a low weight at Chepstow, Miko just chinned gallant top weight Halcon Genelardais to secure the Welsh Grand National by a head. Much later, on another £500,000 Scoop6 bonus day at Newbury, we were to bump into Ginger again and we asked his expert advice on the favourite in the bonus race, but we'll get round to that a bit later. Yet again, The Squirrel suit was packed for a day trackside and Ginger, God rest his soul, was bang on form for us.

Chapter 9

MORE MASCOT MADNESS

The first Saturday in March 2006 saw 269 people achieve their dream of winning the Scoop6, but the dividend was a bit of a nightmare paying just £199 each. We had got the weekend off to a flyer in *The Sun* racing pull-out tipping up a single banker in the first leg and following up with the winner of the second. But on the day, the biggest price of any of the six winners was 5-1. With three winning favourites and three winning second favourites, it was no surprise the dividend was so poor.

Yet the biggest shock of the day was that the Totesport customer from Middlesbrough, who landed £46,341 the week before, failed to add the £97,244 bonus to his haul by not selecting Cornish Sett, the 5-1 favourite that landed the Vodafone Gold Cup at Newbury.

Needless to say, the Saturday after, all *The Sun* readers who followed The Squirrel tip, Victram at 8-1 in the Imperial Cup at Sandown, would have been rubbing their paws after our pick won the race and helped them all to a share of the £120,192 bonus fund. Trainer Ado McGuinness sent Victram over from the Emerald Isle and duly landed the spoils by a neck from Dusky Warbler at 20-1, thus delighting another clutch of *Sun* readers who got more from their share of the bonus than from finding six winners the weekend before. Though having said that, it wasn't hard as there was more than twice as much in the bonus pot than the previous weekend's Scoop6 win fund.

Cheltenham arrived and AP McCoy got Brave Inca at 7-4 up in the Champion Hurdle and trainer Mouse Morris landed the Gold Cup with War of Attrition at 15-2 and the Saturday after, the Scoop6 win fund hit £96,645. That's when professional punter Dave Nevison struck, having had trainer Francis Flood's GVA Ireland under Ruby Walsh at

5-1 favourite, to land the John Smith's Midlands Grand National at Uttoxeter.

A few years later, that was the very bonus race that gave us more than three million good reasons to celebrate. Before then, Dave, who popped up as a guest on Channel 4's *Morning Line* the following week, had the ultra-tricky thirty-runner William Hill Lincoln to crack at Redcar, to unlock a £41,419 bonus fund. Not sure what Dave's bonus pick was precisely, but for certain it wasn't the John Quinn-trained 22-1 winner Blythe Knight, ridden by Graham Gibbons. The six-year-old chestnut gelding was drawn in stall nine and three in the first four came from single-figure stalls that year, so there was no excuse for the James Fanshawe-trained 7-2 favourite Cesare out of the six box.

The Lincoln's normal home Doncaster was undergoing renovations, and the temporary billet at Redcar always did have a slight low to middle bias in our books. It was a very tough nut to crack with just a single selection for a bonus win. Our longshot in that particular renewal was trainer Mark Johnston's Royal Island at 25-1, which was staying on into second at the finish under Joe Fanning; though was never catching the winner on the day. Our banker that week was Spoof Master in the William Hill-sponsored Brocklesby Stakes and Bill Turner's two-year-old duly obliged at 5-2 by four lengths from the favourite for a second winning single banker on the bounce. Mr Turner had a habit of targeting the race and getting his two-year-olds ready very quickly in the season.

Grand National Day at Aintree saw Irish raider Numbersixvalverde's no-nonsense triumph in the John Smith's sponsored big race at 11-1 beating the 5-1 joint favourites, Hedgehunter and Clan Royal, by a tidy six lengths. That win ensured thirty-eight-year-old Glaswegian postie Mark Wylie became the first £2 punter to land the Scoop6 on Grand National Day, pocketing a cool £129,988 on his way into the record books. And the week after, Mark had a shot at a £97,024 bonus at Haydock in the Red Square Vodka Fixed Brush Novices' Hurdle with a bumper field of sixteen runners.

In *The Favourite* pull-out, our bushy-tailed bounder tipped up Royal Alchemist at 9-2 in the opening leg at Kempton as a single banker for our fourth Nap winner in five weeks. But more importantly we gave our new-found friend, Ginger's Cloudy Lane at 8-1 in the 2.55 at Haydock, and he romped home by six lengths from Oscar Park for another near £100k special delivery for the Glaswegian with the golden touch.

Our winning single banker run went to five from six weeks, but April was set to end with The Squirrel competing in the Yorkshire Young Farmers' Clubs Rural Recycling Mascots Steeplechase on a sunny Sunday at Wetherby. Unlike the Huntingdon appearance, we distinctly didn't tip up the Scoop6 Squirrel to land the event against seventy other entrants over a furlong. We warned readers that this Yorkshire adventure was just a prep run for another crack at the Mascot Grand National proper at Huntingdon in September.

Disaster struck at Wetherby with our furry friend suffering a suspected broken metatarsal in the right paw just twenty-four hours after Manchester United's Wayne Rooney suffered the same injury to his foot at Stamford Bridge. With a bandaged paw we limped on, but Doncaster's Desperate Daisy triumphed over the field and a fantastically fit Young Farmer claimed the trophy.

The week after in May, The Squirrel Syndicate was pretty stunned when two punters from Essex and Suffolk split the £44,000 place pool without picking any winners in their £2 and £4 bets respectively. But an even bigger place dividend than their £22,000 each wasn't too far away. It was days like that with bumper place money that highlighted just what a fantastic punt the £2 Scoop6 line was on a Saturday.

On May 20th the 'Scoop6 Squirrel' column predicted that one of our readers would crack the near £480,000 win fund and with our pick Sphinx obliging in the opening leg, it was not a surprise that a player with a £128 Squirrel perm from South London did just that. The man was one of six winners. Along with him was small-staking punter Richard Baker, aged thirty-five, from Borden, Hampshire, who placed a £2 line at his local Coral shop, to land the biggest win of his life. And the boys landed the £203,700 bonus pot when the Michael Jarvis-trained front-runner Borehan at 5-1 made every post a winning one under Philip Robinson to land the Coral Sprint at Newmarket.

Bizarrely, that same weekend a lucky couple from Kent, Paul Painter, aged fifty-eight, and his wife Karen, fifty-two, both placed a £2 line on the Scoop6 and split the win fund with £25,909 each and two free shots at the new bonus of £22,208. Paul explained how he'd placed his bet on the phone, while Karen had done her £2 line on the internet. The pair were happy they'd both picked the same horses as it gave them an extra shot in the fourteen-runner bonus race at Musselburgh. However, neither had selected Jim Goldie's 8-1 winner Glencairn Star under Daniel Tudhope in the Archerfield House Sprint, so that Derby Day the bonus rolled on.

The Squirrel Syndicate members were squeezing their nuts during the big race as that week's banker was the Marcus Tregoning-trained Sir Percy at 6-1, who jockey Martin Dwyer sneaked through a gap in the shadows of the post for a short-head victory over Geoff Wragg's Dragon Dancer at 66-1. Sir Percy took home the first prize of £740,695 and jockey Darryl Holland and the connections of the runner-up had to settle for £280,728, but it wasn't going to be much more than about a year before we were going to get our paws on Scoop6 pots even bigger than both those prizes put together.

The joy of six is certainly something to behold and a seventy-one-year-old Squirrel fan ended June with more than £200,000 after collecting the bonus rollover on top of his Scoop6 from the week before. On the eve of the World Cup final in the Olympiastadion in Berlin, an old friend of ours was running in the opening leg of the Scoop6, the twelve-runner Laurent Perrier Champagne Sprint Stakes at Sandown. We duly made Pivotal Point our single banker. Sent off at 5-1 with Seb Sanders in the saddle, Pivotal proved our point and the Stewards' Cup winner of 2004 triumphed by half a length from 5-2 favourite Benbaun.

We followed that up with the next two winners at Sandown for a tasty 74-1 treble on the day, but it wasn't enough to help a fan of the column unlock the pots. Pivotal was drawn in stall two and the favourite Benbaun was drawn against the rail and one thing we are very keen on at Sandown is low drawn runners, as they have a big advantage in the sprints.

The next day, a lad from just up the road in Tameside, Simone Perrotta, found himself on the winning Italian side in the World Cup final with his teammate Andreas Pirlo man of the match in the 1-1 draw. The game was probably most famous for Zinedine Zidane's half-hearted Glasgow kiss on Marco Materazzi's chest. The extra time head-butt left the Argentinian referee Horacio Elizondo no option but to send Zidane off, and that was the last game he ever played for his country.

Meanwhile back on the pitch, the Italians beat the French 5-3 on penalties to lift the World Cup Trophy, which had replaced the famous Jules Rimet Trophy, named after the FIFA president of that name who passed the vote that initiated the tournament in 1929. The trophy was originally named simply the World Cup, or the Coupe du Monde, but the Jules Rimet Trophy came into being in 1946 and was the trophy that the England team later held aloft after beating the Germans at Wembley in 1966 with the new World Cup introduced eight years later in 1974.

Yet for the 1996 Euros, The Lightning Seeds, Frank Skinner and David Baddiel gave us that great football anthem 'Three Lions' with that sparkling line 'Jules Rimet still gleaming.' Older football fans throughout England have fantastic memories of that marvellous match.

We all remember the photograph of a toothless Nobby Stiles holding the Jules Rimet Trophy aloft after the game, but the yarn behind that image is pretty hilarious. For Nobby's roommate back then in the 1966 World Cup squad was Scouser Ian Callaghan who played for Liverpool. Before the game Nobby came up to him with something wrapped in a handkerchief and, as Ian wasn't playing, he put it in his suit pocket and asked him to hand it over at the final whistle.

Cally couldn't resist taking a peek and when he realised it was Nobby's false teeth, he decided they could stay in his pocket and he never took them down to the pitch. Hence, that iconic image of a near toothless Nobby Stiles with the trophy. Toxteth-born Cally, a Liverpool legend, had to wait more than forty years for his World Cup medal, but in 2010 Nobby's family had put his winner's medal up for auction. Nobby's old team Manchester United's Museum stepped in with a bid of £160,000, a record price at the time for any England World Cup winner's medal.

Talking of teeth, that July we really put the bite on the bookies, as after single banker Pivotal Point we gave another couple of banker tips including Quenched at 4-1 and finished the month making Kahlua Kiss at 11-4 joint favourite a single selection in the 2.10 at York. It was the opening leg of the Scoop6 and Robert Winston piloted William Muir's Kahlua Kiss to an impressive five-length victory over David Barron's 5-1 shot Mistress Twister on the Knavesmire.

The banker run continued into August as single banker selection Jeremy Noseda's unbeaten Bustin Justin gambled into 11-8 favourite under Shane Kelly landed the opening leg of the bet over seven furlongs at Newmarket. Another gamble on the day was our longshot. It was trainer Alan King's Urban Tiger, punted in from double-figure odds to 7-2, and Richard Hughes gave the lightly weighted three-year-old a great ride for a comfortable win at Windsor.

The week after though our luck was out as a £253,980 Scoop6 win fund slipped through our paws and went to another syndicate. They had to tackle the twenty-three-runner Great St Wilfred Handicap sprint at Ripon to take down the £108,848 bonus fund. When Excusez Moi at 10-1 landed the William Hill-sponsored Great St Wilfred for Clive Brittain and Kerrin McEvoy, we knew the bonus had survived.

At the same time, we had been on a single banker winning spree with Burning Incense at 5-1, landing the second leg of the bet for us and trainer Roger Charlton and jockey Steve Drowne. When the opening leg the next week went to Wasseema at 9-4 out of stall two at Sandown, we had taken the single banker run to seven out of eight weeks. We did say on a fair few occasions we should have just been lumping everything on our bankers, but it's more fun slipping six in and those bookie chaps did have a bad habit of closing winning accounts.

That August, Sir Clement Freud's *Sun* column 'A Knight At The Races' was gracing our pull-out on a Saturday. Though by October *The Favourite* article had been rebranded 'Freudian Slip' with a clever play on words referring to betting slips. This had *Sun* racing editor Trevor Clements' fingerprints all over it, as it was a witty headline for a winning column. Also that August, Santander, or rather Abbey as it was then, started publishing adverts in the racing pull-out featuring a red squirrel. Their furry friend was telling of a 'really high rate for regular savers'... seven per cent! Now those were the days. Lots of *Sun* readers were banking good money with our winning tips, and we reckon someone in the marketing department at Abbey had got the winning habit with us.

August ended with some very frightening news... our grey cousins had picked up a contagious killer virus and lots of squirrels were dropping like flies. We were very concerned for our red relatives in Formby and Cumbria, as they had historically suffered enough at the paws of the greys. The fear of the new contagion clearly was playing on our minds and the winning banker run ended in September just as lucky Lennie Gotch, aged fifty-four, from North London, landed £380,240 on the jackpot at Kempton. Travel agent Lennie could certainly have booked some trips with his winnings, but he'd have also probably won the £57,614 Scoop6 if he had entered. For Lennie had done the hard part and picked Killena Boy, the 20-1 winner that knocked everyone out of the win fund.

Sprint king Dandy Nicholls missed the entry stage for the Ayr Gold Cup and at the same time The Squirrel's handler missed the entry stage for the Mascot Grand National. Instead of winning on a consecutive attempt, we were poised to present the trophy to the new winner. As we announced the news in the column with a heavy heart, we at least got back on track with another winning single banker as trainer Neville Callaghan's Excellent Art with Kerrin McEvoy on board beat the 6-4 favourite Helene Brilliant by a short head at Newbury.

The week after we were off to Huntingdon and had persuaded a budding photographer, Jon 'Biddy' Baxter, to slip into The Squirrel suit. The year before, that notorious one-eyed pirate Captain Blade, Sheffield United's mascot, had attempted to spoil The Squirrel Syndicate victory parade with a last-minute rugby tackle attempt as our furry friend approached the post. Inside the suit, Kevin, the former Chaddy the Owl, was waiting for any last-minute antics as he knew just how cut-throat the mascot world could be.

As The Squirrel entered the dying stages, he spotted from the corner of his eye a glint of cutlass and feared the Yorkshire pirate might be attempting to stop his history-making mascot Grand National treble in its tracks, so he sidestepped him with a classy little skip and a jump that wouldn't have been out of place on a world-class rugby field.

Anyhow, the usual death threats followed the Scoop6 Squirrel victory, but we hadn't taken them too seriously. At least Cyril the Swan had wound his neck in and wasn't calling for blood – he'd had enough trouble with that Yorkshire bloodhound we suppose.

When we arrived at Huntingdon, all was calm and dandy, but as soon as Biddy slipped into The Squirrel suit and started to make his way onto the course, all hell let loose with lunacy galore and a large collection of apparently cuddly creatures wanting to thump *The Sun's* mascot. The football mascots' bloodlust had rather shocked the mild-mannered photographer in The Squirrel suit. But he was swiftly told to grow a pair and make the presentation eventually to Mickey the Monkey, from Kick-4-Life, whatever that was.

After the bushy-tailed bounder was so badly abused by some fairly repulsive mascots, we felt it was time to retire from the Mascot Grand National with one run and one victory being the equivalent of getting out on top. On the long journey back, Biddy attempted to moan about the punches that were thrown, but we pointed out that as he was wearing a cushioned mascot costume there was no danger money on offer.

From our time in The Squirrel suit, we knew how rough it could be for mascots. It made Spider recall the episode only the year before at Cheltenham's November meeting when the six-foot tall Paddy Power Gold Cup mascot got assaulted by three yobs. Londoner Pascoe Willis, aged thirty-two, was in the fluffy replica of the famous Gold Cup when a trio of drunken thugs attacked him, picking him up by the testicles, taunting him and roughing him up in front of stunned racegoers.

Pascoe had immediately reported it to the police and then went with the officers to find the culprits. The three clowns made out it was just a laugh, but being picked up by the goolies is never funny. When they found them, the yobs apologised, but Pascoe wanted them evicted from the racecourse. He said: 'I left the police to it – the lads thought it was a big laugh, but they were idiots and they almost ruined a great weekend for me.'

Remarkably, back then just twenty-four hours after the assault, the Paddy Power Gold Cup ran against *The Sun's* Scoop6 Squirrel in the inaugural running of a Special Squirrel Stakes up the famous Cheltenham hill. Must admit, we almost forgot about this, but our sensational Scoop6 Squirrel ran away with the trophy, hot on the heels of his Mascot Grand National success at Huntingdon, but we had tipped it up to *Sun* readers though we went off 4-7 favourite.

Inside the suit was Olympic hurdler Matt Douglas, then twenty-eight, who famously won the Mascot Grand National himself dressed as Freddie the Fox four years earlier. Matt, who was training for the Commonwealth Games in Melbourne the following March, was actually getting into the costume outside the main entrance when the Manchester United owner at the time JP McManus was arriving. Instantly, The Squirrel handler said a cheery hello to JP and told him Scoop6 Squirrel was the winner of the first race which made JP smile, so our man Spider quickly followed up with: 'Are you having a winner today?'

With a twinkle in those Irish eyes JP replied: 'I hope so.'

After a swift look through the card, Lingo was his only runner that day in the Greatwood Hurdle and was trained by Jonjo O'Neill and ridden by a certain AP McCoy. That was a winning combination if ever we saw one and the 10-1 didn't last long after our Squirrel handler told everyone to get on. Lingo duly landed the race at 5-1, but injury sadly curtailed this promising young hurdler's career.

Before racing proper got underway, our Scoop6 Squirrel had made mincemeat of the opposition – five inferior Squirrels from *Nuts* magazine in that sole running of the Cheltenham Squirrel race. That nice chap Paddy Power had gifted us a small box right over the finish line after we revealed the mascot assault.

The Squirrel handler was assisted by his chum Yozza, recruited as getaway driver and bet-placer ahead of the opening contest. His relatively easy chores entailed placing a small jackpot perm. Yozza was handed the money, then given the simple instruction of finding the winner of the twenty-three-runner handicap on the card for which he selected 12-1 Irish raider Hordago that went on to win well.

Unfortunately, it was just after this one won, that Yozza mentioned he had forgot to put the jackpot perm on with all The Squirrel race excitement. The other five legs in the £36 bet had been marked out by Spider and contained all five winners. Rather magnanimously, as they got in his rusty, old Rover for the long trip back to the North West, the pair dismissed the miss imagining the £45,000 pot would have been won by a fair few tickets. When they discovered that it was a rollover the next day, they had to put that down as the £22k each that got away, but on the plus side they didn't cry too much.

A few weeks before in October, incidentally we landed a share of a £500,000-plus win and bonus fund with a couple of dozen *Sun* readers and that chap Dave Nevison, but it wasn't life-changing for any of us. Many were *Sun* readers as we gave some decent winners in the column at 8-1 and 9-1, from memory.

As November ended, a Squirrel fan from Kentish Town, London, landed a £67,000 Scoop6 win fund and followed up with a £115,000 bonus pool on top – 'Thank you my *Sun*'we heard him say. The month closed with at least a dozen more of our fans collecting on the Scoop6 as our winning banker Gallant Approach went in at 7-2 along with another couple of column tips. Unfortunately, a total of fifty-three people had winning tickets that day and the dividend was just £2,073.

The week after, for the third year on the bounce, we tipped up the winner of the William Hill Handicap Hurdle at Sandown in the shape of trainer Dr Richard Newland's Overstrand at 8-1. Once again we gave another couple of winners at 4-1 and 5-2 with the banker, but it was the big race winner that unlocked a decent bonus for five *Sun* readers, who added £9,418 each to their haul from the week before. The same week, seven ticket holders had shared the win fund and two of them were *Sun* readers from Rotherham and London, who collected £8,207 each.

The festive season was special as ever, but we were amazed that nobody won the Scoop6 on Boxing Day when all thirty-three ticket holders still standing managed to omit odds-on King George winner Kauto Star from their perms. Talk about nuts, it was another that certainly got away. We started our last column of the year with Sharp Belline at 11-1 landing the opening leg at Haydock. Then our banker Skippers Burg landed the last leg of the 3.40 at the Lancashire track. Now 2006 had been a fun year, filled full of winners, but not in our wildest dreams could we have imagined what lay in store in 2007.

Chapter 10

HADDOCK BATTERS THE BOOKIES

So here we are in 2007, but we've already told you all about that wonderful winning streak that saw The Squirrel Syndicate net more than £3 million in three weeks. Looking back, we are surprised the brain cells survived to tell the tale, as we consumed some industrial amounts of celebratory sherbets later in the year.

But so much more happened in 2007 that it's hard to know where to begin, so when in doubt, it's just best to start at the beginning.

January was pretty tricky from a Scoop6 perspective to start with, but Venetia Williams was having a decent month. We bankered Venetia's Maletton in the Connaught Cup Handicap Chase at Wincanton with the mudlark under Sam Thomas duly obliging at odds of 5-2. The pools still rolled though with the final Saturday of the month being Festival Trials Day at Cheltenham. We were predicting bumper pots of more than £600,000 and wanted to win it.

Spider, doing his usual Saturday due diligence with extra *Racing Post* form study, marked out possible longshots and had watched the *Morning Line*, like most serious punters did in those days. When John Francome, a fellow *Sun* columnist, flagged up the chances of Martin Pipe's Whispered Secret in the Ladbrokes Trophy Handicap Chase, our chap's spider senses were alerted as he had already marked the 25-1 shot as well worth a bet. From the bookmakers after he'd got on at 25-1, he flagged up the outsider as well worth considering in the final leg over two miles and five furlongs for the perm. His only proviso was that some of the others might be better jumpers.

Our perm had five bankers in that last leg. It was decided at 25-1 to leave the longshot on the non-banker list and not up the cost of the already lumpy perm. Racing got underway and it was all really going to plan with our overnight longshot Simon getting backed into 7-1 and landing the first leg. We were off to a flyer and we got the next three bankers in the perm up. We were cooking with gas and then in the 3.35 at Southwell, a non-banker, trainer Charlie Mann's Haggle Twins with Noel Fehily in the saddle, scored after being nibbled at in the market into 8-1. This now meant we had the first five in the betting at Cheltenham covered in the final leg for a good share of the win fund of £410,000.

Spider was in The Three Tunnes watching with a few other syndicate members, including Walks the plumber, punting Pete and his dad, John. They were supping a few pints of Robbies' mild to calm any nerves, but there was a delay to the race as the Cheltenham officials were worried about low-lying sun. What happened next was about to take the shine off our day, as the stewards decided the race would now just have three fences in the back straight and another on the side of the course, meaning there was not that much jumping for the horses to deal with.

At the bar, Spider was thinking of going and taking some of the 14-1 on Whispered Secret, as his concern about the jumping issues was not so pertinent with four fences out of the race. As he deliberated, Whispered Secret went 12-1 then 10-1, and the chaps with him suggested we had enough covered and not to worry. Whispered Secret went into 8-1 at the off and the fact he didn't have to jump too many was a good thing as he hit the first, blundered at the seventh, but then the four fences up the home straight were bypassed. With just 10st 3lbs on his back and Rodi Greene riding out of his skin, he steered the bay gelding home by half a length from three of ours, led by New Alco at 4-1. We even had Whispered Secret's stablemate the 7-2 favourite in our perm, but Pipey's Vodka Bleu finished last of ten under Timmy Murphy.

To add to the heartache, some other ticketholder had the winner, hence the £410,000 was gone as well. Whispered Secret certainly comes into the 'one that got away' category. The next day a paragraph in a Sunday paper's sports pages revealed that a lucky lady, from Northwich, Cheshire, had won the lot with a £2 ticket. Spider saw the potential for a story and contacted the nice PR man for Betfred, who checked if

Agnes was happy to talk to someone who was set to turn her into, as the newspapers proclaimed: 'Britain's most successful female gambler'.

Naturally, The Squirrel suit came out of mothballs as Spider fancied doing some photos with the lucky lady and our furry friend. The winning punter's name, once again was straight out of the realms of 'you couldn't make it up'. She was called Agnes Haddock and she ran a little shop called The Ironing Board in Northwich. She was a keen fan of her Saturday racing thanks to her dear old dad Angus, a merchant seaman who loved his horses.

Inside forty-eight hours of her life-changing win, Agnes, or Aggie as we came to know her, had met a giant Squirrel at her shop. Of course, the headlines were pretty straightforward –Trev leading the way in *The Sun* with 'Haddock Batters The Bookies.' Aggie had spent just £2 on her line and had made her choices based on nice names. In the first leg, Simon at 7-1 got picked as Agnes knew a nice lad called Simon. As a dance fan, Exotic Dancer at 6-1 was her selection in the second leg. As she went into the Betfred shop to put her £2 line on, the weather was overcast, so Clouding Over at 6-1 was naturally her pick in leg three.

Now Agnes had an extra stroke of luck in leg four as she had picked a mule called Mountain because she was a fan of the rock band of that name. But it was pulled out of the race and under Tote non-runner rules her ticket went instead on the favourite Katchit which won at 2-1. This got her into leg five with the Haggle Twins at Southwell, selected as it sounded a bit like 'Aggie'; yes, really that simple. And the final leg Whispered Secret was picked purely on that mention Mr Francome gave the Pipe horse on the *Morning Line*. It was very bittersweet at the time, as Whispered Secret so nearly got in our bet as a banker. But as time moved on and we met Agnes with her husband Colin at the races, we were rather glad that they had in fact won it on their own.

Yet before we rush ahead, we'd better tell you about Agnes' bid for the bonus the following week at Sandown in the sixteen-runner ToteScoop6 Handicap Hurdle. We studied the form all week and our selection was Taranis for the Paul Nicholls and Ruby Walsh combination - we made it the banker in our column that Saturday. The one we feared was last week's winner Whispered Secret and we suspected Agnes might even pick that as she chased the £278,000 bonus pot.

The first we knew of her selection though was when Agnes popped up on TV alongside Derek 'Tommo' Thompson trackside at Sandown. Aggie had gone with our banker Taranis. She was screaming like a banshee on live telly as her pick hit the front to go half a length clear of Whispered Secret at 12-1 on the line.

Afterwards, Aggie thanked rider Ruby live on Channel 4 for getting the job done and the Irish charmer chirped up: 'Don't forget my cut!' or some such similar riposte. We rang Aggie to congratulate her afterwards and asked if it was The Squirrel's banker tip in the column that had put her on the winner, but nope, that wasn't the case.

In true Aggie fashion, the horse that took her winnings to £688,000 was number thirteen on the race card and that, as she explained, was her birth date. Her 344,000-1 seven-timer with £2 on simply consisted of selections with nice names and a bonus bonanza thanks to the winner being horse number thirteen. Female logic indeed, but not many of us have had a tickle of £688,000 for two quid, so very well done as it clearly worked for her.

The month of February ended with us bemoaning in the column our lack of form, but we promised we wouldn't yet be resorting to the Aggie formula of picking winners with sweet names. We spotted Simon was going again with Andrew Thornton on board and gave him a mention in the article. But even though the then landlord of our once favourite boozer The Three Tunnes was a chap called Simon Howarth, we decided that wasn't enough to put him up as the tip in the paper. You've guessed it, yes John Spearing's charge cosily landed the *Racing Post* Chase at 11-2. We did give the winner of the opening leg of the Scoop6 that day at Newcastle, in the shape of Little Big Horse at 15-2, and followed that with the first Scoop6 race at Kempton with Natal going in at 5-2 favourite for the Nicholls and Walsh combination.

After racing that day, we got a telephone call from Agnes – when the number popped up, we honestly thought she'd won again and she had, but just a £200 pick-up for a place line. Up to this point we were feeling hard-pressed to beat the ironing lady with the golden touch, but perhaps the tide had turned as Punjabi in the last leg had also knocked the final twelve ticket holders out of the win fund.

The weekend after we were hoping to bag the £466,492 pot ahead of Cheltenham, and when Venetia Williams' Green Belt Flyer at 20-1 won the 2.40 at Newbury under Sam Thomas, we were looking good. We had seventy-two of the remaining 102 tickets in our sweaty paws and in the next leg we had twenty-four of those tickets on the second favourite Nozic at 7-2 and if that won, we would have had six on each of the four runners in the fifth leg at Kempton. Then all of that lot on winning favourite Orcadian at 3-1 in the last leg, the 3.50 at Newbury.

Nozic appeared to be cruising to victory after jumping the last in front, but then it went the shape of a pear, as the late gamble on David Pipe's Madison Du Berlais backed from 20-1 to 12-1 paid off, as he just got up to pip our second favourite by a neck. It was particularly painful, but one *Sun* reader the week after was very glad we left it behind.

For Arfyn Archie Evans, aged fifty-nine, from Cwmbran, Gwent, had a single £2 ticket that yielded £695,911. We had tipped up the opening leg winner Albertas Run at 6-1, but the real magic that weekend was Templegate tipping all seven winners at Sandown – including the four Scoop6 races. Templegate's seven-timer paid 14,322-1. But surveyor Arfyn Archie was laughing all the way to the bank with his Scoop6 winnings the equivalent of a 347,955-1 winner and that is what you call great value.

The feature race that weekend was the Sunderlands Imperial Cup Handicap Hurdle at Sandown and 11-4 favourite Gaspara won it comfortably by six lengths for the combo of David Pipe and AP McCoy. A few years later in April 2010 Gaspara was to cost us a small fortune in bizarre circumstances in a race at Newton Abbot.

Father Paddy McMahon was the owner and he officiated at St John's Church in Chorlton-cum-Hardy, Manchester, where Ken Burrell was in tune with the punting parishioners. The priest and the entire parish were plunging on Gaspara at the Abbot. But it was almost divine intervention that got in the way, as a flagman instructed his jockey Danny Cook to go round the penultimate flight, whilst the remainder of the field jumped the hurdle.

Gaspara led all the way and despite the diversion round the penultimate hurdle still held on, but was disqualified for omitting the flight. The year before, Manchester City manager Roberto Mancini had visited St John's for a service, and his Blues went on a winning spree. Legendary

Manchester United managers Sir Matt Busby and Sir Alex Ferguson were both regulars in the pews back in the day, and Fergie may well have had a few quid on Gaspara like us.

Meanwhile, the weekend after his bumper Scoop6 win, Arfyn Archie was back for more. Like a scene from Oliver Twist, he was holding out his bowl for the £333,916 bonus fund and landing that would have made him a millionaire from a two quid punt. All that stood between Arfyn and that wonderful windfall top-up, were eighteen runners and a hell of a lot of fences in the John Smith's Midlands Grand National at Uttoxter.

The previous year's winner GVA Ireland was returning, and The Squirrel flagged up the Nigel Twiston-Davies-trained winner Baron Windrush, backed into 12-1, as that weekend's longshot. From memory, our Welsh whizz probably went with Templegate's top weight pick Ladalko, but there was no repeat joy for the boyo as the Baron bolted in for us by twelve lengths.

The Grand National proper wasn't going to see a repeat of the year before with a Glaswegian postie delivering a fortune on the day – the big race actually went to Silver Birch at 33-1 for up-and-coming Irish trainer Gordon Elliott with Robbie Power doing the steering. Interesting to note his warm-up was the Cheltenham Cross Country race – the same path to Aintree glory plotted by Gordon for Tiger Roll on a couple of occasions.

We tipped Tiger Roll up at 50-1 and 20-1 for those first two Grand National wins, but didn't actually fancy him for the treble in the abandoned race in 2020 as he was up in the weights and down in price. But in 2007 we did fancy trainer Peter Bowen's McKelvey, the runner-up with Tom O'Brien on board and first-time cheekpieces on. We backed him at fancy prices each way in advance, and again at 16-1 on the day of the race.

Spider had actually managed to get some good Grand National hospitality courtesy of legendary PR operative Dave Jones, who did a fantastic job for the Tadcaster-based John Smith's outfit. Smith's and Jonesy were always excellent hosts and it was no-nonsense hospitality all the way.

As Silver Birch sailed past the post ahead of his pick, Spider sought some solace with a story on the big race winner with care homes and pubs named after Silver Birch all battering their local bookies. You couldn't make it up, but it was true and the nearest boozer to Betfred HQ in Warrington really was called The Silver Birch. The regulars in there duly thrashed their local bookies.

The week after Aintree, it was the Scottish National at Ayr and we flagged up trainer Charlie Swan's Irish raider Emmpat at 7-2 as the single banker for the weekend, which put us back on winning tracks, although the Scoop6 pools continued to evade us. As May started, the Scoop6 pools began hitting record-breaking levels with the August 2002 record win fund sum of £1,371,162 in danger of being overtaken. Our longshot Cockney Rebel at 25-1 had won the Guineas, so the Scoop6 pools were still on the up with £1,054,523 carried over from Newmarket and the next weekend they went past the £1.5 million mark.

But before then, that first Bank Holiday weekend in May was special for another reason as our old chum Harry Findlay, then aged forty-four, was set to bank £2 million by landing the Race08 that had been going for 81 weeks without anyone pulling it off. The Race08 bet was basically an extended Scoop6 with eight legs and each had the first seven in the tissue betting numbered 01 to 07, followed by the 08 which was everything else, that is all the longshots lumped together as one pick.

It was no wonder nobody had won it since it had launched, but the £2 million weekend did look interesting. It is another one that got away as Spider had suggested we give it a go that weekend as the pool operators were offering a guaranteed £1 million on the Saturday, with another £1 million on the Sunday. But we decided it was a no bet, especially with such a bumper Scoop6 pool on the horizon to contend with. The Spider logic was that Guineas Day would see Cockney Rebel and some other longshots win - the 08 could be picked as a banker in several of the legs. And then on the Sunday, he fancied all the favourites and second favourites, and that came to pass as well.

Harry took down the two millions in quick succession, but we did at least get the gig to present the cheque for £2 million to Harry at Chester races. The Squirrel suit was dusted down, and with a picnic in the boot of Richard's top-of-the-range BMW, we ventured to the midweek Chester meeting, which also had Sir Alex Ferguson and his

Manchester United team in attendance.

Someone like England ace Wayne Rooney would probably have agreed to hand over the cheque for a sum in the region of £20,000, but the Race08 people arranged for The Squirrel Syndicate to do it for £750. With the benefit of hindsight, we needn't have bothered as we've still not been paid the agreed sum, and we do wonder if Harry ever got his winnings?

We met Harry by the weighing room as he was great friends of a fair few jockeys and he was in a very bouncy and buoyant mood, as we suppose you would be having just won £2 million. He told us how he had backed his promising novice chaser Denman to win £1 million at the Cheltenham Festival, where he beat Willie Mullins's charge Snowy Morning by ten lengths with Mick Fitzgerald on board, to land the Royal & Sun Alliance Chase at odds of 6-5 favourite.

The day for us had started with a jackpot perm as the pool was quite decent at Chester, and we'd had a couple of early winners go in before we met Harry. The Squirrel suit was donned by our pal punting Pete, and we made the cheque presentation on the lawn.

Pete was no stranger to dressing up, as Spider had once persuaded him to don a disguise as a garden gnome and go with him to invade the Royal Horticultural Show at Tatton Park after the organisers banned gnomes. The pair of them took a fishing rod and slipped into their costumes in the toilets after getting through security. They had banners proclaiming 'Give a Gnome a Home' and 'Crackdown on Gnomelessness' and even sat on one of the rockery displays with their fishing rod dipped in a pond.

Protest over, the crusaders for gnomes everywhere went off to the champagne tent for a lobster lunch after pulling off their stunt. At this point, the local TV cameras caught up with them. Pete, who hadn't booked the day off work, had to pop his whiskers back on while dining for fear of being caught on camera.

Harry was more used to publicity and had been in all the newspapers after Spider did up a yarn about his £2 million Bank Holiday weekend. Everybody was congratulating H on his betting bonanza. Always keen to explain that he wasn't a £2 punter, Harry revealed he had spent £61,000 on the Saturday perm and another £82,000 on the Sunday bet. He also admitted before then that the pressure was on a bit, as they had been about £350,000 down on the Race08 since its inception.

We do recall one of the issues with having a crack at the Race08 was that the rules posted on their website said you could only withdraw £10,000 at a time, so we felt our efforts were better targeted at the Scoop6. After Harry headed off clutching the comedy Race08 cheque – probably to his helicopter – we headed to the champagne bar as we had been finding all the winners and needed to celebrate. We landed a share of that day's jackpot, and after some more champers, our minds turned towards the coming weekend's Scoop6.

The initial maths suggested we'd need about £100,000 for a proper go, and Richard suggested we should get Harry on board, but Spider had a wealthy celebrity acquaintance in mind. The pair of us, awash with champers and winnings, agreed that we would try and turn up £50,000 from other investors as Spider had a very interesting web of contacts.

Anyway, on the return journey, he firstly dialled *Coronation Street* legend Ken Morley, who played 'Randy' Reg Holdsworth, the boss of the fictional Bettabuys supermarket on the ITV soap. The call went something like this… 'Ken, I've got a great opportunity for you, would you be interested?' Wheeler-dealer at heart Ken had replied with a tentative yes then Spider went into the explanation of the scheme. There was a pause, as the soap superstar replied: 'What, gamble £50,000 you must be mad! Have you been taking the waters at the races?' A rather tipsy Spider then said: 'Should I take that as a no then?' It wasn't really a question he needed to ask.

His next port of call was an attempt to get hold of comedy legend Bernard Manning, who had often passed on tips for winning horses to Spider and his *Sun* colleagues, but for whatever reason he failed to raise the owner of the World Famous Embassy Club. Bernard, aged seventy-six, sadly passed away in June of that year, so we missed the chance of calling in for a celebratory scoop in his sort of salubrious establishment in Manchester's Harpurhey.

Undeterred, Spider ploughed on. One of the dads from his youngest son's football team was next on the list. It turned out this fella used to take his son Joe to the match and stand on the touchline reading *The*

Sun's Favourite racing pull-out. Only the Sunday after the Guineas, this chap started telling one of the other parents how the 'Scoop6 Squirrel' column was brilliant, having tipped up the 25-1 winner of the big race. Another dad pointed and said, 'See the other Joe's dad over there; he's the one who writes it.'

Shortly after, rugby-loving Nick Blashill, then aged thirty-nine, introduced himself and was very complimentary about our column. He thought it was fantastic tipping, which perhaps it was, or did we just get lucky? At that point, Nick had asked if we could recommend a good trainer. He and his partner Gary Brierley wanted to buy a racehorse, as their business in Bulgaria was going very well. Spider said he'd think on it, and they exchanged numbers.

Just a few days later, Nick took the call from Spider. Unbeknown to us at the time, he was sitting round a table in Bulgaria with three other businessmen. Spider asked if he'd purchased the racehorse and, when that was a no, he added: 'Then better than that is perhaps putting £50,000 into the Scoop6 this weekend as it's a bet to nothing?' Unlike his showbiz chum, Nick played for time saying, 'Can I come back to you?', then he returned the call a short while later saying: 'I cannot do £50k, but can do £30,000?' At this point, Nick was told the money had to be in The Squirrel Syndicate account by Friday in order to be involved in the bet. We hadn't all met the bloke and we were not going to be letting him have a £30,000 line of credit. But, true to his word, the money landed that Friday afternoon.

The next day, Spider was very keen on Wise Dennis at 20-1 in the twenty-nine-runner Victoria Cup at Ascot and Leslingtaylor at 20-1 in the twenty-three-runner Swinton Hurdle at Haydock. He put the pair of them in a Lucky 15 with another double-figure winner and a second, collecting £26,000 from his multiples before the Scoop6 had even finished. He had wisely also told his old schoolfriends Denis and Yozza to get on, and the winnings went around.

Sadly, The Spider had been summoned home for babysitting duties, so he failed to place all his bets. The one he placed with the two 20-1 shots and a 10-1 winner with a second landed him £26,000, but the other four he didn't place would have added another £125,000-plus to his haul as he had selected another 10-1 winner on the day. 'It's only money' as he so often says.

We took that as a sign, and sure enough with those longshots going in, only eleven ticket holders, including The Squirrel Syndicate, had a share of the £1.6 million-plus win fund. It was very fitting that the last leg winner that weekend was our banker James Fanshawe's Firenze at 7-2 in an eleven-runner sprint at Nottingham. The dividend was a tasty £149,715 and as well as The Squirrel's collective, including Blash, two other pub syndicates involving *Sun* readers landed a share of the Tote's treasure.

The coming Saturday was going to be fun with a £1,108,811 bonus on the table. One of The Squirrel-loving syndicates, headed by pub manager Steve Barber from West London, contacted us to see if he could join the party. We were happy to have Steve and the guys on board and we headed off to Newmarket, managing to get more winners from the week before on side. We had about eight horses covered in the bonus race which, from memory, was a twenty-runner Betdirect. com Heritage Handicap at Newmarket.

Things are a bit hazy on this bonus, but if we are correct about the race, then the winner was Nicky Henderson's 14-1 shot Sentry Duty that landed the prize for our eight-strong winners' alliance, netting us all an extra £123,201. The week before when getting on board with us, Steve said: 'I've gone in with The Squirrel. Half a loaf is better than none.' After landing the bonus it must have been lively in his boozer, but the moral of the story is 'Always take the bread if you get a chance to go in with others.'

For pub manager Steve and his Squirrel fans in the boozer, that meant winnings of £272,916, which is not to be sniffed at. By joining forces with The Squirrel Syndicate they'd put themselves in with a proper squeak at landing the bonus. Blash had turned his £30,000 into £100,000 and everyone was in the dough.

With the pools drained we took the foot off the Scoop6 gas for a bit, but at the end of the month Cockney Rebel was back out in the Irish 2,000 Guineas. Steve Harley, from the band of the same name, who topped the charts in 1975 with 'Make Me Smile' ('Come Up And See Me'), had been asked by owner Phil Cunningham if he could use the name for the colt. It turned out Phil landed a few lumpy bets on the Rebel and after the Newmarket Guineas he threw a birthday party for trainer Geoff Huffer, presenting him with a brand new £35,000 silver Audi.

Huffer was full of confidence ahead of the Curragh attempt and we were as well, making Cockney Rebel a single banker in the final leg of the Scoop6 and once again he was to make Harley and all the connections smile. The tip was a delight for *Sun* readers as three of the five winners that week were Squirrel fans, including a Ladbrokes punter from Staffordshire with a £64 perm, and they all collected £36,388 each and a shot at the £77,974 bonus on Derby Day.

None of the bonus hunters were in luck when South Cape at 14-1 won the 2.35 at Folkestone. But once again Squirrel fans were in the money, as we tipped Frankie Dettori on Authorized at 5-4 to land the Derby, but also gave Pocketwood at 8-1, Keyaki at 3-1 and Secret Tune at 4-1 for a tasty 388-1 four-timer on the day.

The month ended with us in the running for a £295,294 Scoop6 win fund with the final leg at Bath. We got through the first five races with our perm, leaving us with one ticket on Potentiale the 5-4 favourite ridden by Darryl Holland, and it turned out Harry had Bathwick Breeze still in at 11-1. Potentiale was travelling well, but when they went behind the trees on the far side, he dropped out of shot and fell back in the race, losing his place about seven furlongs out. Then back in camera shot, he made ground and was back in the thick of things.

Coming round the home bend, Holland took Potentiale wide and once again off the TV screen. Back in picture, Potentiale started to make ground, but Bathwick Breeze held him off by four lengths. Afterwards, the jockey said the John Hills-trained gelding had lost its action.

The £295,294 had escaped our paws and ended up in Harry's pocket. We predicted the following week that Harry would choose the favourite Osiris Way as his bonus pick as that's what we would have done. He did, and that went in landing him the additional £204,529 bonus. With Harry having taken £500,000 from the Scoop6 in the past week or so, we put our paws up and waited until mid-July before having another go.

At that point we asked our new rugby playing pal Blash if he fancied a share of the bet to the tune of £4,000. After getting that £100k from his first go, there was no hesitation this time. Sadly, despite our longshot

Charlie Tokyo storming home in the 48th John Smith's Cup at York on heavy ground for Richard Fahey, we failed to land the Scoop6 and Blash had lost most of his £4k.

Not the same story for massive Scoop6 Squirrel aficionado Adam Phillips, aged forty, from Wick, West Sussex, as he had our long-shot in after reading the column as his two-year-old son was another Charlie. When Jamie Moriarty's magical ride gave him victory on the Knavesmire, just three tickets, including Adam's, were standing in the Scoop6 win fund. Carol Vorderman fan Adam was then cheering on trainer Tim Easterby's 6-1 shot Countdown with David Allan on in the final leg, before dashing off to William Hill's to check his single ticket windfall. Adam quit his £6-an-hour canteen job with Tesco after his £427,434 win. He had only slipped his £2 line on during a shopping trip with his wife, Sue, as he had a spare couple of quid in his pocket.

The following week Adam was on the *Morning Line* and aiming for a £183,186 bonus. In the Summer Plate at Market Rasen, Adam selected trainer Peter Bowen's Iron Man, the 5-1 second favourite. The win was never in doubt as he stormed home by eight lengths under Paddy Merrigan. That took Adam's haul to £610,620 for just £2 – he certainly, like Agnes Haddock, had experienced the joy of six.

The following Saturday, a Coral customer from Liverpool was hoping to take his Scoop6 tally up to £114,567 after using a £16 Squirrel-style perm to land £80,197 the week prior from the win fund when Adam was clearing out the bonus pot. The Liverpool player's luck ran out in the bonus race at York when their selection El Bosque ran unplaced.

It wasn't until the end of August that the Scoop6 got exciting again and it was tax inspector, lucky Lisa Hotston, who taxed the pot with six winners for a £208,361 windfall. The following week, the Hampshire revenue office worker was after a tax-free £212,966 bonus at Beverley, but fortunately for us she left it behind. September was just a month of continuous rollovers.

October with a thirty-five-runner Cambridgeshire to crack on the opening Saturday, started to see the pots swell to tremendous levels and though we tipped the big race winner John Gosden's three-year-old Pipedreamer, the 5-1 favourite under Jimmy Fortune, the win fund rolled again. The year before, we had given Formal Decree at 9-1 to land the Cambridgeshire, and we were happy to have back-to-back winners. A week later, despite The Squirrel Syndicate's winning banker Fonthill Road at 13-2 landing the final leg, the combined pools had reached £1,674,472 – with a bumper £958,743 in the win pot and a further £715,729 in the bonus bin before racing had even started.

The Tote were predicting a £2.5 million combined pot on the coming Saturday October 20th and that looked just about right to us. As previously mentioned, with 107 runners declared overnight and Ken urging caution, it really was probably a no bet, until Spider banged on about soft ground form and a couple of highly likely French raiders.

He suggested a smaller perm with the soft ground types to the fore and the Frenchies both as bankers, highlighting the fact that Barry Hills had a great record in the first leg with longer priced fillies. We asked Blash if he fancied a quarter share for £4,000 and once more the rugby player put into the £16,000 perm that was to help us land a then history-making Scoop6 dividend of more than £1.5 million. Blash was now firmly a part of The Squirrel Syndicate, and his hard-drinking rugby ways went down a storm with all the guys.

It was only many years later when Blashy explained that, on that first occasion in May, the £100,000 had been split four ways. Then when losing in July, one of that four never paid up his share of the losses. Another one of the four, having lost £1,000 said he was quitting while still in front, and we were not to ask him again.

When Leg Spinner landed the win fund for us, the other guy who hadn't paid over his £1,000 loss in July, rang up to say something like, 'Haven't we done well!' to which Blash replied something along the lines of: 'Thanks, WE have done well, but YOU haven't.' The Welcher then added: 'You know I'm good for a grand?' Well, if Blash had given him a third of his £375,000 share of that win, then he would have been good for the grand.

The moral of the story is to pay up if you lose, and then you may be in again on the winning day. With another single ticket Scoop6 win, courtesy of Charlie Swan's Jalmira at 8-1 and then that marvellous Malt Or Mash moment in the November Handicap bonus race, if Mr Welcher had been honourable and paid up, he could very well have had a share of £750,000.

But Blash rightly was having none of this nonsense and stood his ground, splitting the £750,000 fifty fifty with Gary. It was enough for Nick to pay off the mortgage on his vast detached house which backed on to Stockport Rugby Club, where he hobbled out for the veterans on occasional weekends. Our tips on what we nowadays call Malt Or Mash Day probably went some way to helping quite a lot of people land the Scoop6 win fund that day – we even gave old Inchnadamph as a single banker in the final leg.

This is what we told *Sun* readers:

With a rollover a possibility, the suggested perm is 2×2×2×5×2×1 which is 80 lines at £2 each costing £160 – or £16 per person for a ten-strong syndicate. Picking a single banker helps to reduce the cost of the perm and Inchnadamph could win Jamie Spencer the jockey's title and a punter, the Scoop6.

Leg 1	2.05 pm Doncaster: LAKE TOYA (2)
Leg 2	2.35 pm Doncaster: BORDERLESCOTT (2)
Leg 3	2.50 pm Wincanton: KINGS QUAY (2)
Leg 4	3.10 pm Doncaster: MALT OR MASH (5)
Leg 5	3.25 pm Wincanton: ABRAGANTE (2)
Leg 6	3.40 pm Doncaster: INCHNADAMPH (1)

We tipped up Malt Or Mash as we did like it, but recommended others have lots of picks in that race as, if we got it wrong, then they would have around £1.2 million to play for in the bonus fund the week after. Our picks in the opening legs both finished second, beaten in photo finishes, but a fair few people went with two picks there and had found both winners, and then we had given the final four winners in the column.

A clutch of Scoop6 Squirrel fans won that day, and we got a lovely call after the dust had settled from one of them. Bricklayer John Heron, aged seventy-seven, from Cheltenham, dialled in thrilled to say that his £5,000 win had given him the foundations to finally retire. John, who was hoping to land the £70,000 bonus with the winner of the Paddy Power Gold Cup at his local track, said: 'I can't thank The Squirrel enough.' As John was one of thirty-three winning tickets from the week before chasing the bonus, we really did hope he'd get a share of it. Indeed, ten of them did divide it up after the Ferdy Murphy-trained L'Antartique at 13-2 ridden by Graham Lee, landed the spoils by a neck from Il Duce at 33-1.

We did know that a syndicate of Squirrel fans from a pub in Maidstone, Kent, had a share of that £70,000 on top of the £5,000 win from the week before, as landlord Derek Draper called to thank us. Delighted Derek said: 'The Squirrel is a must-read for Scoop6 players – it's just a shame he didn't leave the £1.1 million behind. He gave another couple of winners last week, but we arrived at L'Antartique in the bonus race by taking a vote.'

The Squirrel Syndicate is all for democracy and we can only imagine how many extra pints Deggsy sold on the back of those two wonderful weekend wins. Looking back, November 2007 was evidently responsible for a substantial amount of alcohol-induced liver damage the length and breadth of Britain.

Chapter 11

SUN-SATIONAL DAYS RACING

At the end of November 2007, a retired bank manager from Essex, supplemented his pension to the tune of £80,341, but missed out on the bonus of £34,432 at Lingfield.

Though as he was missing out on the bonus fund, London stock market trader Gerald Kistnen collected £64,974 from the win fund. The following week was the Hennessy Cognac Gold Cup at Newbury with a bonus of £62,278 up for grabs and The Squirrel told readers that Harry Findlay's Denman at 14-1 to win the Cheltenham Gold Cup in the spring could be good value.

Gerald, aged forty, plumped for top weight Denman first time out to do the business and the 6-1 second favourite was impressive, giving 19lbs and an eleven-lengths beating to subsequent Welsh Grand National winner Dream Alliance. A gelding that later had a great feel-good movie made about him called *Dream Horse*. Gerald, no doubt, went on to invest his Scoop6 gains of £127,252 on the stock market, but unbeknown to him and the rest of us, a financial global meltdown was just round the corner in 2008.

After Denman's victory we were surprised Harry hadn't pocketed the win fund, but just a week later Mr Findlay was among eight ticket holders to share the rollover pot. Each ticket collected £22,303 and Harry had four of them. After his win, he called as he was sure The Squirrel Syndicate would be among the other four winners, but unfortunately that wasn't the case though two *Sun* readers had got lucky.

One of them was a Squirrel fan who won with a £32 perm and the other with a straight £2 line, so very well done; with the two remaining tickets held by a high-staking telephone player. The bonus race was the seventeen-runner boylesports.com Gold Cup Handicap. Harry was hoping to add the £76,470 bonus to his £89,212 win fund gains from the week before. But it was another David Pipe second string that came to the rescue of the bonus fund as Tamarinbleu at 22-1 under Denis O'Regan, ensured the roll, beating Le Volfoni at 25-1 and Patman Du Charmil at 20-1, a real bonus buster for Harry.

With Newcastle abandoned just three days before Christmas, two *Sun* readers were among the four ticket holders who collected more than £17,000 each on a truncated four leg Scoop6, on the back of which they enjoyed a fantastic festive season. They were both Squirrel fans as we had given two of the four winners in the shape of Jack The Giant and Cloudy Lane. From there, the bonus and the win funds rolled into 2008 and right through January.

February started with combined pools predicted to smash through the £1.5 million mark with a £651,154 win rollover set to top £1 million and the bonus did reach £508,861. Even Agnes Haddock had joined The Squirrel Syndicate with £20. Aggie was a guest of the Tote at Sandown, where the year before our tip Taranis had gone in and the horse's race card number coincided with her birthday, bringing a bonus race win to take her haul to £688,620 for a £2 stake.

In the column, The Squirrel Syndicate revealed we were certain that *Sun* readers would land a share of the bumper pot and with three winning favourites, including Harry Findlay's Gungadu at 5-2 in the last leg, it was a pretty straightforward Scoop6 with races from Sandown and Lingfield containing just sixty-one runners. At the end of a pulsating hour and a half on Channel 4 we were among nineteen ticket holders in the money - perhaps a bit of Aggie's luck had rubbed off on to our paws.

The dividend was £55,745 and our biggest surprise was that genial Harry, who owned the last Scoop6 race winner, wasn't joining us on the hunt for the half-a-million bonus at Newbury the next Saturday. Our hearts weren't bleeding though, as Harry had been on a damn good run since last summer and he had Denman to look forward to in the Cheltenham Gold Cup, so he wasn't going broke any time soon.

The next weekend was going to be fun at Newbury, but before then we had other winners wanting to join up with us for a combined crack at the bonus fund, including a *Sun* reader or two, as predicted. The most interesting of the nineteen winners was Glaswegian warehouseman John MacDiarmid, aged forty, who had borrowed £20 off his grandad to have a £2 line on the Scoop6 and a few pints of heavy that Saturday.

Funnily enough, John had thought his horse was only placed in the first leg, and he was actually watching the last race wanting Harry's Gungadu to simply place, as he thought it might be too painful to have five from six winners. When John called at the bookies on the Sunday, he was expecting a place payout of £23.60 and couldn't believe it when they apologised and told him they could only give him £600 of his winnings. John, from Govan, took the money and was in a state of shock when he discovered they owed him another £55,145. The opening leg John thought his horse was in, wasn't on TV and the winner was at another meeting and not the first race he'd watched.

The next weekend his Dunkirk veteran grandad, John, aged eighty-nine, turned up trackside, but we were busy tracking down extra members for our winners' alliance and only got to meet him after the bonus race had taken place at 3.20. In the car on the long trek south there was time to expand the group to five ticket holders from the week before, so at least we would be getting a handful of picks in the ultra-competitive twenty-four-runner Totesport Trophy Handicap Hurdle.

Warehouseman John wanted the 7-2 favourite Five Dream for the Nicholls and Walsh combination, but we had never met him before and usually made sure the newcomers to any winners' collective chasing the bonus were on the longshots. But Spider was certain that the favourite Five Dream would finish behind Ginger McCain's 16-1 shot Mohayer. It was fortuitous that the first trainer we bumped into on track was the great man himself. Reminding him of his encounter almost exactly twelve months earlier with a giant squirrel suit in the winners' enclosure at Haydock, laughing Ginger said very helpfully: 'Whatever happens, the favourite will be behind my fella.' We had put Mohayer up as a longshot in the column, so now we were very happy to have our new Glaswegian chum on the favourite that he wanted.

Among those we had been talking to about joining the syndicate of winners was ex-lorry driver Phil Carey, aged fifty-three, from Swansea, South Wales. Now we remember meeting six former Welsh miners down at Newbury as one of their number had a winning ticket. It's really hazy, but we think the group were there with Phil and possibly on the same table as John and his grandad as guests of the Tote.

Another player in with us had selected Gary Moore's 14-1 shot Wingman with the trainer's son Jamie in the saddle off bottom weight of 10 stone, and when he hit the front two out, we were all cheering. The top weight Nicky Henderson's Punjabi at 28-1 emerged from the pack as the only danger, but the weight difference always looked like being too much to overcome and it was. Unfortunately, another ticket holder who hadn't joined our alliance had selected the winner on his own. He took away £254,430.50 and left us the rest as a five-way split.

Trust us, with thirteen of the unlucky players who had gone on their own in the bonus bid going home empty-handed, a further £50,000 per ticket top-up for our feted five was most welcome. We popped up to the Tote hospitality table to buy the chaps some champagne and that's when we met Dunkirk veteran John senior. He confided that he still hadn't had his £20 loan repaid, and we'd better not be putting him in the paper as all his pals at the Glasgow ex-servicemen's club would be wanting him to buy them a drink. On top of that, John told us that he didn't like champagne, so we bought him a whisky – fine Scottish malt if we recall correctly.

It was great raising a glass with the Second World War veteran. He was loving his day at the races with his grandson, who was now £106,500 ahead from that £2 line from the £20 loan. The six Welsh former miners were happy enough with champagne and it was all rather jolly as we celebrated. Before leaving the track, we bumped into a journalist called Steve Jones, who was to become Templegate on *The Sun*, if he wasn't already, so we offered him a lift home, which was a quaint village somewhere in the Cotswolds. Wherever it was, it was on the way back North and saved him using cabs, or public transport, and was very picture postcard as you'd expect for a legend like Templegate.

Back in Scotland, John found himself on the front page of the *Daily Record* and he was very flattering about us. They reported that John said: 'I'd heard about The Squirrel and realised he was one of the best in the business. I'd have been nuts to have turned down his fantastic offer of forming a syndicate. He's an absolute pro and has won millions on the Scoop6 bet, so when a man like that offers to help you out, you know you've got a better chance of winning. I'm usually a shy guy but I was shouting and screaming and all the Glaswegian in me just came out.'

Now we weren't actually there to witness John going nuts, but he had a very thick accent and we probably wouldn't have understood a word of what he was shouting. Instead, we were cheering on Wingman from the stands, and there was more than enough noise in the air to carry the six-year-old to victory.

The Scoop6 was soon enough rolling again, but before we were to get anywhere near it again, there was a duel in the Cheltenham Gold Cup that had racing fans everywhere gripped. The race was billed as Kauto Star vs Denman and we were all firmly in The Tank's camp, as that was Harry's nickname for his beloved soon-to-be champion. With the mud flying, Denman at 9-4 did the job in style putting seven lengths between him and the odds on 10-11 favourite Kauto Star with their stablemate Neptune Collonges a short head back in third. The night before, Spider having had a great Thursday at Cheltenham, had ended up buying champagne in the Queens Hotel and told everyone Denman would do the business.

As the champers flowed, and a contingent from the FA, guests of Betfred, drank a lot of it and departed, Spider met a chap called Martin Hilliard. Martin, a fellow Merseysider, was living in the village of Kill, not far from the Curragh. Martin had not had the best of festivals, so Spider attempting to cheer him up and rescue his Cheltenham, suggested putting everything he had left on Neptune Collonges each way with Mick Fitzgerald on board at the overnight odds of 100-1.

Obviously, if Martin had been a 'Squirrel' column reader, he would have already had Denman at 14-1, but to rescue a losing festival you always need a longshot so one at 100-1 would do the trick. We were to meet Martin many moons later on a jaunt to Doncaster and we bizarrely ended up sharing a cab with him on the way to the racecourse. After all those years, he still remembered that 100-1 rescue mission. He was so grateful that he got his friend to give us a spare hospitality ticket, thus saving us putting folding over on the gate.

Another time at Doncaster station we remember queuing for a cab and suggesting that the nice young man behind us and a couple of ladies dive in with us. The well-dressed youth informed us that his father had a horse running that day, and that he had gone to school with the son of the former *Today* newspaper tipster Henry Rix. When we checked out the horse Tomyris, it turned out that the lad's dad was none other than Kazakhstani billionaire Nurlan Bizakov. And he does have a fair few horses. We felt it was a tenner well spent, as it's not every day you have the son of a billionaire in the back of the cab with you.

Later in March, Dame Judi Dench spoiled what would have been a £1 million rollover Scoop6 when her Mark Tompkins-trained horse Smokey Oakey won the Lincoln at 10-1. Beaten into second was our old favourite Blythe Knight at 22-1 with tragic Jack Lee's heartbreak horse Babodana at 28-1, a stablemate of the winner, back in third. Dame Judi's winner was most welcome on the Emerald Isle, where a Totesport credit customer, back in the days when you could bet on the slate, landed a monster £611,938 win fund.

The next week the Irishman had to find the winner of the fourteen-runner Rosebery Handicap at Kempton, but his pick, Mr Aviator at 13-2, was half a length behind the eventual winner, the warm favourite Philatelist at 5-2. Michael Jarvis had this fine stamp of a four-year-old bay horse in fabulous fettle and when he hit the front inside the final furlong it really never looked in any doubt.

On Grand National Day at Aintree, old Jack Lee was once again in our thoughts as the winner we both tipped in our head-to-head challenge the week before he died, Comply Or Die was looking like going off joint favourite with Donald McCain's Cloudy Lane. The Pipe hotpot duly won the big 'un by four lengths and we were sure Jack would be cheering him on with a heavenly choir.

Two fellow *Sun* racing columnists John Francome and John McCririck tipped the winner. Though Big Mac's column actually flagged up that his selection was that of his long-suffering wife, The Booby; quite magnanimous for the world's leading misogynist at the time. Yet it was no booby prize for owner David Johnson as Timmy Murphy guided his mount over the thirty fearsome obstacles for the £450,720 first prize. With four winning favourites going in during the Scoop6, that Grand

National winner gave Harry Findlay four of the six Scoop6 winning tickets of £24,977 each with the other two being £2 players. Precision engineer Keith Dixon, aged fifty-nine, placed his bet with William Hill at Chelmsford, Essex, just before the local racetrack opened, and the other winner was a Coral customer, from Herts.

The next week the bonus race was the eighteen-runner Bathwick Tyres Handicap Hurdle at Newbury and we recalled Harry doing us with Bathwick Breeze at Bath the year before. We suspected he'd be collecting the £443,522 bonus on top, with a race of that name to sort out. Well, Harry did just that having trainer Tom George's 10-1 shot Majaales with Denis O'Regan among his five picks. As well as Harry taking his winnings past the £400k mark, one of the £2 players added a bumper £88,000 to their near £25k from the week before.

That same week, the 5,396 strong Elite Racing Club's Saturday syndicate landed the £94,853 win fund, which worked out at almost £20 per member. Now the furry fellow did regularly suggest getting together with your mates, but fortunately we have never had that many friends, and a Squirrel Syndicate win was always well worthwhile.

At about this point we had suggested to Trevor at *The Sun* that a Scoop6 syndicate for readers might be fun, but he was happy with the column as it was. *The Sun's* readers were also happy as they had landed literally millions with our perms and tips since we started in 2004. We simply put the wider Scoop6 syndicate idea on the back burner.

Chasing the bonus at Ayr, Elite Racing's syndicate manager Matthew Budden, aged thirty-four, burnt the midnight oil studying the form in the twenty-four-runner race. Not unsurprisingly, Martin failed to find Sean Curran's 66-1 winner Iris De Balme. Predictably the Scoop6 rolled as earlier, Border Castle at 40-1, had landed the Scottish Champion Hurdle and rolling pools were all around as May approached.

After 2007, was it too much to expect May to become a merry month again, probably not as it turned out. The winning formula the year before had entailed a trip to Chester and once again we hit the Roodeye at the same time as Sir Alex Ferguson and his Manchester United were closing in on yet another Premier League title. While Sir Alex proceeded towards the stables on the centre of the course, the track commentator announced the racehorse That Boy Ronaldo was a non-runner and the Portuguese superstar was still with Manchester United at the time. Fergie failed to back the winner Viva Ronaldo at 20-1 in the same race, but did have a cheery look on his face when Championship Point powered home later.

We couldn't help smiling at the races that Ladies Day as some of the outfits were worthy of National Cleavage Day and many of the syndicate are great believers that breast is best. Sir Alex gets a mention, as it was later in the month at Haydock that we were to see him again. He does so love the sport and just like John MacDiarmid and his grandad, Fergie hailed from Govan, which has never been the poshest part of Glasgow.

On May 17th the Scoop6 win fund hit £649,307 after ten tickets on Adrian Nichols mount Cape Royal, the favourite the week before, found themselves missing out in a photo finish. It was Lockinge Day at Newbury and our single banker that week was Godolphin's 3-1 favourite Creachadoir under Frankie Dettori and the maestro got him home comfortably ahead of the Sir Henry Cecil-trained Phoenix Tower with Ted Durcan on board. It was only the second leg when Frankie picked up the prize, but Paul Cole's Strategic Mission at 16-1, landing the London Gold Cup Heritage Handicap at Newbury, put more than ninety per cent of remaining tickets out in the fourth leg.

As Sir Henry's 15-8 favourite Ajaan won the fifth leg, it wasn't too much of a surprise that eleven of us should be sharing the win fund when jockey Jim Crowley got Derek Shaw's 9-1 shot Baby Strange up by a neck in the final leg. While we had one ticket for a dividend of £59,027, Harry Findlay had six of the eleven for a nice touch of £354,162 and that was even more than the bonus £298,956 up for grabs at Haydock the following week.

By race time the next weekend at the Lancashire track for the fourteen-runner bonus race the 3.05 Silver Bowl Heritage Handicap, we had teamed up with Harry and a couple of other ticket holders. Two of the previous week's winners were going it alone. We were pretty confident of finding the winner and when 'The Choirboy' Walter Swinburn's charge Staying On at 6-1 did just that under Adam Kirby it was happy days, particularly for Harry with more than half of our share of the bonus pot with the other £149,478 going to the Elite Racing syndicate of nearly 6,000.

Ahead of the race we got our friend Aggie Haddock into the parade ring and she got a smacker off Sir Alex as she wished him luck. Manchester United's gaffer Sir Alex was trackside once again and we saw him in the parade ring ahead of the 5.15 as he had a share in the Barry Hills-trained Hunt The Bottle ridden by his son Michael. Suffice to say, this wasn't going to be another Rock of Gibraltar, the horse famously gifted to Fergie by JP McManus and the Coolmore crowd, who were at the time the owners of his club Manchester United. Despite a late gamble from 15-2 into 11-2, Hunt The Bottle could only manage fifth behind the Pat Eddery-trained Castles In The Air ridden by his brother Paul.

At least we'd had a winning day and then in midweek it got even better with a nice share of a £1 million jackpot. It's just great when you get your pool betting right. We ended the month with a lovely winning longshot at York. Spider had spotted the lowly weighted Masta Plasta at 33-1 in the last leg of the bet on the Knavesmire and the opening show was 20-1 as he'd clearly got on early. Sprint king Dandy Nicholls had booked 7lbs claiming Mrs Adele Mulrennan, now an *ITV Racing* pundit, and she made every post a winning post for a victory at 16-1. The rollover of £163,944 was on long before our lovely longshot hurtled to victory.

The next weekend was the Epsom Derby and we tipped up Jim Bolger's New Approach at 5-1 – our third consecutive winning tip in the Vodafone-sponsored Classic. The £258,559 Scoop6 had already rolled by then as Holbeck Ghyll at 15-2 won the Epsom Dash over five furlongs for Andrew Balding and William Buick.

We were hopeful of another rolling Scoop6 on June 28th and had tipped up birthday boy Brian Ellison's Chester Cup third Tilt in the race, but out of stall eleven he could only manage eleventh place. It was Tony Martin's Irish raider Arc Bleu at 14-1, who kept on well under Adrian Nicholls, to nab trainer Richard Fahey's 16-1 shot Halla San, under Paul Hanagan, by a head approaching the line. This win helped put a Southern punting syndicate of our acquaintance into pole position to land the £711,831 win fund and when the Michael Bell-trained Redford at 7-4 favourite under Jamie Spencer won the final part of the puzzle – the Toteswinger Handicap at Newcastle – they had the money in the bank.

Must confess though congratulating them on a massive win, deep down we were very keen for them to leave the £305,070 bonus behind the week after. They had to find the winner of the Old Newton Cup at Haydock, which wasn't easy. They went for Luca Cumani's Mad Rush, gambled into 5-2, and when Seb Sanders pushed the throttle in the final furlong, nothing could live with the four-year-old. Unfortunately, for us and everyone else, a comfortable four-length victory took the syndicate's winnings to £1,016,901.

That July on John Smith's Cup Day at York, we tipped up Blue Spinnaker at 12-1 in the opening leg. Then we followed up with John Quinn's Zomerlust priced up at 12-1 in the paper overnight as our longshot, but the six-year-old sprinter sluiced through the heavy ground at the Knavesmire and returned the 4-1 favourite under a mud-splattered Robert Winston. Despite flagging up that pair, it was the Jane Chapple-Hyam-trained Yellowstone at 10-1 in the penultimate leg that knocked the final eleven ticket holders out of the win fund, leaving a rolling £184,578 combined with £68,696 in the bonus fund.

Yet before having a crack at that, we were going for the £685,520 jackpot at Leicester, which was an evening meeting and it was Channel Crossing at 16-1 in the fourth leg that made the dividend worthwhile with a payout of £60,839 to a £1, which we managed to get to 50p.

Our single banker Drill Sergeant landed the 2.20 at Beverley that weekend and then an anonymous forty-something Blue Square customer spoiled our £1,030,837 win fund dream by finding all six winners at Newmarket, Beverley and Goodwood and, in solving the eighty-five-runner puzzle, broke a lot of hearts.

The next week the London geezer was going to Newmarket, where the Nanny Goat, which is cockney rhyming slang for the Tote, had lined up the eighteen-runner Adnams East Green Nursery Handicap at 2.35 for him to solve with his free shot to add to his million. Trainer Richard Hannon's Gal Aloud at 16-1 winning under Ryan Moore gave us all a £459,211 rolling bonus. At the same time, a couple of punters with four-figure perms landed £50,462 each and the week after, one of them waltzed off with the bonus fund to take their winnings to £509,673.

The next week the launch of a new bet, The Super 7 from the Tote, had us all gazing into our crystal walnuts to try and scope out any value. In what was almost an elongated Scoop6, value was far from apparent – so we decided to leave it alone and only play when the pool reached record-breaking levels. This was a reasonably wise move as we went on to land a share of the record-breaking dividend on The Super 7 and the Tote then rather swiftly terminated their new bet.

Meanwhile, that weekend with Haydock abandoned, the Scoop6 became a Scoop3 and our single banker Elnawin at 6-4 favourite landed the first leg and we even gave the winner of the third and final leg at Kempton Premio Loco at 2-1 with Clive Brittain's Hattan at 16-1 landing the middle leg to enhance the dividend. We took a share of the £157,784 win fund and the £48,272 place fund, but with 440 tickets sharing the former and a further 3,498 getting the latter it wasn't anywhere near even a small fortune. The win dividend paid £358.60 and the place payout was £13.80.

As the first anniversary of our £1.5 million Scoop6 win with Leg Spinner in the Cesarewitch approached we encouraged *Sun* readers to have a go at the best bet on the planet. We gave them Kite Wood at 9-4 as a single banker and even Heaven Knows at 5-1 in the last leg, but the rolling pools turned up at Newmarket.

Twelve months on the Scoop6 even had seven more runners declared overnight, with 113 contestants as opposed to 106 runners the year before. We gave Ron Harris' talented four-year-old sprinter Judge N' Jury at 11-2 as that week's banker in the fifteen-runner Totescoop Catterick Dash and that went in. At that stage, the two remaining win fund ticket holders were evidently not Squirrel fans and the bet rolled. The final leg was the Cesarewitch and last year's winner Leg Spinner was top weight off 9st 10lbs, but this time the second from 2007 Nicky Henderson's eleven-year-old Caracciola did the business at 50-1, beating Tony Martin's Pitman's Derby winner Arc Bleu by three lengths. We seriously hadn't thought lightning might strike twice.

The pools were building and the November Handicap loomed with that anniversary of £3 million in three weeks on our minds but, despite giving the first two winners in the Scoop6 Harry Patch 4-1 and Les Fazzani 7-2, things were going to change as the pools rolled on towards

£2 million. The final leg at Doncaster saw 33-1 shots Invincible Force and Barney McGrew fight out the finish with that hardy jockey Franny Norton almost lifting the former over the line to prevail by a head.

Michael Jarvis' two-year-old sprinter Harry Patch was named in honour of a chap of the same name, known as the last fighting Tommy from World War One. At this point, little did we know that we were actually going to get the bullet long before Harry himself passed away at the grand old age of 111 in July 2009.

Chapter 12

A £3.1 MILLION AFTERNOON

The telephone call was pretty apologetic and came a week after the first anniversary of our £3 million in three weeks. To be fair it wasn't exactly what we were expecting.

Racing editor Trev very rarely rang, if ever. Here he was explaining that, with cutbacks galore as a result of the drop in advertising revenue due to the financial crisis, he had a difficult choice to make.

Apparently, it was either the Scoop6 Squirrel, that furry bundle of fun, or Sir Clement Freud, who at this point was father-in-law of *The Sun* owner Rupert Murdoch's daughter Elisabeth, wife of his PR guru son Matthew Freud.

It probably would have saved Trev a bit more money axing Sir Clement with his reputed £5,000-a-week column, but we fully understood how it was The Squirrel Syndicate getting the chop.

Life as the punters' furry friend had been fun and we had no real intention of giving up, as we were just starting an online Scoop6 syndicate called AggiesNags with our chum Agnes Haddock. Out of the goodness of our hearts we continued supplying the column to the online edition of *The Sun* without actually mentioning we'd sort of had the tin tack. Anyway, it carried on making a weekend appearance for months. The following April our former colleague Sir Clement, a one-time Liberal MP, died, but at that point we had no plans of going back into print.

Funnily enough, the first week without the 'Scoop6 Squirrel' column in the pull-out saw Templegate step into the gap with six losers under the headline: '£3 Million Scoop6 – Templegate's Guide'. It was a massive week with record-breaking pools on the horizon after we believed nine weeks of win fund rollovers, but Templegate suggested ten weeks was the number. We both agreed the win pot would hit £2 million and the bonus on top would be another £1 million.

The column we supplied to *The Sun* online that same Paddy Power Gold Cup weekend at Cheltenham gave a certain 13-2 winner Imperial Commander as the banker in the sixteen-runner feature race - it was business as usual for the bushy-tailed bounder. Lest we forget, Imperial Commander was to become a standing dish at Cheltenham and even won the Gold Cup a couple of years later for trainer Nigel Twiston-Davies.

It was the following weekend when the win pool hit £3,496,088 and eight ticket holders led by our friend Harry Findlay landed it for a return of £437,011 per ticket. Among the winners was Nick Gliddon, aged forty-three, from Kingsclere, near Newbury. His eight-year-old daughter Ellie was set to join him as he chased the bonus in the Hennessy at their local track. The Squirrel suggested Air Force One at 5-1 was the one to beat and the bonus hunters did have him and the 9-2 favourite Island Flyer in their picks along with Ellie's selection, the last fence faller, Big Bucks. Yet once again it was David Pipe and Tom Scudamore with Madison Du Berlais at 25-1 that came to the rescue of another big Tote pool as the £1,529,525 bonus fund rolled after their three-length victory.

With a rolling bonus we went into battle the following week tipping Araldur 11-4 favourite as a winning banker in the 2pm at Sandown, and it was no surprise when two tickets split the win fund with a dividend of £128,359 each and a crack at the rolling bonus of £1,639,547. The bonus race the following Saturday was the 3.20 at Doncaster. Ray Stubbs, aged forty-nine, from Bebington, Wirral, and Lawrence Ireland, fifty-one, from Bedale, North Yorks, having staked £2 and £16 the week before, were now chasing £1.6 million. It was very exciting for them, but the bonus rolled when the Tom Tate-trained Charlie Crab at 12-1 won under Keith Mercer.

With Cheltenham abandoned, it had become another Scoop3 and though there were seven winning tickets collecting £7,386 each, none would be playing for the rollover of £1,709,969. Though the Scoop6 was proper value as the winning treble would have paid just 519-1.

The Welsh National was a heck of a race at Chepstow that festive season and the year before we had tipped up winner Miko De Beauchene and this season we really fancied Venetia Williams' eight-year-old Mon Mome en route to the Aintree equivalent, but the bay gelding hit the second fence and the favourite did well to stay on into eighth. We did have Jim Dreaper's winning Irish raider Notre Pere at 16-1 in our perm and as it transpired the final leg of the Scoop6, the Desert Orchid Chase at Kempton, was to be particularly painful for us.

We and Harry Findlay had fourteen of the nineteen remaining Scoop6 tickets going into the last leg and the win fund of £393,673 was well worth sharing, but the real prize was to get another crack at the £1,808,264 bonus pot. We each had a ticket on the Nicky Henderson-trained second favourite Petit Robin at 2-1 and, with Barry Geraghty booked, he looked the likely winner as they came over the last with German raider Fiepes Shuffle at 16-1 under Jamie Moore the danger.

Well, we had met up in the Leg Spinner room in The Three Tunnes for a beer and a cheer ahead of the last race having had the first five up. Then in the last hundred yards it was like watching slow motion. Barry was doing his best, but the Hun horse seemed to have the impetus and did us in the shadows of the post. We at least had beer to cry into, but it was hard to take after such a rollercoaster of a day with Mon Mome backed at fancy prices failing to deliver when favourite.

Little did we know just how far that bonus was going to roll, nor who we would be meeting when we eventually won it on a day when we actually didn't back Mon Mome in the bonus race. The New Year came and 2009 was going to be special for so many reasons. As we quaffed champagne at Squirrel Towers on New Year's Eve none of us knew of the other fine Krug-glugging moments that lay ahead.

At the end of January with combined pools of £3.5 million, a syndicate of our acquaintance from East Sussex, landed a lovely win fund of £1,541,739 and we had tipped up 6-1 favourite Jass in the penultimate leg at Donny. They now had a free crack at the bonus fund of £2,469,009 in the eleven-runner William Hill Top Team Football Prices Handicap at Lingfield but failed to find trainer Jim Boyle's 15-2 winner Formation, making for yet another rollover.

On Valentine's Day we had our hearts broken when a Suffolk punter landed the £669,465 win fund with winners at 18-1, 16-1 and two at 11-1, including future Gold Cup winner Jonjo O'Neill's Synchronised. But the week after, this particular winner earned a place in all our hearts when he pledged to give the £2,755,923 bonus fund if he landed it to the Royal British Legion, which was a fantastic bit of philanthropy.

It reminded us of our Thomas Russell Cancer Trust days, but on an absolutely massive scale. The usually iron-hearted Tote even had their hearts melted and offered the charitable chap a charity bag of sand on the winner of the bonus race at Kempton whatever happened. Tom George's Nacarat at 10-1 won the bonus race, which meant the mystery punter could still make an £11,000 donation to the Royal British Legion thanks to the Tote.

The pools carried on rolling and it was the weekend ahead of the Cheltenham Festival with £999,702 in the win fund when we finally got a ticket to give us a shot at the record-breaking £3,184,369 bonus pot. Everyone with a winning ticket in that win fund landed more than £58,000 each, so we were all well ahead, but the big prize was the bonus in the John Smith-sponsored Midlands Grand National.

For the post-festival trip to Uttoxeter, we invited as driver Patrick Shields, who years later was to pop up on Channel 4's *Morning Line* looking like an extra from *The Godfather* with dark shades and a black overcoat – he really just needed the violin case – after winning a share of £226,000 with us. But this was a practice run for that trip to Warwick when he wouldn't be driving, although that's another story. With Patrick at the wheel, we decided to invite new boy Blash, a legendary beer monster, along for the ride. He had landed lumps with us in the past and could act as minder if we got too merry with a cheque for £3.1 million.

Now before race day we'd already been in touch with Harry Findlay and knew he possessed four of the seventeen tickets and we had one. Between us we managed to find another nine ticket holders who were happy to come on board. Just three tickets were going it on their own in a bid for the full £3.1 million, or a share of that, or potentially bugger all. It was high stakes for them, but if we managed to get that pot amongst us, without having to split it, then each ticket was worth

£227,455 and the rest of us thought that was good enough. Two of the punters away from the track were happy with Harry helicoptering in and signing up on their behalf to our winners' alliance. As ever, we knew we'd be more than happy to hand Harry a cheque for £1,364,770 if we pulled it off.

But before then, we had some new faces on board and one of them had a remarkably wonderful story to tell. For building site foreman Bob Blackhurst was advised by his surgeon after open-heart surgery on a double bypass that he should avoid excitement. So after going under the knife, Bob's first trip out after his life-saving op was to place a small bet on the horses. Incredibly, Bob, aged sixty-four, saw his £2 line on the televised Saturday Tote Scoop6 bet come in. This landed Bob more than £58,000, but his heart was in for even more strain that weekend when we met him as he colluded with ten other winners to try and collect a share of that record-breaking £3,184,369 bonus dividend.

Construction site manager Bob, of Winchester, told us before the big race: 'It's only three weeks ago since I was having a double bypass. My GP referred me to the specialist after I was short of breath and suffered a pain in my chest. Within a few weeks, I was on the waiting list and then I was being operated on. My first real expedition out after the surgery was to place a Scoop6 bet on the telly races and some ante post bets on Cheltenham at Ladbrokes. I really couldn't believe it when my Scoop6 bet came up. I'd placed an order for a car for my wife and was due to collect it at the end of this month, but with being off work after surgery I was worrying about how I would pay for it.'

Anyhow, Bob's financial dilemmas were soon to be solved with The Squirrel Syndicate on the bonus race winner Russian Trigger at 8-1 to land the biggest ever Tote dividend, breaking our own record from November 2007. Bob, along with nine other winning syndicate members, had cheques for £227, 455 presented to them by The Squirrel within minutes of the winner passing the post at Uttoxeter.

He said: 'I am so grateful to The Squirrel and Harry Findlay for helping us and they even had a doctor in the syndicate who checked my racing heart after the horse won. It was so exciting, but I didn't overdo the shouting and cheering, nor the champagne supplied by the Tote.' Bob's stunned wife, Marguerite, aged sixty-three, said: 'I can't believe he's won and there's a doctor on hand to check out his chest. The heart surgeon has obviously done a good job. But he had told him not to get too excited, so Bob didn't tell him he was planning a trip to the races to take his winnings to more than £285,000.'

Fellow winner and syndicate member Dr Shivaji Jadhav, sixty, from Blackburn, Lancashire, who also collected a total of more than £285,000 for his winning £2 line on the Tote Scoop6, told us: 'I've checked Bob's heart after the race and it was in good order – they've clearly done a fantastic job on him.'

The syndicate had the majority of the field covered, with only rank outsiders Always Waining and The Dark Lord left out. The three other ticket holders plumped for Hold The Pin, Gidam Gidam and Kilcrea Alsa, meaning that they would have shared the bonus with the syndicate had one of those three won. We had sort of popped into the Tote box without an official invite, but it was very jolly and our friend Dug the Tyre, from Hazel Grove's famous Milesmore Tyres empire, was actually in the adjoining box.

Jovial Dug was a guest of Always Waining's owner Peter Douglas, who founded a very successful Staffordshire engineering business – the PJD Group based at Castle Donnington, near Derby. Charming Peter came across and told us not to bother backing his lad in our bid for £3 million, as he wanted better ground. Now that was very nice of Peter, as it echoed what we thought.

As we chatted, Peter laughed that his trainer Peter Bowen hadn't told him not to back it, but suggested we didn't read anything into that as apparently, he never told him to back the horse even when it won. Another one we almost left out was Venetia Williams' Mon Mome, now Spider had already told us when the Aintree Grand National weights came out that this French-bred horse was well worth a bet for the big race. In fact, he'd been banging on about Mon Mome since before the Welsh National.

Anyhow, his thoughts on the Midlands Grand National for the French-bred was that it was just a prep race for the big 'un at Aintree. And Spider wasn't wrong as the nine-year-old never got in the race. As the mud flew, Victor Dartnall's gelding Russian Trigger battled on gamely to bat away Flintoff by two-and-a-quarter lengths, with Hold

The Pin back in third. The ten punters who all held a single ticket got £227,455 each, with Findlay's four lines scooping him a total of £909,820.

We vividly remember that day as it was another superb Scoop6 record-breaking dividend and we were all smiling ever so broadly writing more than £2.9 million worth of cheques from our Squirrel Syndicate's account.

Richard told the newspapers afterwards: 'I was delighted to write out cheques for more than £2.9 million as they're a great bunch of gamblers. I'm not the type of punter who ever thinks he can win it on his own – it's always so much better winning with other people. The three punters who missed out made a very definite choice, but the odds were stacked against them. I do all my punting by looking at the mathematics of it and when the numbers stack up then you have a bet.

'Harry Findlay is a real punter and he's happy to take a profit any day. Nobody was ever going to win the Scoop6 bonus on the John Smiths Midlands Grand National on their own and we know this from experience. It's great that smaller punters get the chance of some big returns and the looks on the faces of everyone in the Tote's box at Uttoxeter racecourse were simply full of the joy of winning.

'It's what a day at the races is all about and incredibly, less than eighteen months ago, we picked up some other record-breaking dividends worth together more than £3 million in the space of three weeks.'

Among the other stunned winners were auctioneer and valuer Richard Rood, from Portsmouth, who placed his initial £6 bet on his fifty-fifth birthday and landed an enormous present; water board worker Ian Howard, aged forty-two, from New Romney, Kent; retired coach painter John Johnston, seventy-five, and his lorry driver pal Norman Dunnett, forty-seven, from South Queensferry, Fife, who staked a pound each to land their £285,000 haul. Being Scots, we had to write those boys a cheque each for half their share. One not wanting the other to get the benefit of the extra interest no doubt – canny Scottish chaps indeed.

The Tote had the top team of Mary Coyne and ever-efficient PR George Primarolo on hand and even telly's Clare Balding made a flying appearance into the box. Not the first or last time she's been in a box, but it was great to see her.

As the cheques were being written out, Mary from the Tote, asked Spider to give the winners a share tip as his stock market punts during a period when he actually had very little money were golden. Between serious slurps of champagne, Spider suggested everyone should lump the lot into Barclays Bank shares and before the year was out, if anyone had actually listened their fortunes would have been worth more than £1 million as the bank's shares boomed.

When Spider did get a few quid, he tried the same trick with Lloyds shares only to see them go into freefall, then bailed out by the Government. He became the very reverse of a millionaire, but as we all know gambling on the stock market is nowhere near as profitable, or as much fun, as gambling on the horses.

Totepool spokesman George even chipped in a golden line, or two, to his media mates, saying: 'Although the record-breaking Scoop6 bonus fund has finally been landed, it couldn't have been won by a nicer mix of punters and they've all pocketed a serious amount of money. To have a seventy-five-year-old who won the bet with a single £2 line standing toe-to-toe with legendary punters like Harry Findlay and The Squirrel is what the Scoop6 is all about and goes to show you don't have to invest a huge amount to pocket some serious cash.'

It was the first time the Scoop6 bonus fund had been won since 30th August 2008 and had reached £3,184,369 before the record-breaking dividend. That Saturday's Scoop6 was not won, meaning £83,506 rolled over to the following week. There were four winners of the place dividend, each of whom won a massive £11,929.50.

Before hopping in his helicopter, happy Harry Findlay told the media: 'This is what racing is all about – there is no better bet on the planet than the Scoop6. It was a pleasure to share the winnings with so many wonderful people.'

We managed to eventually get back to The Three Tunnes with Patrick roaring into the car park. He was more than ready to throw a fair few pints of Robinsons' mild down his neck after being unable to consume industrial quantities of champagne like the rest of us at the races. It was funny how the year flew after that, and the next big 2009 highlight for one of our number was to be the Grand National at Aintree.

Now Spider had two punts at big odds when the weights came out earlier in the year. Irish Grand National winner Butler's Cabin at 33-1 backed into 7-1 favourite for the big race, plus Mon Mome at 40-1, which he had backed with a best odds guaranteed bookmaker.

Although that wasn't quite the order of the day when he tried to collect. He'd had large each way bets on both. Blash and a few others listened to him, and after the glorious victory at odds of 100-1, they all commissioned paintings of the winner from a wonderful watercolour artist called Ian Fennelly.

We have one of his somewhat abstract images of our £3 million winning weekend winners in all our homes, but Spider has Mon Mome hanging beside the stairs because, before that win, we'd only ever heard of Foinavon winning the Grand National at 100-1. The remainder of 2009 was nothing to write home about for the syndicate, but we did have another record-breaking win just around the corner.

The Squirrel Syndicate in the parade ring with Albatross Club pals ahead of Oi The Clubb Oi's run at the Cheltenham Festival in March 2019.

The champagne was popped after Russian Trigger won the Midlands Grand National at Uttoxeter in March 2009 – landing us a bumper cheque for £3,184,369 – what a super Saturday afternoon that was.

OTCO at Nottingham racecourse with former Champion Jockey Jim Crowley in the saddle – the pair were two wins from two runs at the track.

Above: Lots of headlines in 2007 with those remarkable wins that added up to £3 Million in three wonderful weeks.

Right: The Squirrel catching up with the *Racing Post*

Chapter 13

ANOTHER RECORD DIVIDEND

The Tote Super7, wasn't really that super, nor very magnificent… it was a very tough bet to get right as it had one leg more than the Scoop6. Just imagine the true odds of having a 50p accumulator on all those winners and then trying to land it most days… you'd go broke.

We probably had a couple of goes at winning it ahead of what could well have been a record-breaking dividend in January 2010, but we shared the pool and carried off £326,042 for getting it right.

The year before on January 15th 2009, Dave Nevison missed out on a £360,000 Tote Super7 after jockey James Davies fell off Neil Mullholland's Topless when well clear inside the final furlong. He must have felt a real tit.

Nevison and his business partner Mark Smith had staked £84 and were counting their cash when Topless jumped the last in the 3.50 Carlsberg UK Handicap Chase over three miles and three furlongs at Taunton. The eight-year-old pulled five lengths ahead and then the mare drifted left. Davies tried to straighten her with a slap of the whip, which made her jink right and him unseat.

We suppose if Carlsberg did rollovers, then it probably had to be something like that, as second-placed Pangbourne then won the race. We actually all probably remember their near miss, more than we recall our win, as you do tend to dwell on the ones that get away. We had something equally painful on Grand National Day a few years ago, but more of that later.

The Tote engaged a new PR person that January in the shape of George Primarolo, who landed himself in the Tote Super7 crosshairs on his first morning in the office. Very honestly, George said: 'The Super7 is a young bet and the idea at the moment is to grow the pool so that someone gets a big jackpot out of it at some point.'

Honesty is, of course, the best policy, but it didn't stop him getting both barrels from Nevison, who launched a broadside at that comment, saying: 'That means they're picking the days that it won't be won and it offers no value.'

And that was pretty much the case, hence us only getting involved now and again. We believe the bet was terminated at some point in 2010, possibly not long after the first Irish winner, a chap from Athenry, landed 110,000 euros for his two-euro line placed in a local Ladbrokes shop. At that point the Tote Super7 had only been won five times since it launched in September 2008 and was rightly canned in our opinion.

Meanwhile, 2013 had ended with a Christmas to remember for a couple of lucky ladies, who each won the Scoop6 with £2 lines and a crack at a £419,067 bonus that had been rolling over since August 31st. Sally-Anne Clayton from Wishaw, North Lanarkshire, and Sheila Stephenson from Lincoln, each won £24,511 for their two quids. They had a big hill to climb in finding the winner of the bonus race in the Welsh Grand National and when Mountainous passed the line in front that left £437,340 in the bonus bin.

Shotgun Paddy hit the target in the Betfred Classic Chase at Warwick two Saturdays later and an electrician from South Yorkshire with a £2 line sparked a £178,426 payday for his couple of quid. Even more exciting though, he had a shot at the now rolling bonus of £495,536, but he left that behind when his 8-1 pick Night Alliance was pulled up in the Peter Marsh Chase at Haydock.

February started with six tickets chasing the now £600,000-plus bonus in the Betfair Hurdle at a rain-sodden Newbury, but when Splash Of Ginge at 33-1 went in for Nigel Twiston-Davies, that was yet another roll. One of the six was £2 player Mark Turner, who had the third, 6-1 favourite Irish Saint, for a three-way split of a small fortune. On the plus side his wife, Lynne, at least had a tenner on the winner with the Tote and collected £437. Let's hope Lynne never used those immortal words of all wise wives: 'I told you so!'

Yet it was to be a day for the ladies, as a dramatic conclusion in the pursuit of that afternoon's win fund saw two tickets left in the finale. One was on Rigoletto, who was withdrawn after bursting out of the stalls. That ticket was transferred onto the favourite My Kingdom, who duly went on to win and land grandmother-of-nineteen Geraldine Hughes a £54,782 windfall. And Geraldine's day was to get better as she placed her £2 bet at the Betfred shop beside the Wetherspoons in Hoylake near her Merseyside home, so she qualified for a £100,000 bonus on top from Fred Done. They don't call him the Bonus King for nothing.

A little like Agnes Haddock eight years earlier, Geraldine used nice names and her brother Paddy's ginger hair to help her land £154,782 with a free shot at the bonus of £702,010. Liverpool fan and great-grandmother-of-four Geraldine, aged sixty-seven, had watched the Reds' 5-1 demolition of Arsenal at Anfield on TV with her family as her first five winners powered home in the Scoop6.

When she switched on for the final leg at Lingfield, she thought her £2 punt was sunk when Rigoletto wriggled out at the front of the stalls. Mum-of-six Geraldine later said: 'I was delighted with the Liverpool result, but we had the family round for the game, so I wasn't able to watch the racing. I kept up to date with my picks via text on TV, and when I got the first five up I had them all watching the last leg with me.

'The biggest priced winner was Splash Of Ginge in the big race at Newbury at 33-1 and I only picked that as my brother Paddy had a lovely mop of red hair when he was a boy. He's seventy-six now and it's receding a bit, but that winner left just seventeen tickets in the bet. It had gone from around 100,000 tickets in at the start to just two left in the last leg. Mine was on Rigoletto and the other was on Hadeeth that finished nearer last than first.

'When mine burst out of the starting stalls before the race I thought I had lost, but it was withdrawn and classed as a non-runner, so my ticket automatically went on the 5-2 favourite My Kingdom and that won. It was fantastic and I've not been able to sleep since the win.

'It is unbelievable, and what made it even more incredible was when my husband Wally rang me the next day to tell me that I'd had a £100,000 bonus added to my win as we'd put the bet on with Betfred – he'd read about it in the *Racing Post*.

'He was on his way to Richard Fahey's stables in Malton with our sons, Stephen and John, when they spotted the article with news about the Betfred bonus prize. They each had to read it twice, before they rang to tell me. I wondered who was ringing so early in the morning, but it turned into a very pleasant surprise.

'The day before, I went into the Betfred shop on Hoylake High Street to place the £2 bet and then came home to watch the match. I've had four winners before, but never had all six. My best wins before this have been a few hundred pounds on the Placepot.

'This is life-changing for us and now we've got another bonus to aim for on Saturday in the Grand National Trial at Haydock Park and that is £702,000 and I really cannot believe that. I thought they were kidding when they told me I had an extra £100,000 bonus on Sunday and now a free go for another £702,000 this week in the bonus fund is mind-boggling.'

We'll let Geraldine explain her win in her own words, as it's pretty unbelievable: 'The first horse to win was on Channel 4 at Newbury and I'd picked Upswing as we're just round the corner from Hoylake Golf Club, so I put the 11-4 favourite in my bet and that won leaving 24,084 tickets in the win fund.

'The second leg was Gregori at Lingfield at 11-4 leaving 8,156 tickets in and the next was 11-4 favourite Indian Jack at the same track with 1,816 tickets on it and I picked them both as they are boys' names and I like horses with boys' names. I then went for Splash Of Ginge at Newbury and just seventeen tickets went through on that and my brother Paddy's hair helped me pick it.

'Then in the fifth leg at Lingfield I had 8-1 shot Rivellino – with a name like the Brazilian footballer, who's a year older than me, then I had to have him and that left just two tickets in the bet. And then I got the biggest bit of luck when my horse burst out of the stalls and I ended up on My Kingdom.

'In William Shakespeare's play, Richard III once said 'my kingdom for a horse,' but for me My Kingdom was the horse. I'm a big fan of Elvis - he's The King, but we're not going to Memphis as we're all off to Cyprus for my grandson Jake Painter's wedding to his fiancée Rachel. It will be a great day in the sunshine later this year. Now that's what we need for the rest of the week, so that Haydock Park dries out and they can race... it will be a bonus.'

Geraldine was speaking at the two-up two-down terraced home she shared with her husband, Wally, a seventy-two-year-old retired electrician. He was a bit of a wag as well, saying after her win: 'Gerry's the real bright spark in our family pulling off six winners in the Scoop6. I'm just keeping the ticket safe until Saturday when she gets her free bonus pick in the big race.'

Even Betfred boss Fred Done, who created Britain's first betting shop millionaire when Stuart Bolland from Cadishead, Greater Manchester, won the Scoop6 in October 2004, was on Geraldine's side.

Fred said: 'Our biggest ever female Scoop6 winner was Agnes Haddock who landed £688,620 after placing her £2 Scoop6 in the Betfred shop in Northwich, Cheshire, in February 2007. But if Geraldine lands the bonus, like Aggie did, then she will take her crown as Britain's most successful female gambler on the horses and all for just two quid.

'Geraldine has already collected a £100,000 bonus for placing her £2 bet directly with Betfred in the shop and now she's looking at an even bigger bonus with a free pick in Saturday's big race at Haydock, weather permitting. But I am known as the Bonus King, so wish Geraldine well with her bonus bid. And if Gerry pulls it off, she'll be the first winner, man or woman, of two bonuses in the space of a week on the Scoop6.'

The six winners on her Betfred slip and tickets left in the win fund on each one:

Leg 1 – Upswing 11-4 favourite 1.50 Newbury 24,084 tickets left

Leg 2 – Gregori 11-4 2.35 Lingfield 8,156 tickets left

Leg 3 – Indian Jack 11-4 favourite 3.10 Lingfield 1,816 tickets left

Leg 4 – Splash Of Ginge 33-1 Newbury 3.35 seventeen tickets left

Leg 5 – Rivellino 8-1 3.45 Lingfield two tickets left

Leg 6 –My Kingdom 5-2 favourite 4.20 Lingfield Geraldine's single

Unfortunately for Geraldine, her luck ran out at Haydock when 16-1 shot Rigadin De Beauchene landed the £42,712 prize in the Betfred Grand National Trial, but that was another story as she watched the race with thirty-nine members of her family at the track.

Geraldine, wearing a glittering outfit with shimmering accessories, said: 'It is unbelievable – I am all shook up at how well I've been treated. The night before, I heard the cover version and that was it, I was picking Merry King. I am a massive fan of Elvis and the horse has such a lovely name. I even got to meet jockey Tony McCoy and trainer Jonjo O'Neill – I am a racing fan and that is a priceless picture for my mantelpiece. I haven't really spent any of last week's winnings, but I plan to let the kids, the grandkids and everyone have a little.

'A £702,000 bonus would have gone a long, long way. It is absolutely astonishing that anyone can win so much money for just £2 and I'll carry on doing the Scoop6.'

Winners like Geraldine are just what the Scoop6 needs, and it was for people like her that The Squirrel and friends set up their online syndicate. We were sure we'd get more super wins, which we did, and we'll come to some of those in a bit.

As the Scoop6 win and bonus rolled, it got very exciting at the start of March for a sixty-year-old £2 Coral punter, from Nuneaton, who landed £412,691 when Headly's Bridge won the Greatwood Novices' Limited Handicap Chase knocking five other ticket holders out. He lined up a shot at a bumper £878,564 bonus fund with a crack at the seventeen-runner European Breeders' Fund William Hill 'National Hunt' Novices' Handicap Hurdle Final at Sandown. On the day he plumped for Brother Brian who finished fourth behind 20-1 winner Brave Vic.

Towards the end of April, the rolls were reaching levels never seen before. Spider suggested we set up a tented drey outside Haydock Park racecourse to try and drum up even more interest in the pools that were set to hit £4 million. We even got invited on to the Channel 4 *Morning Line* for a chat on the day of the races, but we had to do the interview by phone. We were simply too busy to get trackside as it took a full morning working on the perm and studying the form.

Elections were in the air around this time and as we headed back from Haydock through posh Wilmslow in Cheshire - we spotted then UKIP leader, fifty-year-old Nigel Farage. Nigel was foraging for votes on Grove Street, one of the main shopping thoroughfares, so we parked up to have a chat.

Now David Cameron was Prime Minister at the time and as we headed towards Nigel wearing a seven-foot-tall Squirrel costume we had visions of his security detail decking us, rather unceremoniously. Yet far from that, Nigel's slightly puzzled look initially, changed into a beaming smile.

Mr Farage extended his hand and told The Squirrel: 'I know all about gambling.' He then duly posed for pictures, while passing pedestrians scratched their heads as we both looked a couple of nuts, but Mr Farage wished The Squirrel Syndicate well with our punting and we duly promised to buy the beer-drinking party leader a pint if we won.

Seeing an opportunity to promote The Squirrel's SuperClub.com party, we told the waiting media, after our impromptu meeting: 'You don't have to be nuts to join Nigel's party, but perhaps it helps. He came across very well, most people spotting a near seven-foot-tall squirrel in the street might run a mile.

'Though we suppose we were dressed as the traditional British red squirrel – not as the North American grey variety that is taking jobs off our true native-born squirrels. We have lots of members of our online syndicate in Scotland, next thing you know the Scottish National Party will be signing up to get extra funds to buy votes for their independence campaign.

'Punting and politics don't generally mix, but members of all parties are among our online syndicate. Once you start mixing squirrels with politics some might say that's the first step towards madness... on a personal level we think they are all nuts. Perhaps, if we win this week-end's Scoop6 I can stand for the Save Our Squirrel Party? People would be nuts not to vote for me and join up online.'

'We don't want four million members, just this weekend's £4 million Scoop6. Though a place on the Brussels gravy train for a British red squirrel could see those all-important EU funds diverted to our nation's woodlands to help endangered species.

'Saving small furry creatures could be a campaign slogan, though I'm not sure if UKIP's Mr Farage would be covered by that description. We will keep our promise and buy him a pint if we win, as any gambler knows you have got to be as good as your word... something politicians would do well to adhere to.' That last point we were particularly proud of, but sadly for us none of it appeared in print as the media seemed to have a bit of a downer on dear Nigel.

We even got Agnes Haddock on the campaign trail as a SuperClub member. Her comments running on the newswires must have been one of the most surreal party-political moments of the campaign. Aggie said: 'I know which one I'd like to see running the country. But I am glad Mr Farage knows all about gambling – we'd be happy to have him join our online syndicate to win this weekend's bumper pots. I've seen The Squirrel in action and he's a smooth operator.

'I'd love to see him stepping out of the doorway at 10 Downing Street. He wants to spread warmth and winnings around the nation – it would be good if the Government were as big-hearted towards the electorate. The Squirrel has the feelgood factor.'

Unfortunately for us, we were not feeling too good after the penulti-mate leg that Saturday when Angel Gabriel flew home to win at Ripon. Our tickets were among the final sixteen to bite the dust. This triggered a rollover of £2,096,863 in the win pot and £1,777,220 in the bonus. This would build to £5 million on the table that first Saturday in May.

That meant all-time record pools since the launch of the bet on July 24th 1999. We had a record-breaking number of memberships in our online SuperClub with 2,428 memberships in the series, almost treble the previous top figure of 857. Each series ran for four bets and a membership cost £20, which was the same cost as a one-day syndicate membership.

Members could purchase as many memberships as they were comfort-able with, and any returns are proportionately returned to the members. The Scoop6 Squirrel made his page three debut that weekend – in the *Racing Post*, not *The Sun*, so he got to keep his kit on. The bet's organ-isers, Betfred, expected punters to plough around £2m in the pools that afternoon, which would see the dividend for a single £2 winning ticket hit £2.9m and the bonus reach £2.1m.

Betfred's odds were 4-11 that the bet would be won and 2-1 it would go begging and they took one punt of £12,000 on a rollover. The final leg of the bet was the colts' Classic and 40-1 outsider Night Of Thunder eliminated the one remaining ticket in the QIPCO 2000 Guineas. The final ticket holder plumped for Noozhoh Canarias in the decider and had a great run for his money as the Spanish raider led going into the final furlong on the far rail only to be struck down late on by Thunder.

The shock result set up the mouth-watering prospect of a £7.5m Scoop6 the following Saturday, the likes of which had never before been seen in Scoop6 history. An incredible £3,427,714 was ploughed into the pools by punters across the country, which left a total of £3,296,563 in the win fund and £2,291,377 in the bonus.

The week after lightning struck again, if not thunder, as Ballyglasheen stayed on dourly to win the Pertemps Network Handicap Hurdle at Haydock, thereby setting up a £10 million Scoop6. The Evan Williams-trained four-year-old was the solitary uncovered horse in the race and eliminated the last 207 tickets in one swoop.

Turnover was once again incredibly strong, with a remarkable £3,653,178 – up £225,464 on the previous weekend – invested by Scoop6 punters in the hope of becoming an instant multi-millionaire. The rollover was the tenth on the bounce and meant punters could set their sights on a win fund of £4,575,175 and a bonus fund of £2,839,354 at the start of business the following Saturday May 16th.

Betfred odds on the Scoop6 going were 4-9 – yes, and 13-8 – no, but no lumpy £12k on this day as two betting shop punters made it through to the final leg of a £10.7m Scoop6. An £8 Ladbrokes customer was double-handed in the finale, with Escape To Glory and Justonefortheroad carrying their hopes at Thirsk, whilst a £2 straight line punter in Ireland relied on the Kevin Ryan-trained Capaill Liath.

It was the Ladbrokes punter who came closest to landing the monster £6.8m win fund as eventual runner-up Escape To Glory was unable to reel in Llanarmon Lad, whose victory set up a spectacular £15m Scoop6. There were 765 winners of the place fund, which returned a dividend of £1,717.40 - not a bad consolation prize.

Totepool revealed a staggering £6,569,058 was pumped into the pools that weekend and the win fund was £6,874,345, with the bonus pot now standing at an all-time high of £3,824,712. Like so many others we did dearly want to get our paws on that little lot. Yet it wasn't to be. We placed two perms, one with the first five winners in, the other with the last five winners and we needed an extra £17,000 to weld those two perms tightly together. We were £11k short of immediate funds on the day to enable us to have the final leg winner Chatez in both perms.

Eight punters though were celebrating after becoming millionaires when Chatez won the final leg of a colossal £16m Scoop6. A rollercoaster afternoon began with 16-1 outsider Bear Behind eliminating nearly ninety-six per cent of the ticket pool in the first leg. The remaining 238,627 tickets were whittled down to 122 going into the final leg, where Fergus Sweeney guided home the millionaire-making Chatez to win by half a length. Each ticket holder collected £1,342,599 and were to play for a further £5,481,763 in the bonus race the following Saturday.

Three of the eight were betting shop punters. One of those was £2 Betfred customer Craig Brazier, aged thirty-nine, from Mansfield, Notts, who cleaned bins for a living. After the win pool went, Betfred boss Fred Done said: 'In recent weeks I've done the conga when the Scoop6 has rolled. Tonight I'm dancing with joy after making eight millionaires. That's what the Scoop6 is all about. I can't wait to meet them all next weekend when I take them racing. I wish them the best of luck going for the monster £5.5m bonus fund.'

A history-making £11,047,002 was staked on the Scoop6 that day, which was an increase of just under £4.5m on the previous weekend. It was no wonder Fred was so delighted with a thirty per cent takeout for organising the pool. There were also 7,327 winners of the place dividend which paid £301.50, and we got a fair few of those.

It was multi-millionaire gambler Bernard Marantelli, then aged forty-three, who won a British record Tote dividend of £5,481,763 after offering bin cleaner Craig the chance to double his £1.3 million win from the week before. Craig who was already a new millionaire from his two quid punt decided to go it alone, and his pick Tumblewind gave him a good run.

But it was Bernard's selection Top Boy at 10-1 that did the business in the sprint on the Knavesmire. The pair had shaken hands and wished each other well before the race. Craig then headed to the Tote box, which had a fine view overlooking the finish line at York. However, as the race unfolded jockey Adam McLean, aged twenty-two, got Top Boy up on the line. Speaking on Channel 4 after riding the winner, McLean said: 'I had no idea there was a ticket for £5 million riding on the horse.'

We'd met Bernard a few years earlier at Cheltenham, where he was laying favourites on Betfair for six-figure sums and having a fantastic festival. In those days he was still a junior banker and gambling was just a highly profitable sideline. We estimate Bernard, probably by this stage at York, had landed around £20 million in Tote pool bets and had even set up his own football betting pool Colossus.

The London-based father-of-one graduated with First Class honours in biochemistry and worked in the biotech field for several years before completing an MBA at London Business School and trading equity derivatives for four years at Deutsche Bank. Bernard, the son of an Australian bookie, was also punting as a hobby and quickly cottoned on to UK pool bets and applied his purely mathematical approach to profit. After reading articles about the mathematics involved in landing the pool with perms, Bernard embarked on a sensational winning spree in his spare time having set up computerised 'bots' to place his winning bets.

Some of his biggest rewards came from harvesting millions on the Tote Scoop6 and jackpot. Shrewd Bernard holds the record as the only punter to ever land win and bonus funds three times in succession. It breaks our hearts sometimes when we think how it was our articles about the maths that brought Bernard into the Scoop6, as perhaps we had given too much information away.

Though The Squirrel Syndicate never really held on to our nuts - good luck to all in the game we say. As Blash once famously said, after recounting the story of gun-wielding Bulgarian mafioso trying to shake him down in Sofia: 'I've spent fortunes on drink, fast women and fast cars. The rest I've just wasted.' We do recall Bernard telling us at that first meeting at Cheltenham in the Betfair tent, that he could be run over by a bus and his 'bots' would still carry on winning money for him. It was most disheartening at the time, but Bernard has dodged lots of London buses since that day.

After his record-breaking win, Bernard said: 'We tried to get every-one to collude all week. In the end there was my ticket and two other syndicates, but we never heard from Craig the binman. It's the biggest ever pool win for us, but we were down on the series until this. I have won £1 million a couple of times previously, but sports pool bets are the most exciting betting products out there. Instead of winning £1.8 million today for a third of the bonus, I'd have been happy with £1.3 million for a quarter of it and Craig could have doubled his winnings from last week. But he managed that initial £1.3 million for just £2, which was a lot less than we staked on the bet.'

Magnanimous Craig welcomed Bernard into the Tote box after his win to congratulate him and toast his triumph. Craig was straight back to work cleaning bins on the Monday. Afterwards Craig said: 'Good luck to them. I have enjoyed every minute. It's been absolutely brilliant and for a few seconds it looked like my pick Tumblewind had a great chance. I'd backed the winner too many times on the all-weather with no luck, so I'd never have picked it. They did well and we're all happy.'

Chapter 14

BRAZILIAN GONE WRONG

A head of Bernard Marantelli landing that record-breaking Scoop6, we had suggested his new football pools company Colossus Bets should drop the minimum stake from £2 to 20p, making it easier for small punters to get involved.

Richard made the call to Bernard one evening from The Grapes Hotel in Hyde, where former world boxing champ Ricky Hatton was having a knockout session at the bar. Bernard did listen to the idea, and that June the World Cup offered an opportunity for a crack at his flagship £10 million Colossus pool, requiring seven correct scores in some football matches.

We had hoped Bernard would launch the bet and include the quarter-finals, semis and final in a Colossus. He did exactly that, and we placed a 20p perm aiming to get to the later stages, which we did, and we were all hoping to get some wages that way.

We liked the prospect of a £500,000 win to 20p and not the £5 million to £2, as the outlay was less, and we also had a chance of consolation prizes. We would then get a free go for a further £500,000 if we got it right.

The extra £500k was in the shape of a bonus correct score pick, something Colossus had taken on from the Scoop6. Bernard had also taken to offering a cash out opportunity. Though really not something we'd agree with, it could offer a chance to get out if circumstances had changed and your original bet looked bad value.

We were cooking with gas as our Colossus perm covered the quarter-finals, semi-finals and final with every score up to 2-1 either way. On 4th July, France played Germany in the first quarter-final at the Maracanã stadium in Rio de Janeiro and a Hummels goal in the thirteenth minute was the only one of the match, and we were off to a great start. That evening Brazil beat Columbia 2-1 and the next day Argentina beat Belgium 1-0 in Brasilia, then the Netherlands and Costa Rica drew 0-0, so we were more than halfway there.

The Dutch beat the surprise package of Costa Rica 4-3 on penalties and we marched on to the semi-finals. We liked the look of the German team for the first semi-final on July 8th against the home nation Brazil at Belo Horizonte, but this was a World Cup semi so we, along with the rest of the planet, were expecting a tight match.

What happened in that stadium was totally shocking, Germany played like the home team. After eleven minutes Müller put them a goal up, but then Klose scored and Tony Kroos bagged a brace, and Khedira got the fifth well before the half-time whistle. Our £1 million win was not on the cards any more.

After half-time, the Germans got a couple more for good measure. It was 7-0 going into the final minute when Oscar got the consolation goal for the host nation. Shocking in the extreme was the score of 7-1 and the next day the Dutch and Argentinians managed a 0-0 bore draw, before the Argies went through on penalties. The final was another nil-nil affair at ninety minutes, with Germany eventually breaking the deadlock in the 113th minute, so we'd had six of the seven results correct, but sadly the Huns had done us for £500,000 on our 20p perm.

We decided that general football score predictions were usually too tough, but carried on with the Colossus for a bit. We did have high hopes of the Euros and the 2018 World Cup, but Bernard never nailed the £10 million on the closing stages again. We had taken our shot and were outgunned by the Germans, which we suppose makes a change as they never managed to outgun us in two World Wars.

After our close call on the £10 million Colossus, we had to have a crack at the £1 million HDA15 when Bernard launched that. Once again, we went almost all the way with our home wins, draws and away wins taking us to fourteen out of the fifteen correct on our first go at that.

England goal-scoring legend Michael Owen was an ambassador for Colossus Bets, and the BT Sport presenter very kindly helped a young man wearing The Squirrel suit off the stage at a London venue when we told the waiting media: 'Just because the figures look enormous that doesn't mean the £10 million prize is out of anyone's reach – a £2 player like Agnes Haddock could get lucky and land the lot.

'But we're playing the Colossus as a syndicate and want to land a big pool that will spread out very well around the members. We take our hat off to Bernard's innovation as his baby was just what the football betting world needed. But most punters are not yet shrewd enough to realise what great value it offers. It is only a matter of time before it really takes off as more and more bookmakers come on board.

'We've already been one result away from the £1 million HDA15 and one off the £10 million Colossus – that's what we call knocking on the door and we know it can be done. But just like the Scoop6, it isn't easy, though with skill and judgement you can narrow down your odds and put that massive win within reach.'

Colossus was shortlisted as the Digital Gaming Innovation of the Year that September in the Global Gaming Awards 2014 in Las Vegas.

A few weeks later SuperClub member JRN placed a small 20p perm and pocketed a whopping £5,100-plus on a £230,000 rollover PICK4 of Champions League matches. At the time we said of JRN's joyous result, with a very late Gunners' goal on Arsene Wenger's sixty-fifth birthday: 'You'd be nuts not to play these pools. We think the people at Colossus Bets are defining the future of football betting, and our chum Bernard Marantelli is using his Scoop6 winnings to give footie fans a great run for their money. We know we keep banging on about it, but it is true and we're now getting winning members who are the proof of that pudding.'

Meanwhile, in June while the World Cup was rumbling on, a big-hearted betting shop punter from Kirkby, Merseyside, who won £139,665 for £2 and got a free shot at a £119,713 bonus – pledged to give half of any bonus bonanza to a cancer charity. The dad-of-two, who lost his thirty-eight-year-old sister Julie eight years earlier to breast cancer, wanted half of any future fortune to go to Macmillan Cancer Support.

The forty-nine-year-old driver, who placed his Tote Scoop6 ticket in his local William Hill shop, said: 'When my sister died eight years ago Macmillan were marvellous, and I've brought up her young daughter as my own ever since. Without them I'd have probably cracked and I very much appreciate all that they did.

'I have lost a good friend this year to cancer and Macmillan were doing the same great job for him and it is hard work at a very difficult time for people. They deserve all the praise and when I spotted a race at York with Macmillan in the name, I thought it was an omen and what I've never had I won't miss.

'My luck changed about ten days ago when my boss told me that my part-time job was going to become full-time. Then a couple of days later, I won the Scoop6. The £139,665 will enable me to buy our house and secure the future for us. It won't change me, but it will make a massive difference to us.

'The bonus is a hell of a lot of money, but what I've never had I won't miss and if I can put some of it towards a good cause then that would be great. I'd be happy to do that as I am not a horseman, I just picked the six winners the week before as a bit of craic with my dad. He watches them on the telly, because he doesn't really get out of the house.

'I cannot afford to gamble, but had a couple of quid spare at the weekend. I'd urge anyone to give a couple of quid to Macmillan if they're going racing this weekend. There are a lot of people worse off in this world than me, so if I can help then I am happy with that.'

The Kirkby gent and another seventy-one-year-old punter, from a Ladbrokes shop in Barnstaple, Devon, who both shared that weekend's Scoop6, each played for a further £119,713 with a free pick each in the bonus race – the Betbright Charity Sprint – at York. The Kirkby punter plumped for Charles Molson and even Totepool spokesman Andrew Griffiths was cheering on his pick in the bonus race, but See The Sun rained on his parade by winning on the Knavesmire.

In February 2009, a Scoop6 punter from Suffolk pledged a £2.75 million bonus to the Royal British Legion, but when his bid failed, he still made a £200,000 donation to the cause from his earlier winnings of £669,465 to a £2 stake. And in November 2007 we donated a portion of our shares in the £3 million winnings in three weeks to the Thomas Russell Cancer Trust Fund. Gamblers can give as good as they get, but our generosity was about to come and shoot us in the foot.

The week after that bonus rolled, we had put our selections up on the SuperClub website about thirty minutes ahead of the first race, which we did as a rule around that time. Nowadays they go up pretty much at the last minute, as a direct result of what happened on this day. The Scoop6 card was four races at Royal Ascot with a couple of sprints from Ayr. We decided that the Royal Ascot races were easier than the 4.15 from Ayr and made four picks in that tough race to give us more of a chance, with just two and three selections in the first few races from Ascot.

Well, we had a shrewd member, fifty-three-year-old Kiwi Mike Brown, of Canton, Cardiff, who ran a furniture shop called Branches of Bristol opposite Temple Mead railway station. He saw our selections online, but piggy-backed our perm with one of his own that had some extra runners at Ayr.

Now Mike slipped in Burning Thread at 12-1 in that 4.15 and his pick beat our selection Bear Behind by a nose in a photo, so heartbreak for us and the key to a single ticket £163,696 Scoop6 for him after our selection Baccarat won the final leg at Royal Ascot. Mike placed his £576 bet via totepool.com, which meant he also collected a £250,000 Betfred single ticket bonus on top. The Scoop6 is a game of skill, so it was fitting that Mike hit the jackpot with Baccarat.

Then it got really spooky, as it turned out that Mike's first big Scoop6 win was thirteen years earlier on that same Royal Ascot weekend and he went on to land a share of the bonus when Franny Norton got Paul Cole's three-year-old up to land The Pitmen's Derby in 2001.

Ahead of the bonus race on June 28th, Mike explained to Spider: 'I heard them talking on the radio about the assassination of Austrian Archduke Franz Ferdinand in Sarajevo on June 28th 1914 and couldn't believe the coincidence. As exactly thirteen years ago I won the Scoop6 on the final day of Royal Ascot then landed a third share of a special £200,000 bonus when a horse called Archduke Ferdinand, trained by Paul Cole, won the Northumberland Plate at 12-1.

'That win was also watched by a group of lads from Scotland who named their band Franz Ferdinand after discussing the assassination, but to find myself going back to Newcastle for a second chance of a massive win in the Northumberland Plate has to be a sign.

'My first win in a Scoop6 bonus race was back in 2001 and I picked up a total of £73,000. Then I went on to win the Scoop6 on my own in February 2004 and got £208,000 that time, but if I get the bonus on Saturday, it will take my Scoop6 winnings over the £1 million mark.

'But to win it thirteen years to the day is an astonishing coincidence and last August when I won, I shared an extra £50,000 with another chap as we'd both placed our bets in Betfred shops. With the £250,000 bonus for placing my bet direct via the Totepool website I feel I've already landed the bonus, so this weekend is just an extra bonus of £189, 869 - I feel no pressure and am totally relaxed about the weekend.

'The win was a real stress reliever. Like a lot of small businesspeople up and down the country, cashflow has been an issue for the past six years since everything went haywire in the global economy. The first £100,000 of my winnings goes to securing the future of the business. The Betfred bonus I won this time, with the one last year together with that first Totepool one, adds up to around a third of a million – now that's a real bonus.

'People don't need to win £2 million on the National Lottery at odds of 14,000,000-1 when you can win £400,000 to £600,000 on the Scoop6 at odds of about half-a-million to one. They say lightning doesn't strike twice, but the coincidences are incredible and I am hoping it does in the Northumberland Plate as picking up my second bonus on the race would be fantastic.'

Needless to say, Mike had our pick Angel Gabriel in the big race and landed that bonus of £189,869 to go with the £413,696 from the week before. All that on the hundredth anniversary of Archduke Franz Ferdinand's car stalling on Franz Josef Street in Sarajevo, Bosnia, five feet in front of assassin Gavrilo Princip, who fired twice into the vehicle killing both the Archduke and his wife. The event was the catalyst for World War One which cost 16.5 million lives.

Fred Done said after the race: 'It is an absolutely astonishing coincidence that Mike has already landed a share of a £200,000 Scoop6 bonus on a horse called Archduke Ferdinand and now he's back on the hundredth anniversary of the fateful assassination to do the same again in the SAME race. Talk about slaughtering the bookmakers! I've got Mike down as the Scoop6 assassin – he keeps sniping off our massive bonuses.'

Mike, clearly delighted with his success, added: 'The Angel of the North was certainly shining down on the North East for me today. The Pitmen's Derby has been lucky for me in the past, so I had a funny feeling it might be my day. The race couldn't have gone any better and I'm absolutely delighted to have hit the bonus.'

The remainder of that summer saw the Scoop6 turn into rollover central with eleven rolls taking the bet up to £4 million in the combined pools by mid-September. And nineteen punters were celebrating after Dance of Fire's victory in the 5pm at Doncaster, which saw them richer by £153,429 each on the Scoop6.

The next week they all got together with each of the nineteen tickets selecting a different horse. Well over half of the Ayr Gold Cup field was covered, including the eventual winner Louis The Pious. The winning ticket itself was one of several belonging to a large staking syndicate, which meant each ticket holder added £65,755 to the £153,429 they had banked the week before.

And Louis piously lined up an £11k win for another twenty-nine punters who got all six right in the Scoop6 that weekend. After that, the win fund went on rolling over until the start of November, when a single ticket picked up £750,920 with a crack at a £263,598 bonus pot if they got the winner of the Betfred November Handicap at Doncaster. A race with such happy memories for us, after that great afternoon in 2007 cheering home Malt Or Mash.

November ended with retired magistrates' clerk David Lawrence, aged fifty-eight, of Ramsbottom, Lancs, placing a £16 perm in a Betfred shop and solving the biggest case of his betting career when winning £158,139.30 on the Scoop6. A week later David failed to add the £100,552 bonus to his haul, but he is proof that crime doesn't pay.

In January 2015 our Scoop6 SuperClub offshoot, the Football Colossus Club, scored in the record-breaking £561,031 PICK4 with Swindon's 3-0 triumph at the Ricoh Arena landing members £22,038.48. A return of more than 110,000-1 for our 20p winning line was a great result and just 2.545 tickets got the four scores correct.

This took the Football Colossus Club returns since the start of the Premiership season to the £60,000 mark and we felt we were getting into the swing of things with our soccer bets.

We recruited Spider's respected journalist chum Nick Walker as the Football Ferret to aid with our footie form study and it went okay for a while.

Eventually we realised that we were never going to win these big pools on our own, and other forms of pool betting eventually eclipsed Colossus for us.

We'd still not put anyone off playing for 20p, or even £2, as you could just get lucky and land a big one. It could make watching the matches more exciting, though not always for us, as we did generally have all seventeen possible outcomes covered.

Chapter 15

GOING TO THE DOGS

With saturation coverage always useful, it does remind us of the time we won a then history-making greyhound jackpot at Sheffield's Owlerton Stadium back in July 2009.

It was Spider who spotted the record-breaking pot was going to smash through the £100,000 mark. Just how hard could it be to get the six winners in six dog races with a maximum field of six? Still, we weren't initially sold on the idea as we saw the number of the Beast 666 in what we had just been told.

While Richard was working out a possible perm, Spider was despatched to do some due diligence and find out if Sheffield was a fair track, as we didn't want to be sharing it with everyone on trap one six times in the jackpot races.

Spider slipped off to see Dug the Dog, or more accurately Dug the Tyre, at Hazel Grove's leading rubber emporium. His three-wheeler, just like Del Boy Trotter's, was parked outside bearing the immortal slogan: 'Milesmore Tyres New York, Milan and Hazel Grove.'

Well Dug told him that Owlerton was a really fair track, and he'd been trying the jackpot himself for a few goes without success. But even better, Dug said that a website 'We Love The Dogs' took the jackpot bet online. We wouldn't even have to go over the Pennines to place the perm.

This, it later transpired, was to become a real blessing in disguise as unbeknown to us, two punters from the South of England visited the dog track with almost £47,000 in plastic bags to place a massive bet perming every single greyhound in the six races... and they managed to lose.

The barmy gamblers targeted the British record-breaking £101,110.39

jackpot – but ended up out of pocket when our syndicate and another punter shared the prize with them.

The men had journeyed hundreds of miles from the South of England on a gambling adventure they believed would net them a small fortune. They stunned staff at the dog track when they opened up their plastic bags to reveal thousands upon thousands of pounds.

The pair had £46,656 to cover every permutation of the six dogs in six races won by Magna Flintoff at 8-11 favourite, Farloe Titan 4-1, Droopys Peaches 3-1, Derryhogan Chick 9-4, Razldazl Rosie 5-1 and Cill Dubh Light at 9-2.

But their cunning plan came unstuck when two other ticket holders also covered all six winners to split the pool three ways and land £33,703.46 each, which meant a loss of nearly £13,000 for the high-rolling Southerners. They returned home with an even smaller fortune than they arrived with and most likely their tails between their legs.

Sheffield dog track MD John Gilburn told Spider: 'The two men arrived at the track before racing saying they wanted to play all the permutations on the jackpot and produced a carrier bag stuffed full of money. We took them into the cash room, and it took us an hour to complete the count.

'The two men had travelled up from the South of England. I don't know if they were part of a syndicate or what, but when they came for their money at the end, they were very philosophical about the situation.

'One other winner was a local punter who wished to remain anonymous, while the third bet was placed on the internet. Our total must be the biggest achieved in this country. But it's back to square one and we will be starting with £1,000 again.'

Anyway, it was now January 2015 and after six rollovers, the Totepool Greyhound Sky Sports jackpot stood at a record-breaking £141,003, so after the success from that time and an anticipated pool of more than £600,000 this time we were once again going to the dogs.

This time it was Hall Green in Birmingham on a Tuesday evening. Spider was on a mission to let Sky viewers know where we were at coming up to the final leg, while Richard remained at home placing the perm and cheering on from his sofa.

We had started doing jackpot perms with the SuperClub the previous September. We did that as we felt it was right to share even more pool wins with our members if we could.

The bet at Hall Green consisted of races three to eight broadcast live on Sky Sports with the first race of the jackpot scheduled to start at 7.43pm and it would finish with the Prestige Final itself at 9.08pm.

Right enough, we got all six winners, but no bumper dividend this time as it emerged that lots of other people did the same. Though thanks to that Sheffield win on our other greyhound jackpot bid, we were still well ahead on the dogs. But we'd be barking to be doing that bet every week, when the starting pool is pretty poor and this record £609,583 pot was split too many ways for a proper profit.

Mid-March was memorable as we had our fourth SuperClub crack at a bumper jackpot, and like the earlier ones we got all six winners.

This time the venue was Carlisle. Spider had flagged up Just Cameron against the odds-on favourite Duke Of Navan in the second leg, and he got that absolutely right. He also pointed out Purcell's Bridge at 25-1 in the third leg as a worthwhile longshot. The latter horse, which may well have helped us get a single ticket win, led over the last but got nabbed in the mud on that long uphill run to the line in Cumbria.

We then got potentially a very decent result for the club in the penultimate leg as Age Of Glory at 25-1 beat Copt Hill at 12-1 with Surprise Vendor the 3-1 favourite back in third. This meant we had a £1 ticket on the very warm favourite in the last leg. Including our money, there was a total of £6.50 on Palypso De Creek and the only other horses with money on were Nowurhurlin and Wayupinthesky, both with £1.50 on.

There was £427,924 to be paid out and we estimated the return would be just over £65,000 if the favourite won. We suggested savers on some of the others if members fancied it, but we've never been so loud cheering on a 4-6 favourite. Palypso de Creek came good, beating Nowurhurlin at 8-1 and Dica at 14s.

'Happy days and nice one, Squirrel' was the message from our SuperClub members. Just Cameron beating Duke of Navan was a key part of the dividend being decent. Purcell's Bridge holding on would of course have meant a £427k payout, but a win's a win and member

Mr Broadley gave us his heads-up on the hunter chase. It meant the only favourite we doubled up on was the last one.

We must admit we do have some very shrewd members and we want to keep on winning with them. The dividend was £65,834.40, so a wonderful win with bumper Scoop6 pots on the horizon.

But the Scoop6 wasn't going to plan in March and April, seeing us hit the side netting twice with five out of six winners in the bet. On the second occasion April 4th, the £762,121 win fund was collected by someone and that pool was back to square one.

The bonus of £382,513 looked pretty secure as they had the Grand National at Aintree to solve. Many Clouds provided a silver lining for Scoop6 players as his win in the big race meant the bonus rolled as expected.

Mid-May saw a three-way split of a £628,556 ToteScoop6 win fund after Spark Plug motored home to win the last leg at Newbury. A retired Warwickshire couple with an £8 punt at their Coral shop in Lutterworth landed £209,518 and the other tickets were held by syndicates. They had a £570,741 bonus to look forward to and the syndicates took it down when Seamour at 15-2 beat Totalise at 20-1 in the 2pm at Haydock.

By the end of June, the Scoop6 was back up to £630,487 and we landed it, but with 107 other tickets so a poor dividend of £5,837.80 each. Thanks to Fred Done and his £200,000 bonus we managed to get the winnings into five figures as about forty tickets shared that extra wedge. It was the last time Fred fancied paying out the £200,000 bonus, unless it was going to a single ticket holder.

Basem won the bonus race the following week at Sandown and forty tickets got a share of the £198,286, so another £4,957 for each of them. We teamed up with club member Rachel Horner and picked a couple of longshots in the hope we might land the bonus with just a few other ticket holders. We felt it was the right thing to do for a syndicate of around 200 members.

That was the end of our Scoop6 wins for that year, but in August we launched our fifth jackpot syndicate and managed to show a profit from a £192,041 pool at Brighton on a sunny Sunday. Fred Done, that autumn, decided to change the traditional single meeting jackpot and really confuse everyone with cross card pots, which were generally very tough. Also, they really were not easy to sell at all at the track. Fred did a lot of things very right, but this wasn't one of them.

The joy of the jackpot was always watching all six races unfold before your eyes. Richard will never forget Spider ringing him one Saturday as he was on a coach trip to Haydock in May 2012 with his pals from football and the rugby club.

They had asked him to study the form and come up with a perm. The rugby lads reckoned £20 per man would be good, so he had a full bus and picked out an £800 perm. Anyhow, as well as the rugby guys, who all went in with their wives, there were thirteen youngsters who asked if they could get on the bus to fill the seats and twelve of those went in on the bet.

Spider stood at the coach door, but his knowledgeable mates from football said nobody ever won the jackpot and he'd already won it more times than anyone should. He was £400 short for the perm and rang Richard to see if he fancied it, but Squirrel rather foolishly told him that it would roll over and they'd win it that Sunday instead.

Quite cockily, Spider explained he planned to do it Saturday. Spider decided to go all in himself as he fancied the perm that relied on Red Merlin at 13-2 or Arab League at 16-1 winning the big race the Swinton Hurdle. This was the very race that he'd tipped up Leslingtaylor to win at 20-1 five years earlier and that helped us land a Scoop6.

Anyhow, they had Arab League for a single ticket win of £250k or Red Merlin for around a tenth of that. Arab League led at the last, but was badly hampered and Donald McCain's Red Merlin ran out the easy winner.

The next two races were seven-runner affairs and he had six covered in each race. The kids had disappeared after paying in their money and only one had decided not to pay; from memory, every £20 paid in was now worth around £700. The kids in particular were thrilled as they hadn't otherwise had a winning day, but soon discovered they'd got enough for a fortnight in Benidorm for their troubles.

The coming Thursday, Spider was off to York and had told everyone Judge N' Jury would win the opening sprint. At double figures it was well worth lumping on. Richard called to see him as he was slipping his lucky tie on and suggested they do the jackpot.

Just for him, the syndicate would have Judge N' Jury as a banker in the first leg. Sure enough, it won without another horse getting past him and we landed the jackpot, so two jackpot wins in just six days for Señor Spider.

He splashed some of those winnings on a new Skoda Yeti motor for his long-suffering wife. Then that following Saturday he was invited by Betfred for a spot of hospitality at Haydock. He helped himself big time with winner after winner and exacta after exacta, both at that track and the away meeting at Chester.

It was a pretty decent day for both Spider and racehorse owner Dr Marwan Koukash by all accounts. After that little lot, he decided to use some of his ill-gotten gains to buy himself a brand-new Jaguar, just like the ones that were to feature in that year's Bond movie *Skyfall*. We had seen the new Jag at a launch in Manchester's Urbis Museum after a day at Chester races not long before.

Meanwhile, ahead of the 2015 Bond premiere of *Spectre*, once again starring Daniel Craig, we decided to have a go at the cross-card jackpot. This proved to be an error as the Ludlow, Plumpton and Kempton three-way puzzle proved too tricky for us.

With a pool of £224,229 we managed five from six winners, so that was the end of our SuperClub 100% record with jackpots that had seen us land six from six on every previous attempt. Though with *Spectre* set to launch soon after, we couldn't resist opening up SuperClub jackpot Syndicate 007.

The year ended with a Boxing Day Scoop6 win when we had one of the forty-four tickets taking down the £1,169,494 win fund for a fair profit, even though the return was only around £27,000 per ticket.

Then the beginning of January 2016 presented an unusual opportunity for The Squirrel Syndicate in online form to try out the National Lottery as that weekend's £58 million draw presented good value.

For the record, this isn't something we ever felt we'd say about any lottery. We were all initially highly sceptical about the introduction of extra balls in the National Lottery. But the fourteen consecutive rollovers with the new rule that any rollover of £50 million or above must be paid out on the next draw provided tremendous value for that coming Saturday.

The higher cost of the £2 lottery ticket was another negative at first. Then the introduction of extra raffle prizes, and the making of more millionaires made it slightly more appealing, but the rollovers are what really rock our boat.

The biggest bonanza for players though, was the rule change that meant the prize money would spill down to other entrants if there was no outright winner, so you didn't need all six balls to get a massive win. This virtually guaranteed that the lottery that Saturday night would pay out more than it received, unless turnover increased more than fivefold.

We estimated that each National Lottery entry had potential value of around £3.65 compared with the £2 cost of a ticket. This assumed that Saturday's turnover was approximately double the figure taken on Wednesday, when the final rollover before the guaranteed payout occurred.

On the basis of this mathematics, for the very first time, our online syndicate would tackle the monster Lotto pool. We were hopeful we might get a decent return and it had to be worth a go. We lined up Shane at the Spar by the Fiveways pub to let us place the tickets in bulk on the Friday night, and we adjourned to the boozer to start filling in the slips.

It was funny as a few Squirrel Syndicate members were in the bar. Among them was John Whittaker and plumber Martin Walker, who had splashed out after earlier Squirrel Syndicate wins when we operated out of The Three Tunnes.

Everton fan John, not someone traditionally with luck on his side, came over and asked what we were doing. We explained it was a National Lottery syndicate and they could both sign up. Steel stockholder John explained it was his fiftieth birthday that weekend, so Spider suggested they should also both get involved in the Scoop6 syndicate, as he was pretty sure we could win that ahead of the National Lottery on Saturday night. We do like such optimism and as it turned out he was very right.

Before the Wednesday night lottery rollover, the punting highlight of the week for our members at www.Scoop6superclub.com was the anticipated £1.2 million in the combined pots on the Scoop6. Those events featuring the Welsh Grand National would unfold on Saturday afternoon prior to the enormous Lotto draw in the evening.

The Boxing Day £1 million-plus Scoop6 would have been a bonanza for members if we'd not had to share the pool with forty-three other ticket holders, and that was our second Scoop6 win of the year.

Unlike in previous years, we had to split both the pots with other winners. The year before, we got returns of more than £206,000 for our members on all bets, but the real value was in an outright single ticket win, and that evaded us.

Spider had a feeling that things would only get better in 2016, accordingly we attacked that January 9th Scoop6 with gusto using our five from six banker perm. This relies on either all six bankers, or five bankers, plus one non-banker for us to land the win. All six is a win, but it's the non-banker that generally knocks enough other tickets out of the pool to make a good dividend.

The opening leg, the 1.10 at Chepstow, went to non-banker Peter Bowen's Awaywiththegreys at 10-1 ridden by his talented son Sean. Straightaway we were up against it and now needed five bankers to follow up.

Incidentally, this is just what happened when Miss Lucifer won that fateful opening leg in 2007 and Leg Spinner landed us £1.5 million all on our own. So it might just be a great start, but we'd have a nail-biting couple of hours racing, sweating on the bankers.

Just 17,375 tickets were standing after the first leg. Next up was banker Mountainous at 9-1 under Jamie Moore for trainer Kerry Lee. The bay gelding won his second Welsh Grand National and that left just 1,698 tickets in the win fund. We had a banker one-two in the next leg from Lingfield as Twin Point 7-4 favourite beat Perfect Alchemy at 3-1 and that left just 651 tickets still in play at the halfway stage.

The next three legs were all from Kempton where Spider had a strong fancy for a longshot in the final leg, but more of that later. When our banker Venetia Williams-trained Yala Enki, 11-4 favourite under Charlie Deutsch, scored in the William Hill Lanzarote Hurdle just 122 tickets were standing and we had nine of those. The next leg saw another banker one-two as Kruzhlinin the 5-2 favourite beat Le Reve at 7-2. Just twenty-nine tickets were left in the bet, and we had three of those.

Our best result in the final leg was Spider's longshot Mr Fitzroy, now a massive gamble from double-figure odds into 11-2 with just two tickets on him, then Hollywood All Star had six tickets on and finally Tara Bridge had seven tickets on board.

In that order, if we had the winner, the tickets we had were worth approximately £215k, £70k and £60k, enough for a good winning day. It came to pass that the gamble on Mr Fitzroy was a solid one, as he beat our other banker Hollywood All Star the 5-1 favourite. In so doing he landed us £214,733 and about another £12,000 in place lines.

Spider rang birthday boy John Whittaker to wish him many happy returns and to tell him each £20 was worth around £1,100, but then got a surprise as he'd actually taken out two memberships, thus landing more than £2,200 from the £226,387 pot. A fishing trip to Florida was duly booked by the delighted angler.

We were really hoping that his luck would rub off on the National Lottery, but that wasn't to be. It also turned out that we hadn't factored in the new-fangled Lucky Dip aspect of the National Lottery that left us posting up random numbers twice a week for the rest of the month; and believe us that was a real chore. We eventually paid out a paltry £418 on January 31st, though it felt like forever at the time. It was a good way short of £58 million, and miles away from the Scoop6 win we achieved with half the stake.

Yet before then, we had a £766,818 bonus fund to play for and it would be the Betfred Classic Chase at Warwick the following weekend that we had to crack. We got a pile of Tattersalls tickets for SuperClub members to join us for the party at Warwick.

Club member Dave Nielson was keen to go, as he'd heard we'd be having members interviewed on Channel 4's popular *Morning Line* programme ahead of racing. Dave was prepared to fire his Aston Martin up for the journey, but first we invited him down to the Fiveways for a Friday evening audition ahead of the trek to Warwick. Back then they had a library room in the pub and Spider was sipping a pint with plumber Martin when Dave appeared for the SuperClub equivalent of the casting couch.

Dave was going to need a drink as Spider had a large, blue velvet bag by his side. Dave quipped: 'Have you got a body in that?'

'Not quite,' came the reply as Spider pulled The Squirrel mascot suit out. Dave, to his eternal credit, looked suitably shocked.

Dave explained that he had hoped to appear on the *Morning Line* as himself, but he was advised in no uncertain terms that that wasn't going to happen. His shot at *Morning Line* fame would be in a giant Squirrel suit, or not at all. Spider had already lined up our two representatives for the gig: our driver from Uttoxeter, Pat the Builder, along with Phil the Milk, who at the time was Hazel Grove's answer to Benny Hill's 'Ernie'. They were the ones destined by the circus ringmaster to make appearances trackside at Warwick and on camera for Channel 4.

As the *Morning Line* was on telly early, it had to be a dawn departure for most of the team, but Richard was hanging back to place that Saturday's perm and would be joining them later.

On the way down, Spider texted Micky Quinn as he'd delivered a giant FA Cup in the shape of a pie to his Newmarket stables ahead of the Wigan V Man City Cup final for bookies William Hill. He'd had the idea as Mick played for Wigan and his biography was catchily entitled *Who Ate All The Pies?*, penned by a man who would later become an award-winning journalist called Oliver Harvey, brother of *ITV Racing's* Luke Harvey.

Spider at some time afterwards roped Micky into judging a national pie contest for a Sunday newspaper – a job that the pair would later blame for their expanding waistlines. Mick gave the boys and our bonus bid a shout out on his *talkSPORT* show while they travelled down the M6.

Patrick had dressed for the occasion as a Mafia hitman, just without the violin case, and Phil looked like he'd been sleeping rough for a week. The Channel 4 team had no idea what was coming their way. Spider had suggested that a milk float and Bob the Builder outfits might make the appearance memorable, but Channel 4 never really had a sense of humour.

Tom Lee got the job of interviewing them, or the short straw as it became known on set. Before then, there was even more bad news for The Squirrel Syndicate team, as Channel 4 didn't want our seven-foot Squirrel in the parade ring during the interviews. What did we say about having no sense of humour?

They had actually conducted an interview over the phone with the furry fellow just over a year before as that £4 million Scoop6 was galloping on. Not so great for Dave either, as Spider now had him stalking round the outside of the parade ring in order to get into camera shot.

He pulled it off really well, and when Dave had done his shift, he shed the suit. Richard had landed at the track, and after a few beers he was next to be furred up and escorted round the track in The Squirrel outfit. In costume, he bizarrely bumped into Mr Blobby with another group on a stag do. Jolly japes indeed.

Back to the TV screens and Patrick was asked how much he'd won, looking so much more debonair than Phil the Milk, who suddenly became the centre of the interviewer's attention when he revealed he won £4,500 with us and didn't know the back end of a horse from the front. The joy of The Squirrel Syndicate.

Though later we had some outraged members getting in touch asking how we could let a couple of total balloons, who knew nothing about racing go on TV? The answer was simple, they were the best advert for the syndicate ever… you just had to look at them and you knew they knew nothing, yet had turned their £20 memberships into thousands.

The comedy was to get even better as Phil, still unshaven after his TV appearance, kept saying throughout the afternoon that a lot of people at the track that day must drink in the Fiveways, or The Three Tunnes, as they were all wishing him good luck. He didn't recognise some of them. It hadn't dawned on him that virtually everyone at Warwick would have seen him in their living rooms that morning as they tuned into Channel 4.

We did get a couple of dozen members along to the track, and Spider had arranged for them to call him when they arrived at the gate. This was another moment of hilarity. Having never been to Warwick races before, he was unaware that the two entrance gates were on completely opposite ends of the viewing area. Oh, how we laughed from our perch in the stands as we saw him scuttling from one end of the spectator area to the other with tickets for members.

Totepool spokesman Mark Pearson was at the races and informed Channel 4 viewers: 'The two bonus tickets are on Houblon Des Obeaux and De Kerry Man.' Neither horse did much, with Houblon running on all too late after trainer Kerry Lee's Russe Blanc won the race.

Not bad for Patrick, as he told us after the race that he'd backed the grey winner at 33-1. Kerry's brother Tom had done the Channel 4 *Morning Line* interview and had suggested to Pat that it had a great chance. Oh well, at least he didn't tell us beforehand when we were chasing that £766,818 bonus!

We did have a great turnout of club members; many we had not met before. One even yelled the club's name on TV and that earned him a hospitality ticket to Aintree that April.

Among the regular Squirrel Syndicate throng were John and Edna Carroll, who had taken the train to join the party. Blash and his chum Banks of the Nile, or Neil Banks to give him his Sunday name, were both on board.

We were staying over and the bonus was just that. We still had almost a quarter-of-a-million good reasons to celebrate and we were hopeful of landing that bonus at some point later as the year moved on. Our perm that day secured four of the twenty-four place lines for a return of £4,393.60, so it was not a total disaster and most importantly the bonus rolled. Although a few weeks later, Venetia Williams fitted Houblon Des Obeaux with cheekpieces for the first time and he romped home. In the interview afterwards, Venetia explained the headgear had had the desired effect... if only she'd given that a go at Warwick!

Chapter 16

A SHARE OF £2 MILLION × 2

Missing that £766,818 bonus hadn't stopped us enjoying our curry and ales in Warwick, but it had meant we cut back on the champagne; though we did always feel we deserved to get our hands on that rolling bonus. It continued rolling right up to the Cheltenham Festival, and on that opening Tuesday in 2016 we really quite fancied our chances of landing it.

Spider's pal Professor Graham was doing his doctorate at Oxford at the end of the 1980s and they happened to go to the festival for the first time in the year that Norton's Coin won the Gold Cup at 100-1. He's been to the Cotswolds every year since, pandemics and foot and mouth apart, for the very finest racing in the world, and 2016 was to be no different.

That year, Blash and some of the boys from the rugby club had invited themselves down for a couple of days. Spider found them some sumptuous accommodation in the dungeon, err sorry, basement, of a rented palatial property. It came complete with a fine penthouse suite which Spider, as the arranger, had bagsied for himself.

An incident ahead of racing slightly marred the visit. We shall call it Basingate as it involves a plastic washing-up basin and a steaming pile of turd fresh from Egypt, where Blash had flown in from. Apparently, the toilet was broken! Not like any normal person was he going to use the loo and then the basin to flush it away. No, the rugby fan, on a visit from his new home in Cairo, decided to use the basin, not the bog. The mind literally boggles, but the day was going to take another turn on the punting front that had us almost in tears.

Fast forward to the racetrack, we had discussed the perm and Spider liked Ballyalton in the final leg, trained by a chap called Ian Williams, who The Squirrel Syndicate rated. Anyhow, we had to cut our cloth accordingly for the perm and instead of having five bankers in the final leg, we settled on four, leaving out Ballyalton as we had to prune somewhere and this one was double-figure odds.

The first leg was the 1.30 Supreme Novices' Hurdle and the Cheltenham 'roar' made Spider's spine tingle trackside. A few minutes later as they came up the hill, our two bankers Altior and 15-8 favourite Min were fighting it out and we were all cheering as Nico De Boinville sent Nicky Henderson's charge Altior seven lengths clear at the line. The 4-1 shot beat the favourite and our non-banker Buveur D'Air at 10-1 finished back in third, which was a great start to the Scoop6 perm with £270,619 in the win fund and that bonus we left behind at Warwick was now at £1,068,508. This sent all six of our perms through to the second leg and we had 1,524 of the 38,309 tickets still standing.

We knew the second leg was going to be tough as it was the ultra-competitive Ultima Handicap Chase and another seven-length winner as non-banker Un Temps Pour Tout at 11-1 under Tom Scudamore put trainer David Pipe on the scoreboard. Our banker Holywell at 8-1 was back in second with two more non-bankers in third and fourth – Young Master 14-1 and Morning Assembly 10-1.

Of the 1,979 tickets through we had forty-eight of them in our surviving perm. We now needed four more bankers to land a share of the win fund and another crack at that bumper bonus.

The third leg was the Champion Hurdle and it was a bit of a sweat for a while until Ruby Walsh on the Willie Mullins-trained Annie Power asserted and hit the line four-and-a-half lengths ahead of non-banker My Tent Or Yours at 10-1 and another banker Nichols Canyon in third at 15-2. Banker Annie was 5-2 favourite – it was the year before, when her final obstacle tumble in the Mares Hurdle cost punters an estimated £50 million in profits from first-day festival accumulators.

The next leg was that very Mares Hurdle and we had plumped for Vroum Vroum Mag at 4-6 favourite as our single banker – a near three-length win from a pair of rags at 66-1 and 40-1 took us into the penultimate leg.

We now had to rely on amateur riders to get the job done as this was the four-miler National Hunt Chase and having a good jockey on board always made a difference. Our main fancy was Minella Rocco at 8-1 with a Mr Derek O'Connor in the saddle, one of the best. He did the business by just over a length from our other banker Native River at 7-1.

At the track Spider had agreed to meet the new CEO of Tote Ireland, Tim Higgins, as we were contemplating dipping our toe into the pools on the Emerald Isle. We weren't sure if meeting him ahead of the final leg was a good thing as we had the first five in and should have been fully focussed on that next race. Anyway, their meeting went ahead. As a result, we were then on a course for some cracks at the Irish Super Pick6, their flagship Sunday pool bet.

Meanwhile, the twenty-runner Close Brothers Handicap Chase was upon us and, as they went off, we were all worried about Ballyalton with Brian Hughes on board potentially spoiling the party as late money saw him backed from 16-1 into 12-1. That was going to happen as Hughesy, headed over the last by another non-banker Paul Nicholl's Bouvreil under Sam Twiston-Davies, battled back to win by half-a-length with our best banker Double Shuffle back in third.

Spider was gutted as were the rest of us as Ballyalton was so close to making the cut. The gallant nine-year-old bay gelding was owned by a chap called John Westwood and a few years later we ended up having a share in a horse with his professional golfer son Lee, who likes the occasional Bloody Mary in the morning!

The next day we decided that the bonus chasers would almost certainly have Diamond King, the paper favourite in the morning, among their picks in the Coral Cup. Spider thought the Gordon Elliott-trained eight-year-old was well in and with Davy Russell on board wouldn't be lacking in assistance from the saddle in the twenty-six-runner handicap.

With that decided, we put on a small Scoop6 leaving Diamond King out of the bet, but amazingly none of the other three winners had him in. The bay gelding drifted to 12-1 and Davy duly did the business by just over a length from the Dan Skelton-trained Long House Hall at 16-1 with his brother Harry in the saddle. From memory, we seem to recall a bonus hunter was on this eight-year-old in second, but on the plus side, the £1 million bonus was rolling on.

Unbeknown to all of us at the time, John Westwood's son Lee, who coincidentally we were to own horses with later, was going to help line up a £2 million win fund for us that June on the opening day of Royal Ascot.

Firstly, we did come close again to landing the Scoop6 on the final day of the festival. This was in part down to one of the rugby chaps, a gentleman called Keano, having the cops called out to him on a matter that he's since always insisted he was innocent of. It was an issue over the central heating at the digs which, shall we just say, he didn't handle too well, especially so soon after Basingate.

But this meant the boys had to move back into town for a couple of scoops. Spider suggested that superb Sam Smith's watering hole, the Circus Bar, just beside The Queens Hotel. Cheapest pint in Cheltenham and they managed to get seats at a couple of tables in a booth right opposite the bar.

Anyhow, a couple of slightly older couples turned up and Spider offered them his table and the chance for the ladies to take the weight off their feet. They got chatting and it turned out the chaps came originally from Achill Island off County Mayo on the West Coast of Ireland. Now Spider's wife's cousin Brian holidayed annually on Achill with his family and the silver-haired chaps suggested they must like the wind and rain.

Being educated Irish folk, they clearly knew their horses and, noting The Spider's slight Mersey twang, asked if he attended Aintree. When the reply was a definite yes, John from Achill, revealed they had a runner Voix D'Eau being aimed at the Topham that April.

Spider then asked if they had anything going at the festival and it transpired that they had one running on Friday. They mentioned that their jockey suspected the favourite wouldn't get up the hill and Spider chimed in that he'd agree that Barter's Hill could be found out by the climb to the finish. Now he had identified the right race, the Albert Bartlett Hurdle over three miles, but still hadn't got the name of their runner at 25-1.

Trying to process all the clues as they chatted, he then had to ask his new Irish acquaintance John the name of the horse, and it was revealed to be Harry Fry's Unowhatimeanharry. Keano hadn't said a word, but by the time the couples had departed, the 25-1, 20-1 and 18-1 were all gone, leaving Spider and the boys with a best price available of 16-1. It was only a little later that Keano confessed to mopping up all the great value around, but we suppose, if the cops hadn't been hunting him, the group would never have reached the Circus.

Yet that chance meeting was going to be helpful the upcoming Friday, as we had attended a fabulous Your Golf Travel/Racing Breaks Cheltenham preview ahead of the meeting with AP McCoy and Micky Quinn among the esteemed panellists. Spider had remained relatively sober that evening and made a good note.

We were as a result all over Don Cossack for the Gold Cup and a few others along the way, including Ivanovich Gorbatov, the 4-1 favourite, who beat Apple's Jade at 12-1 in the opener with our other selection, Footpad at 5-1, back in third. We had placed a very small perm for us of around £100 on the day and had bankered Unowhatimeanharry plus Don Cossack. After that first leg, 5,178 tickets were still going along with us. The second leg, the County Handicap Hurdle, saw our pick Superb Story at 8-1 beat 33-1 shots Fethard Player and Sternrubin. There were now 769 tickets left in the win fund.

At 2.50 it was the Albert Bartlett and a great win for John from Achill Island and the Harry Fry Racing Club. Unowhatimeanharry, backed into 11-1, beat Fagan at 33-1 with Champers On Ice at 20-1 back in third.

After that, just nine tickets were left in the win fund and we had five of those. Six of the remaining nine tickets were on Don Cossack and we had five of those riding on our second banker!

At 3.30 the Gold Cup was turned into a procession with Gordon Elliott's Don Cossack asserting after the last for a comfortable win from 9-2 shots Djakadam and Don Poli.

We had five of the remaining six tickets and we had gone all in on the JP McManus-owned grey Squouateur that was backed in to 9-4 favourite in the 4.50 and had been flagged up at bigger prices by AP at that preview evening.

Sadly for us, seventh wasn't quite good enough in the Martin Pipe Conditional Jockeys' Handicap Hurdle, which ultimately went to Ibis Du Rheu at 14-1 for Jack Sherwood and Paul Nicholls. It turned out that the other ticket on the hot favourite was held by one of our members, London-based Jonathan Grant, going it alone as well as with the club.

On the plus side the final leg, the 5.30 Johnny Henderson Grand Annual Chase, went to the longest priced winner of the meeting, Solar Impulse at 28-1, meaning the win and bonus funds rolled on. That winner was funny for us at the time, as Blash and Banks Of The Nile had moved to Cairo in a bid to install solar panels on the Pyramids, or some such renewable energy caper.

That Scoop6 bonus rolled all the way to June 2016 and, on the Saturday ahead of Royal Ascot, three tickets went into the penultimate leg, the 3.45 sprint at Musselburgh. That's when Lee's runner Hoofalong came to the rescue for us.

We had his Hoofalong at 16-1 in as a non-banker and none of the other ticket holders were on him as he beat our banker Thesme at 10-1. Sadly, we went out even for place money in the final leg at York, but the Tote's Mark Pearson was already saying 'You could live like a King if you win the Scoop6 at Royal Ascot.'

It was the first time the ToteScoop6 had donned top hat and tails for Royal Ascot on Tuesday with more than £3m waiting to be won in the combined pools. The win fund stood at £1,233,974 after eight rollovers, while the bonus pot we had missed out on at Warwick in January had now reached £1,792,585. The total prize fund of £3,026,559 was the sixth biggest in Scoop6 history and we fancied a slice of that.

Five legs were to come from the Royal meeting, with the St James's Palace Stakes missed out. Thirsk's abandonment on the Monday meant the 4.05 at Stratford was drafted in as leg four instead of the original plan of an earlier race from the Yorkshire course. Betfred, originally with the race from Thirsk in the bet, made a rollover odds-on at 4-7. While it was 5-4, the win fund was plundered, but those odds changed with the introduction of the 4.05 at Stratford to 4-6 and 11-10, respectively.

We reckoned that we had a decent chance of bringing home the bacon and by the start of racing, the win fund had hit a fabulous £1,809,528 with £287,777 in the place pool and a further £1,998,140 in the bonus – more than £4 million in combined pots.

The opening race was the Queen Anne Stakes and we had bankered 2015's American champion mare Tepin at 11-2 and Roger Varian's Belardo 9-2 joint favourite and the pair of them fought out the finish, ahead of our non-banker Lightning Spear at 20-1 in third. The US raider triumphed for trainer Mark Casse over the Varian horse and took 107,557 tickets through to the second leg, the Coventry Stakes.

In this, we had bankered the two Irish raiders at the top of the market; Caravaggio 13-8 favourite and Psychedelic Funk 9-2 as the going was soft and the mud was flying. Ryan Moore steered the Aidan O'Brien-trained favourite home ahead of Frankie Dettori on our non-banker Mehmas at 8-1 with Funk finishing third for us.

It looked like those drawn low had an advantage and we pointed this out to members on our website following the progress of the syndicate bet. The third race was the King's Stand Stakes and we had Clive Cox and Adam Kirby on our side with Profitable at 4-1 and they just held on from the Charlie Hills-trained Cotai Glory at 33-1, with George Baker in the plate, and Goken at 50-1 was back in third. With the favourite out of the frame, we knew that would enhance any place payout, but we were still cooking with gas on all the perms at the halfway stage.

Over at Stratford for the fourth leg, they had suffered eight non-runners, leaving just a field of three, but our banker Rossetti at 11-8 favourite beat non-banker Sword Of The Lord at 3-1. All the non-runners meant 3,523 tickets went through with ours in the win fund and just 18,600 place tickets were still standing.

The penultimate leg was the Ascot Stakes over a marathon trip of two miles and four furlongs and Spider had a fancy for Charlie Appleby's longshot Qewy. At around 50-1 in the morning, we couldn't have him in as a banker, but we did have Irish raider Jennies Jewel at 6-1 as banker material. Jarlath Fahey's gallant mare prevailed by a neck from Qewy at 33-1 with non-bankers Mill Springs 25-1 and Moscato 18-1 filling the minor placings.

This left 511 tickets in the win fund and we had twelve of the twenty-two runners covered in the final leg. Ideally, we wanted a non-banker here for a decent dividend and we were looking towards Ardad out of stall one to run a big race from what we thought was the ideal berth.

The favourite under Pat Smullen was Mister Trader, battered into 11-4 and well-drawn in stall four, but fortunately for us the colt ran flat and finished back in twentieth in the twenty-two-runner field.

Meanwhile, up front John Gosden's bay Ardad had burst into the lead as the final furlong approached under Robert Havlin and put them to the sword by more than three lengths. In second was 100-1 shot Savannah's Dream and another non-banker Pedestal at 14-1 was third.

It was a great result ahead of Father's Day with fourteen tickets sharing the win fund and we wanted to get together with some of them to try and take down the near £2 million bonus; the one that evaded us at Warwick was now back in our sights. A whopping £1,644,440 was invested by punters into those first day pools and the place fund returned £777.70 and was pocketed by 370 tickets and we had a fair few of them as well.

ToteScoop6 leg breakdown – 14/06/2016

After Leg 1 – 2:30 Royal Ascot: Tepin – 107,557 tickets remaining

After Leg 2 – 3:05 Royal Ascot: Caravaggio – 45,269 tickets remaining

After Leg 3 – 3:40 Royal Ascot: Profitable – 8,837 tickets remaining

After Leg 4 – 4:05 Stratford: Rossetti – 3,523 tickets remaining

After Leg 5 – 5:00 Royal Ascot: Jennies Jewel – 511 tickets remaining

After Leg 6 – 5:35 Royal Ascot: Ardad – 14 tickets remaining

We had a couple of ales to celebrate in The Three Tunnes as we had already collected £129,252 plus the place money. Yet, there was no rest for the wicked as the serious business of getting together a winners' alliance to take down that £1,988,140 bonus was now underway and we had less than twenty-four hours to sort it out.

The bonus race was the twenty-eight-runner Royal Hunt Cup at 5pm at Royal Ascot the following day. With the one hour prior to race time Tote rule we had until 4pm the next day to register the selections. We would also need to sign agreements with any other winners keen to share with us.

When James Doyle steered Godolphin's third winner of the day

Portage at 10-1 to victory in the Royal Hunt Cup for trainer Mick Halford, he was more than a length ahead of our other bonus pick Librisa Breeze and we were now ready to celebrate properly. Our share of the bonus had actually yielded more than the first day win, and over the two days we had tucked away around £288,000 for our members.

We then followed up that day with twenty-four place lines, but Frankie Dettori with that Sandringham Handicap win on the 11-4 favourite helped three ticket holders to land £87,546.60 each. They were chasing a reset bonus of just £7,556 on the Thursday, so we went out to party even though we also had about a fortnight of paying out members to tackle; and that needed a clear head.

Our next attempt at a tickle was the £10 million Colossus in the Euros of 2016, but as Portugal beat Wales 2-0 in the first semi-final our hopes had gone sooner than the Welsh team were on the plane to Cardiff. The other semi saw Germany knocked out by two French goals to nil. This set up a bore draw final of Portugal v France and with no goals at full-time it was Eder in the 109th minute who broke the deadlock and gave victory to the Portuguese.

Scoop6 pots were falling left, right and centre, but Spider's contact with the Irish Tote supremo had yielded a rapport and we, and we believe the Israelis, were about to begin getting involved in the pools on the Emerald Isle.

We launched a jackpot syndicate 013 to tackle what turned out to be the biggest Super Pick6 pool in Irish Tote history. The Sunday in question the pool rocketed to €2,196,764 and Spider was entrusted with The Squirrel mascot suit for a trip to Ireland. He was warned off from wearing the red squirrel outfit trackside, as his new-found friend Tim wasn't sure how a British invader might go down with the Irish faithful.

Upon hearing this news, Spider went AWOL a few days ahead of the big meeting, taking in the Ring of Connemara (Connemara is a place incidentally), the Sky Drive on the Wild Atlantic Way and countless pubs and pints of Guinness during the journey. We were surprised he hadn't floated into the Curragh after his drinking expedition and he had told anyone who would listen, that the purpose of the trip was to take home a chunk of the Curragh's Tote Super Pick6 millions.

The race day arrived and he was joined by his wife, Anne, her much-loved cousins Aidan, Chris and his wife, Marian, for what would be an epic day at the races.

The opening leg saw non-banker Vociferous Marina at 14-1 get us off to a shaky start, but we still had six perms alive and kicking and needed four out of five bankers to land a win. In the 2.20 we had Pat Smullen on board single banker Eziyra at 5-4 favourite and this put us back on track with five perms still going and every horse covered in the next leg.

In the 2.50, single banker The Happy Prince made us very happy indeed under a regal Ryan Moore ride. We were now through to leg four with the field covered again and €211 of our money in live 50 cent lines among the 9,074.34 euro units through.

Our third single banker Capri romped home in the 3.25 with 5,487 tickets on it and we still had three perms going strong. Once again, we had the entire field covered in the 3.55 and banker Theo's Well won it at 8-1, carrying 434.50 tickets 9.5 of which were ours.

We now had the entire field of nineteen runners covered to 50 cents in the last leg. The poorest dividends would have been 03 with 52.5 tickets, or 13 with 52, but we had some real crackers covered with 7.50 euros or less, to share the pool with. The 4.30pm came and non-banker Tithonus at 12-1 won, but it wasn't a great one as it carried twenty-two tickets on it. We landed a return of €34,948.50, making for a bit of profit. The second horse Rattling Jewel only had fifteen tickets on, and another half-length back in third, Primo Uomo at 33-1 only had five tickets on. If only that had come in, we would have landed a tenth of the pool with our 50-cent ticket.

It wasn't the end of the world, and we were probably lucky; earlier that month one Irish punter imagined they had 432,400 euros virtually in the bank at the Curragh. His single ticket in the final leg of the Pick6 was on 1-7 favourite Order Of St George on Champions Day, but the script went awry as Wicklow Brave at 11-1 under Frankie Dettori held the hot favourite off for a half-length win in the Irish St Leger.

Following another roll at Gowran we had proclaimed, 'Forget Brexit, the SuperClub is now going global; well, starting with the pool in Ireland which should be a record-breaker.' After an annoying run of five from six winners on the Scoop6 and managing all six winners in our perms the weekend before, but we only achieved twenty-four place lines for returns of £1,574.40 as the winners were on different lines.

We had spotted this pot of gold across the Irish Sea and our jackpot syndicate 013 wasn't unlucky at all. We had already landed returns of more than £536,000 on the Scoop6 during the year. A winning jackpot was most welcome even if it wasn't the massive amount of euros we were after.

Tim Higgins, CEO of Tote Ireland, told the media ahead of our arrival: 'We know all about The Squirrel and will be very keen to avoid him getting his hands on our nuts, but we cannot stop him playing with his syndicate. It will be very exciting and getting extra funds in from the UK will be unusual, but we are expecting punters from around the planet to jump on the opportunity of landing such a massive pool.

'We've had red squirrels in Ireland since before the last Ice Age, but none of them are about seven-feet tall, so this incomer from England should stand out. Though I am sure he'd be welcomed with open arms at any of our racecourses.' Perhaps Spider had misheard, and we were now set for a fun period chasing pools on both sides of the Irish Sea.

Chapter 17

LADY LUCK AND HORSE OWNERSHIP

The Scoop6 kept avoiding us at the start of 2017 and the jackpot opportunities were nothing to write home about. We had even taken to doing Lucky 15s with syndicate perms as the pools hadn't really grown to our liking. In May, a sixty-year-old William Hill shop customer from South London, with an £8 bet landed a life-changing £235,626, but missed out on the bonus of £343,453 when he failed to find the winner of the Al Zubarah London Gold Cup at Newbury.

Meanwhile, 2017 was to become a year for the ladies after a single mum using nice names won £246,238 from a £4.52 bet at Glorious Goodwood... despite one of her selections being disqualified after crossing the winning line in front. Bookmaker William Hill had a first past the post policy and paid out on Dark Red at 12-1, but the five-year-old grey gelding was placed second to the Queen's horse Fabricate at 20-1 after a stewards' inquiry in the opening race of the prestigious Goodwood meeting.

And amazingly, three of the other picks won for the thirty-something mum-of-two. They were Thechildren'strust at 100-1, Breton Rock at 50-1 and El Astronaute at 33-1. Her final selection Darkroom Angel led to just over a furlong out and would have landed her £1 million – the bookmaker's maximum payout but the three-year-old filly ran out of puff and finished in tenth.

Her bet included a 1p each way five-timer and, if the fifth horse had won, the accumulated odds would have paid her more than £3 million, but that would have been capped by the maximum payout rule. The Cheshire housewife bought a new house for her and the children as the win came at the point when she was searching for a new rental home in Ellesmere Port, Wirral.

William Hill's first past the post policy meant her 5p each way four-timer came in along with extra doubles and trebles and that landed the lady £201,330 that would have been lost with the disqualification at many other bookmakers.

The woman also took 80-1 on Thechildren'strust, but William Hill had a best odds guaranteed offer and, with the odds drifting to 100-1, that meant the lucky lady landed a whopping £47,869 extra. Her bet in full was ten × 10p each way doubles, ten × 10p each way trebles, five × 5p each way four folds and a 1p each way fivefold, for a total stake of £4.52.

In November, another housewife with Lady Luck on her side, landed £574,278.41 for a £1 bet on the football after suffering for years with her husband and son watching TV matches every weekend. The fifty-nine-year-old burnt the bookies with her astonishing twelve-team accumulator and only started doing her £1 weekend bets about six years before because she reckoned, if she couldn't beat the boys to the TV, she might as well join them.

The woman's 574,277-1 girl power winner at bookmaker William Hill was landed after her thirty-year-old son read out the games and she picked the names of twelve teams that she thought sounded nice. Incredibly, eleven of the teams were odds against outsiders – including Burnley at 4-1 away at Southampton – and only one of the matches, Sheffield United to beat Hull, was odds-on at 8-11.

The housewife's likely favourite scorer was Cherries defender Steve Cook who headed in Bournemouth's winner in the 90th minute. Her fifty-eight-year-old taxi driver husband and their son were both Tottenham fans, but the shrewd female punter swerved Spurs in her weekend betting bonanza. The lady clearly liked teams beginning with B, for as well as Burnley, she had Brighton, Barnsley, and Bolton all doing the business for her, along with Bournemouth.

Betting shop manager Carli Faulkner, aged thirty-eight, had paid out hundreds of thousands of bets in her eighteen years in bookmaking, but confessed there was nothing quite like that, after settling the flutter at the Leysdown-on-Sea branch of William Hill on the Isle of Sheppey,

Kent. The Squirrel Syndicate do love a bit of girl power, especially when the ladies kick the bookies in the balls like that.

As the year wore on, we were hitting the crossbar more times than a relegation team. Even a €447,757 Super Pick6 at the Curragh – which saw a 16-1 shot of ours, Muirin beat 2-5 favourite Sizzling in the third leg – was not enough for a bumper payday. Once again, we shared the pot with too many shrewd Irish punters. The return for us was 8,248.15 euros, which was very disappointing after getting a 16-1 shot in. We still had hopes of hitting the target with another nice tickle in Ireland, but literally had to wait for New Year's Eve before the Emerald Isle was golden again for us.

Before then, we decided The Squirrel Syndicate should put something back into racing with a share in a racehorse. Spider's chums Ross Marshall and Andrew Harding had set up their business Your Golf Travel with their credit cards around a decade earlier, and they had invited him to tear up the fairways with them a few times.

Their fantastic YGT Fairway To Furlong events were legendary and they've now set up Racing Breaks, so that's brilliant and we use them for wonderfully organised race trips these days. Spider's not exactly Tiger Woods – his Waldorf Golf Society handicap is presently 36 – so not sure what these proficient golfers make of his game. They did do a jaunt to Turnberry before President Donald Trump bought it, and nobody purchased Spider's swing in the charity auction… apparently, he made a donation himself – out of shame.

On one trip, they went to Newbury and their trainer at the time, Michael Wigham, was plotting a path to the Cambridgeshire with their bay gelding Credit Swap. Well, former jockey Wiggy was pretty tight-lipped and it was Ross who revealed the cunning and ultimately stunning plan. Back then we tipped their five-year-old bay gelding up for the big race in October 2010 at 66-1 on a short-lived Aggies Nags website we set up with our chum Agnes Haddock.

The boys battered the bookies that day when Wiggy just got him in the race off 8st 7lbs and they thrashed him in the betting at all odds down to 14-1. We recall the Scoop6 that Saturday was in the region of around £500,000 and if we'd known how well Jim Crowley was going to ride him, we'd have bankered Credit Swap and mopped that massive pot up.

Ross and Andrew, along with some other horseracing chums – including Johnno Spence and Lee Westwood – set up a new racing adventure with their Albatross Club just at the time we had decided to dip a paw into racehorse ownership. We had wanted a share in a flat horse with potential to be dual-purpose performer and, with a bit of good fortune, we got involved in a gorgeous grey, unraced, two-year-old called Oi The Clubb Oi's.

The trainer was none other than Ian Williams at the Dominion stables in Alvecurch, Worcestershire; the very chap who trained Ballyalton to win at the festival when we stupidly left him out of our perm as a banker after getting the first five up – horseracing is a small world. The colt was by Champs Elysees out of Red Boots, so had stamina and looked ideal for our scheme to be in a partnership with a dual-purpose runner. We fell in love with him the moment we saw the WhatsApp images from Ian's place, but he's much more impressive in the flesh.

That autumn, Spider had booked a Your Golf Travel and Racing Breaks trip to Ireland and they were taking in the Munster National at Limerick, as well as the manicured greens at Trump Doonbeg, Lahinch and Dromoland Castle. Canny Spider had even booked a short break to Lisbon the week before with his wife, Anne, to ensure he was in the good books.

But as they often say, the best laid plans can come unstuck. Spider had been on a fitness regime. As a result, he tore the rotator cuff over his left shoulder playing football just a week before the Portugal trip and was in a deal of pain. We all knew this, as the next day after the tear, which he hadn't had diagnosed at that point, we were going racing to Doncaster.

Our first port of call in Yorkshire was to see Richard's Nottingham University chum Dr Marcus Bicknell and his delightful octogenarian mum Dorothy, who had prepared a fine buffet and champagne for our arrival. Asking pain-riddled Spider to do the YMCA dance shapes shortly after tipping up in the family's sun-drenched garden near Rose Hill, Marcus immediately diagnosed a rotator cuff tear and described it as a long haul to recovery. And Dr Bicknell wasn't wrong. Spider had a gammy arm for more than six months, so no golf or football, though fortunately his drinking arm avoided injury and, as luck would have it, he needed that a fair deal in the coming months.

Ahead of the St Leger meeting, Spider had interviewed George Baker who landed the Classic the year before aboard Laura Mongan's Harbour Law at 22-1. The race, inaugurated in 1776, is the oldest of Britain's five Classics and is steeped in history, but no St Leger winning jockey had endured more drama in the months after winning the race than George. Inside a month, his thirty-year-old wife, Nicola, had given birth to their first child – a gorgeous daughter, Isobella. Inside six months of that joyous occasion, George was in hospital himself after a life-threatening pile-up on the ice at St Moritz. Winning the St Leger on Harbour Law was undoubtedly the highlight of his racing career – his first Classic among four Group 1 wins. But that horrendous accident at St Moritz for his mount Boomerang Bob, trained by Jamie Osborne, saw him placed in an induced coma and his career put on hold at the age of thirty-four.

It was a rollercoaster of emotions since the previous September with events like those happening in George's life, but over lunch at the track, he revealed he would never forget that day, or the elation when Harbour Law won. George is not alone as jockeys, as a rule, are amazingly resilient. The good times keep us all going as many found out during the recent Covid-19 pandemic.

After the accident, this articulate and intelligent man told us how he had been on a hospital floor with people, who looked the same, sounded the same, but had lost their long-term memory. They were, George explained, in effect, different people as their personalities changed. George told us when he came round from the induced coma he had been placed in, that he was lucky inasmuch as he still knew he was a jockey.

Jovial George laughed as he told us that he remembered telling the medics he was riding Quest for More in Dubai in a week's time. He was apparently fixated on it, but he explained that you can get fully focussed on little things when you are in a place like that. Apparently, one doctor said: 'How do you think you will get on George? You can't walk at the moment.' But George wasn't giving up and told the doc: 'It might not be pretty, but I will have a go.'

Falls in flat racing are not something many prepare for. Something that 30mph crash into the ground – after the horse's hoof found that sixty-centimetre crack in the ice – did for George, was give him a tremendous appreciation of what he had. He told us that before he would watch jump racing and take his hat off to the riders, as those guys knew they would be falling off at some point. George went to see fellow jockey Freddy Tylicki who was paralysed in a four-horse pile-up at Kempton the November before, only a few weeks before we met. He told us how Freddy was inspirational and such a positive person. George added that through the whole thing, since the crack in the ice led to his fall, he had taken the positives out of it; like getting to spend time with his family and seeing a lot of Isobella, which wouldn't be possible if he was riding, as he'd be out every day.

George was in hospital for quite a long time after the fall, but while his short-term memory wasn't good, he still had long-term memory and Harbour Law's win remained unforgettable. George told us how he suffered post-traumatic amnesia, meaning Nicola and his family saw the worse of what happened. He was airlifted to hospital in Switzerland and was there for eight days, then flown back to London, but George didn't remember that and self-effacingly explained how the family saw all the bad stuff.

After the accident in February, George forgot how to walk, and his balance was affected. He went to the Injured Jockeys Fund's rehabilitation base, Oaksey House in Lambourn, three times a week. As he lived in Didcot, that meant he could walk to the gym on other days. He told us it was strange going racing as a spectator when he was used to being in the saddle and when we met that was his plan; to get back to the day job. Unfortunately, George never made it back to race riding, but that afternoon as a special guest of William Hill's affable publicist Rupert Adams, he proved to everyone round that table that he had a great eye for the horses and read the form supremely well.

On the fairway front in Ireland, 'crippled' Spider failed to find a replacement for himself on the golf jaunt and headed off with the chaps to enjoy the Guinness as his ability in the 19th hole was not impeded.

Highlight of his weekend, as a non-player, was likely to be the JT McNamara Ladbrokes Munster National Handicap Chase at Limerick.

John Thomas McNamara was an Irish amateur steeplechase jockey, as tough as nails, like George and all the boys and girls who do this potentially very dangerous job. JT won more than 600 races during his career, but sadly sustained a serious back injury and a broken neck after a fall on Galaxy Rock at the first fence in the Fulke Walwyn Kim Muir at the 2013 Cheltenham Festival. John Thomas was left paralysed and using a wheelchair and in July 2016, after suffering complications, JT died at home in Croom on the West Coast.

Limerick was where he was born, so the big race was named in his memory and Total Recall 2-1 favourite for Willie Mullins and Ruby Walsh turned the race into a procession with a seven-length win in receipt of 16lbs from Mouse Morris' Alpha Des Obeaux.

Ahead of his trip, Spider had placed a tenner each way double on the weekend's two golf tournaments, thinking he might be stuck in the 19th hole as the guys played the various courses. When England's Tyrell Hatton won the Dunhill Links for the second consecutive year at 20-1, it made up for a disappointing day at the races. Spider then had a fair few quid on Brendan Steele at 33-1 following up with a second consecutive win in the Safeway Open in the States.

Just like other Squirrel Syndicate stalwarts, he's a big fan of horses for courses, or in this case, golfers, on tracks they've won on before. By all accounts, Spider got a bit merry and was buying drinks for all and sundry in the 500-room hotel. His bar bill was somewhat sobering the next day, but seeing that comprehensive Munster National victory was to prove helpful in a couple of months as we began the chase for another £500,000-plus Scoop6 bonus.

It was the last week in November, Saturday 25th, when we had a decent crack at the Scoop6 with races from Ascot, Lingfield and Haydock on the menu. The prospect of a win was mouth-watering, a massive £652,905 win fund, a £93,947 place fund and a not-to-be-sniffed-at bonus of £500,648. We decided to use our favourite five from six banker perm. Just like the previous January and that fantastic £1.5 million win fund day in 2007.

The opening leg, the 1.25 at Lingfield, went to non-banker Music Major at 20-1. Banker Pink Ribbons at 4-1 was back in second with another non-banker Beepeecee at 10-1 in third. From 268,421 tickets in at the start, just 4,666 survived after that lovely longshot.

The next leg was the 1.50 at Haydock and we managed a winning banker as Limited Reserve at 9-2 beat Man Of Plenty at 20-1 with our other banker Clyne 9-4 favourite just battling past our Lucky 15 pick Chti Balko for third place. Just 964 tickets were alive in the win fund now and we had seventy-two of those. It was down to Ascot for the third leg, the 2.05, and another winning banker as Top Notch at 5-2 joint favourite beat Double Shuffle at 12-1 with Frodon in third at 8-1. Only 321 tickets survived and we had thirty-six of those.

Now it was getting exciting, and the 2.25 at Haydock saw another winning banker as Sam Spinner at 6-1 beat three non-bankers, The Dutchman at 12-1, then Theo's Charm at 16-1 and No Hassle Hoff at 8-1 in 4th. This was our best banker win and just fifty tickets remained with twelve of them ours.

The 2.35 at Lingfield was sort of a nailbiter, as there was a stewards' inquiry, but we had a banker one-two with 3-1 joint favourites Loveatfirstsight and Jack Blane fighting out the finish, ahead of Black Truffle at 12-1. We would have settled for the result being reversed as Jack Blane was our Lucky 15 pick and also had seventeen tickets, rather than eighteen, on the first past the post. Either way, we had tickets covering four of the nine runners in the final leg. The result stood and we had four of the remaining eighteen tickets.

The light was fading and it was a marathon chase at Haydock at 3.35 that would decide our fate. It wasn't looking great when our banker pick Baywing fell at the first and another banker Henri Parri Morgan unseated on the opening circuit, but we also had last year's Betfred Midlands Grand National winner Chase the Spud at 6-1 among our bankers. Paddy Brennan's mount got them all at it and non-bankers Robinsfirth 10-3 and Cloudy Too could only bring up the places. Once again, this solid stayer showed his stamina to land us, and another ticket holder, £326,452.95 each.

We had to tell our members to be patient again. We wanted to start the payout the week after when we knew our fate following a bid for the £500,648.25, courtesy of the bonus fund to be played for, on a selected race that coming Saturday.

Before then, we were going to be busy, but not tracking down the other bonus chaser as we got a call from them after they read the news on our website homepage. Spider though had a crusading lawyer friend, Nick Turner, who was battling bowel cancer, and we both thought a trip to the gallops to watch Oi The Clubb Oi's in action might be a great tonic for him. Nick, who lived in Worcester just half an hour from the stables, loved the idea and we were going to take him for a fine lunch.

Spider, as number one Squirrel handler, sorted the trip and we thought it might be great to get a giant red squirrel on the back of our galloping grey. We had no idea how trainer Ian Williams would react to the phone call but, though many a stuffy old sort may have given the request short shrift, Mr Williams warmed to the idea almost immediately. Knowing him now, we suspect he just thought Spider was bonkers - he wasn't too wrong there.

Master trainer Williams even offered to put our lad out last lot meaning we could catch him in action, though this still meant a dawn departure for the pair of us from an icy cold Cheshire. We met with Nick in his vintage vehicle ahead of driving into the yard, but his noisy Triumph Dolomite car engine was in danger of upsetting the horses.

With Spider clutching a large, blue velvet bag containing The Squirrel suit, we were ushered into a waiting room. Horror of horrors, the entire right-hand wall had a picture of the Cheltenham celebrations from a couple of seasons before when Ballyalton won and cost us a shot at the £1 million bonus. We looked at each other and rolled our eyes and laughed and thought 'Good on them – we wouldn't mind a slice of that one day.'

Funnily enough, while we were there, Ballyalton's owner John Westwood, with his wife and a couple of friends, called in carrying a large selection of cakes for the staff. They were on their way back from a cruise that had alighted at Southampton. Ian was a great host, though not so keen on either of us sitting on the horse wearing The Squirrel suit, so he lined up jockey Robbie Walsh to slip into the outfit. As Robbie got to grips with the paws and the kit, he explained that he wouldn't mind being a quid behind Ruby Walsh, but informed us that they weren't related.

Firstly, we got to see our grey OTCO put through his paces on the gallops, with a few of Ian's string, and he was moving very well indeed.

His run style reminded us of that game stayer Sergeant Cecil; just the one run in him, but he gallops on. Solicitor Nick was grinning and enjoying his day out with a difference, and we were a very jolly party.

Work done, we managed to get Robbie on board the grey gelding. Our boy, OTCO, was so placid, it was untrue. Some thoroughbreds can be highly strung, but our lad is so docile, very strong and a real galloper. Spider told us how he once went to interview Clare Balding at the stables of her father, Ian, and had wanted to do it on horseback. Mr Balding senior had suggested that wouldn't be happening, so he ended up astride a gate instead with Clare on Grey Shot nuzzling into his notebook.

The highlight of his trip to Park House stables at Kingsclere, near Newbury, Berks, was apparently sitting in the seat the Queen generally used when popping into the kitchen for a cuppa after watching her horses on the gallops. Not being au fait with Cambridge-educated Clare's sexuality at the time, our man on the gate actually asked her if there was a young man in her life. Very helpfully, her response to that was a no.

After our OTCO stable visit, which was a good way to take our minds off that £500,648 bonus, we decided to go somewhere local for lunch. En route we found a place called Winyates, near Redditch, and felt we had to have a picture with Spider beside it, as his surname is Yates. We also felt it could be a sign ahead of the weekend Scoop6 bonus attempt.

Lawyer Nick was chortling as we took the photographs, and we felt we should share them with our chums at the Albatross Club, as we were meeting some of those for the first time at a Christmas feast in London that coming Thursday. We discovered a delightful eatery not too far away called The Orangery and all enjoyed a beer with our lunch.

It was great craic and Nick regaled us with some of his curious cases involving police corruption, which was pretty much his specialist subject. We promised that we'd do our best to get him along when OTCO was running. As it turned out, that never panned out. Instead we ended up sponsoring a SuperClub Chase at Uttoxeter, inviting Nick and his family as guests of honour, but more of that later.

Before then, we had an Albatross lunch in the capital. We sat at a table with a fascinating chap called Tim Dykes, who was the son of a local newspaper editor and owned a few horses. Tim told us how he'd got a Lucky 63 through the card at Sandown up for £1 million, but had gone over the odds as a couple of his earlier winners had drifted. We understood just what he was saying. Tim could have risked a smaller stake to land the capped £1 million, due to the best odds guarantee. Tim's final leg winner was his own horse, Ishikawa, which went off 5-2 favourite as Coral took evasive action and crashed the price down.

It's very nice when a plan comes together like that. We had been studying the weekend card at Newbury hard and felt trainer Nicky Henderson's stayer Whisper might have a big shout in the race. Fortunately for us, Nicky was a guest at the lunch, and we would be picking his brain – with a little luck.

On the train on the way down, sipping Richard Branson's G&Ts, we clocked that Willie Mullins also had Munster National winner Total Recall entered in the big race. Spider had suggested Whisper might just have too much weight, and when we tapped up Nicky over a glass of red, that's precisely what he said – that he might just be too high in the handicap. This probably clinched it for us, as Whisper was put on the bench and Total Recall with another runner American were looking the most likely two bonus picks.

Our livers were on the way to being pickled ahead of the weekend following a fantastic steak dinner washed down with a fair few fine reds. We enjoyed the company once again of jockey George Baker, who was with his pal Dominic Elsworth, of Mr McGoldrick fame, among others in the bar afterwards. The train journey back was a blur, but Spider had the Liverpool Press Club Christmas Lunch the next day. The damage to his brain cells was going to be exceptional, but with Sir Ken Dodd as the guest of honour, he wasn't going to miss that.

He even reported back how Sir Ken, who famously won a court case with the Inland Revenue, had cracked a gag about tax self-assessment saying, 'I think I invented that?' Sir Ken also had them rolling in the aisles with another joke about the taxman asking for you to estimate your annual income. Doddy said: 'I always guess that. The bigger the figure, the better. The best part is when you send off the form, never fill in your name and address – remember, if you've done your bit by guessing your annual income, then it's only fair they get the chance to guess who sent the letter.' Comedy genius indeed, but we didn't need to worry about the taxman as any Scoop6, or jackpot, winnings were always tax-free.

We had used Racing Breaks to book ourselves and Squirrel Syndicate member Rob Smith into The Lodge at Newbury and Dave Nielson was also heading down in his Aston Martin. Dave had booked a posher pad down the road, but we wanted to be trackside. We arrived just as the parents of connections of big race contender Braqueur D'Or were parking up and we wished them luck in the race.

Spider was given the short straw of having to wear The Squirrel suit. He had it in the big, blue velvet bag and was resplendent in his shirt, tie and jacket enjoying a coffee at The Lodge ahead of racing. The first trainer we spotted was Nicky Richards, but the night before we'd seen Arnold Schwarzenegger was back on the small screens for a re-run of *Total Recall* and we saw that as a sign.

We were blessed, as in the cafe at the same time was a group of wannabe police officers, who Spider recruited as a guard of honour to help him find his way to the parade ring. Several other police officers en route gave The Squirrel and his entourage some funny looks, and one or two possibly considered getting out their Tasers which would have made most of us laugh, if not The Spider. He rode his Scouse luck to the outside of the parade ring and then down from there to the rails.

We knew it was thirsty work inside the suit as you have very little vision and it gets pretty hot. He was purchased a fine ale to wet his whistle. Before getting to wet his parched lips though, a gaggle of young ladies came up and asked for pictures with The Squirrel. He was happy to oblige, but as is often the case at the races, one of the girls grabbed The Squirrel's nuts and was grinning away for the photos.

When The Squirrel head came off, that first pint hardly hit the sides and from memory, one of the Albatrossers – Wimbledon AFC's commercial director Ivor Heller – had tipped up Gold Present at 13-2 as a winner in one of the earlier Newbury races. Ivor scored a fair bit with his information, almost as often as his football team.

At about this point, another of the Albatross members, Chief, had spotted us on the rails and invited us up to the Sporting Index box to watch the race from there. Almost at the same time, a Newbury security guard had accosted us and suggested The Squirrel needed escorting off the premises. We swiftly explained that the owner of the racecourse had just invited us up to his box, as Chief was almost that, so put forward the proposal of a guided tour into the main grandstand and up in the escalator, and we would thank him profusely for his good work in front of the boss. Alternatively, our new-found companion could throw The Squirrel out, we would call up to the hospitality box, and then the racecourse owner might have another view of the security operative.

Thankfully, good sense prevailed and as we got in the lift another bemused passenger asked what was going on. We explained that we were chasing the £500k bonus and he wished us well, telling us he had a runner in the Ladbrokes Trophy. We asked the horse's name and it was none other than trainer Hendo's Whisper.

Well, it was rather jolly in the box with Chief, or rather Sporting Index's Karl Suntay, hosting with a fair flock of Albatrossers in attendance. Enough time to say our hellos, then it was out onto the balcony to watch the race. Spider slipped The Squirrel head on for luck and was jumping up and down as Whisper hit the front over the last then, in the shadows of the post, Paul Townend drove Total Recall up. Luckily for us, the colours were completely contrasting and we all thought the red and white of Total Recall had got up by a neck on the line from the blue and white of Whisper.

Spider was of a similar view, despite the tunnel vision of staring down the snout of the costume. It was tense for a while, but the photo came through the right way for us, with Regal Encore at 66-1 in third and Braqueur D'Or at 33-1 back in fourth. When the result was announced, we could raise a glass and that neck winner had taken our haul to £576,766.

We had arranged for the nice chaps from Betfred to bob up with the comedy cheque for that sum, and all the boys in the box were keen to get a picture with it. Among them was horseracing PR par excellence Johnno Spence and Albatross Club chairman Ross, who had a family emergency, so he was unable to join us afterwards for the Moscow Mules in the VIP hospitality area outside.

We had met fellow OTCO owner Jamie Moyes in the box and his

film producer pal Nick Sercombe. When Spider heard Jamie was a film financier, he instantly realised he was used to handling large sums, so handed over our comedy cheque and asked him to look after that while he slipped back to The Lodge to dump The Squirrel suit. Upon his return and yet another round of Moscow Mules with Nicky Henderson's delightful daughter Camilla now in the company, the comedy cheque had disappeared. Fortunately, we didn't have to take that to the bank to get paid.

The guys were moving on to The Queens at Lambourn and we were on board for the expedition. Chief flagged down a car park-owning friend in a Range Rover Overfinch, who offered them a ride to Lambourn, with Spider in tow. Richard and Rob followed on in a cab. We ended up supping in The Queens and purchasing a fair few pints. Spider slipped into the disco with Jamie who performed his party trick of balancing a pint of ale on his head while dancing to that farming classic by The Wurzels – 'The Combine Harvester'.

At this point we spotted the Betfred bumper cheque. It turned out that, of all the pubs in all the world, we had actually ended up in the same pub as the group of young girls who had nicked our cheque from the racecourse. Spider let them have their fun, then popped over to ask for it back, but they claimed it was their cheque. We then stumped them with a daylight shot of The Squirrel at the cheque presentation, so they handed it over with even more selfies taken.

It was all a bit hazy, but trainer Roger Teal handed us a card and we spotted fellow trainer Warren Greatrex having dinner in the pub restaurant. Somehow, we got back to Newbury Lodge, but the next morning Richard realised he'd misplaced his phone. His eldest son Thomas, or Techy Tim to those in the know, put a 'find my phone' trace on it and it showed up in a street near Highclere. Turned out that he'd left it in the taxi on the way home. It delayed our departure for a few hours as we had to wait for the cabbie to wake up. It was still fun and Spider had to get back to Cumbria for yet another pre-Christmas gathering. He made it to the home of the red squirrel just in time for dinner with that bumper cheque on his back seat.

The next three weeks ahead of Christmas were spent paying out Squirrel Syndicate members. Our scheme to have them all weighed in in time for the festive season was successful. It took such a lengthy period as the bank electronic payout limit per day was £20,000, meaning it was time-consuming and we had to double-check every payment. For some of the bigger ones, we delivered cheques by hand; like the £31,000 and £20,000 ones. Others further afield were paid bumper sums by cheques sent in Christmas cards with a nice message. Though a few weeks later, one member Roger, to whom we had sent a £16,000 cheque in the post, called asking after his share. We were horrified, but when we told him it was sent in a Christmas card, he was cool. For it turned out he had moved house and simply hadn't opened the cards from his old address, which was the one we had in our Squirrel Syndicate system.

It had been a great end to 2017 and pushed our returns on the year up towards £750,000 from memory, but it was New Year's Eve and 2017 was far from over for us. Over in Ireland there was a fantastic Pick6 at Punchestown with a gross pool of €961,349 and we wanted some of that. With a party on the horizon to see in the New Year at Squirrel Towers Drey or Spider's Web, we got to work on a perm.

The opening leg was the 12.35 and we had a banker one-two as Monbeg Notorious at 8-11 favourite beat Augustin at 15-8. We had heard just on the off that one of our three bankers in the final leg She's Made It was a non-runner. As a result, we were highly delighted that we had put on three extra perms just ahead of the tapes going up, single bankering Monbeg in the opening leg with three extra picks in the final leg at 3.15.

In the second leg at 1.05, we had a banker one-two-three with Robin Des Mana at 7-1 romping well clear of Thirsty Work at 4-1 and Mount Brandon at 11-2. Of our five bankers here, it was the second best one, carrying 37,966 tickets through to the third leg. In the 1.40, it was another banker one-two-three, but the 9-10 favourite Killultagh Vic was a bad result for us, carrying 15,116 tickets through to leg four. Runner-up Ex Patriot at 7-2 was carrying 8,478 tickets, and the third 6-1 shot Diamond King only carried 4,233 tickets. Either of those might have put us in place for a single ticket win.

The fourth leg produced another banker one-two-three with our second best of the five bankers Veneer Of Charm winning to take 2,506.5 tickets through to the penultimate leg, where we had every horse covered. We just needed one more banker in either of the final two legs, or two of our supplementary horses which were covered in the extra perm. The 2.40 saw non-banker Returntovendor at 25-1 beat our extra perm pick Brave Out at 8-1 with banker Miles To Memphis at 14-1 in third.

We now needed a banker in the last leg, where just 32.50 euros were still alive in the pool. The 3.15 was exciting with our banker Urbanist backed into 3-1 clear favourite beating Glen's daily double at 20-1 with our other banker Oakfield Rose 3-1 co-favourite back in third. We landed a sixth of the near million Euro gross pool - a great finish to the year. The non-runner money went onto Oakfield Rose and instead of three euros like the winner, that pick had 16.50 on.

The dividend to 50 cents was 112,157 euros, making for a great end to 2017, but we imagined it would take the first week of 2018 for us to make the payout. We did give our Squirrel Syndicate members one last bit of advice to celebrate the New Year and that was they should see it in with warm beer followed by chilled champagne. We do all like our champagne moments.

Chapter 18

BEGINNER'S LUCK

While we had some wonderful wins at the end of 2017, it was also the time Oi The Clubb Oi's was heading to the racetrack.

His first day out was December 13th at Kempton. OTCO was 28-1 and ridden by Richard Kingscote, but finished nearer last than first in tenth spot with just two behind him. The winner of that mile race was trainer David Simcock's odds-on favourite Highbrow, under Jamie Spencer, a clear seventeen lengths in front of our lad. Though the best horse on show in that two-year-old novice race, other than OTCO, turned out to be Ed Walker's Caradoc, back in fourth. Sired by Derby winner Camelot, Caradoc went on to win four races. Up to now, he already has career earnings of £111,647.

OTCO was then taken to Wolverhampton on December 27th and at 100-1 under Tom Eaves his education continued. This time OTCO, going left-handed, showed a bit more promise and finished solidly in mid-division. In sixth place, OTCO was almost as near the leader John Gosden's 6-5 favourite Antonian as he was ahead of the last-placed runner, trainer Luca Cumani's Mayer. Antonian never won another race, so it would be fair to say OTCO emerged as the best on show in that ten-strong field.

On 2nd February 2018 as a three-year-old, he went back to Wolverhampton and under Fran Berry at 40-1 finished a little over fourteen lengths behind Ed Walker's 5-2 winner Petruchio. Once again our boy was to develop into the best of the twelve runners on show, and canny Mr Williams was bringing him along slowly yet very nicely.

His next outing was May 21st at Leicester and he'd been dropped into a seven-furlong maiden, so perhaps not ideal for an upcoming stayer. At 100-1 under Paddy Mathers, OTCO finished just over twelve lengths behind Godolphin's Arabian Coast the 5-2 favourite – another horse to only ever win one race. Shamefully, up until this point we had never managed to get along to watch OTCO run, but that was going to change, so more of that later.

In January at Cheltenham Festival Trials Day, twenty-one-year-old Ryan Davies, from Tewkesbury, Gloucs, almost had a life-changing tickle for a £2.50 each way six-timer with William Hill. Electrical wholesaler Ryan had the entire bar at Cheltenham cheering on his sixth selection after five magical winners at 6-1, 8-1, 7-1, 9-2 and 9-1. A large section of the Club Enclosure at the track were following young Ryan's fortunes with his final pick Our Merlin at 10-1 set to land him a life-changing sum.

The gallant six-year-old bay gelding led the entire field coming round the final bend, but despite battling on, 20-1 shot Remiluc and Huntsman Son at 8-1 both passed him on the gruelling Cheltenham uphill finish. Instead of winning £763,010 Ryan landed just £713.20 for the place part of his each-way bet. He had planned to pay off his parents' mortgage if he won, but instead he straightaway sent £700 over to his mum's account.

Ryan said afterwards: 'My pals from school James Colbourne and Robbie Perkins were with me at the races and couldn't believe I had the first five up. We had a great day out and they were really gutted for me at the end, but I still came out with winnings so it's not all bad. My electrician mate Lewis Knox had told me to back Apple's Shakira in the first race, so I actually had the first six winners before Our Merlin's race had started. It's not my biggest win. That came a couple of years ago at Cheltenham when I put a quid on with William Hill and collected £2,700 as all four I backed won.'

When Cheltenham proper arrived, Spider was by the parade ring with his eldest son Charles to wish Ross, golfer Lee and the boys well with their Albatross Club runner Western Ryder in the opening race, the Sky Bet Supreme Novices' Hurdle. With Richard Johnson on board, the Warren Greatrex-trained six-year-old was no forlorn 20-1 shot. But being hampered two out and badly impeded put paid to any chance of a win. The battling bay gelding did well to manage sixth, but with many bookies paying five places each way it was heart-breaking for the team.

However, the day was going to get a lot better for Lee as he landed a share of the jackpot and a cool £20,678 for picking all six winners. His good form continued on the Wednesday, and by the end of racing he had backed eleven of the first twelve festival winners, which is a champagne start to any Cotswold expedition.

Spider had tipped up Tiger Roll for the Grand National ante-post at 50-1 when the weights came out, and victory at 7-1 in the Glenfarclas Cross Country Chase at Cheltenham saw the price for Aintree massively contract. The following day, Squirrel Syndicate member Jonathan Grant just missed out on a superb six-figure Scoop6 win. We had been doing Lucky 15s for members alongside the Scoop6 during the festival, and in the final leg on that Thursday we had backed Warren Greatrex's Missed Approach. In the same race, Jonathan had one of the two Scoop6 tickets riding on the Irish grey Squouateur. This raider from the Emerald Isle finished seventh on Gold Cup Day 2016 with the club's final five remaining tickets on it – at least this time Jonathan got the third place with the 5-1 shot and was able to lay his pick to ensure a profit on the week. Our Lucky 15 selection in the race, Missed Approach at 8-1, won well enough from 4-1 favourite Mal Dini and helped us to returns of £3,699.13 on the day. The Scoop6 was once again on a roll.

After the festival, we were faced with a potentially joyous jackpot at Lingfield the following Monday with a pool of £955,970. The first leg at 2.20 went to non-banker Air of York at 10-1 beating bankers Showdance Kid 6-1 and unlucky in running Malaysian Boleh at 9-2. This sent 90,090 tickets through in the win fund and we had a fair few of those as we had placed more than 36,000 lines in our combination of perms.

The 2.50 saw a banker one-two-three as Critical Thinking at 9-4 favourite beat Herm at 5-1 with Big Amigo at 7-2. There were 20,502 tickets through, and we had lots of those. In the 3.25 our winning single banker Cliffs of Dover the 1-2 favourite beat non-banker Age Of Wisdom at 5-1. This left 10,728.50 in at the halfway stage from 941,582 in at the beginning.

We had plenty of cover left, and our best result would be two out of the three bankers with a nice non-banker longshot. The 3.55 saw a banker one-two as Beautiful Memory at 4-6 favourite beat Sportswriter at 11-8. There were 6,332.50 tickets through in the jackpot and we had loads of those. We would, however, have preferred Sportswriter as the winner, as just 3,855 tickets were on that one. Funnily enough, he had finished just three-and-a-half lengths ahead of OTCO at Wolves back in February.

The penultimate leg at 4.25 saw us land a banker one-two-three-four as In The Red at 13-2 beat Pour La Victoire at 9-1 with Cyrus Dallin at 8-1 back in third. This left 825.50 tickets going into the final leg, so those three winning favourites were going to ensure a poor winning dividend. It was very disappointing as the pool rolled to nearly £1 million and we just needed some of our longer priced bankers going in to make a big difference to the dividend. We did at least manage a non-banker one-two in the 4.55 as Dorian Gray at 8-1 beat Four Fifty Three at 6-1 with banker Miniature Daffodil at 3-1 joint favourite in third. There were fifty-eight units on the winner and our 50p line paid £8,421, so we won a share of a near £1 million pool with six winners and showed a loss. It was extremely disappointing. We could only ever get the six winners, and as is often the case we just needed a few at longer odds instead of the favourites.

At Aintree in April, we put on some hospitality for Squirrel Syndicate members at McCoy's, which is the old weighing room. Our members were all in good spirits as Spider had tipped up Tiger Roll at 50-1 and the compact bay gelding was now vying for Grand National favouritism, with several of the party having got stuck in at the earlier fancy prices. It was a very jolly day with the group backing five out of the six winners and filling their boots.

The Grand National saw the Scoop6 win fund swell and with 111 horses entered on the day in the selected races, we got very close to landing the £369,000-plus prize. The opening leg was the 1.45 and all six races were at Aintree. To get us off to a flying start we had David Pipe's Mr Big Shot the 7-1 favourite with Tom Scudamore on board as a winning banker.

The second leg at 2.25 saw another banker Black Op at 3-1 get home in front, and then at 3.40 Thomas Patrick the 3-1 favourite kept up the banker run. We got a non-banker in when Identity Thief was gambled into 14-1 and won well for Henry de Bromhead under Sean Flanagan in the hurdle.

The week before, we had explained that if getting all six correct that

Saturday, we would have Tiger Roll as our bonus pick in the Grand National. In an exciting finish, gutsy Tiger at 10-1 out-battled Pleasant Company at 25-1 to land the big 'un, with Bless The Wings at 40-1 in third and Anibale Fly in fourth. Our old friend, Ladbrokes Trophy winner Total Recall had gone off 7-1 favourite and was pulled up. Another notable runner was Ross O'Sullivan's Baie Des Iles placed in twelfth at 16-1 with his wife, Katie Walsh, on board.

Just three tickets were now alive in the final leg, and we had two of those. We had one of the tickets on 4-1 favourite Michael's Mount trained by none other than Ian Williams and our other ticket was all alone on the John Nash-trained Scheu Time. After the Grand National win, a small band of Squirrel Syndicate members joined landlord Finbarr Tuite in The Three Tunnes to watch that final race. Our lucky Leg Spinner room was already packed out, so we took a right turn into the posh front room.

We had felt 5-1 shot Scheu Time was well in, and the horse appeared to be galloping all over them at the last, but immediately after the final flight he jinxed and jockey Katie Walsh fell off. We did wonder if without that Grand National ride, we might have seen a different result. But it was what it was, and £369,000 had just gone out of the window. The group was stunned into silence, but a few pints of Robbies later and we were thinking about the next week and a potential £1 million Scoop6. By the end of April, Katie at thirty-three had announced her retirement from the saddle after a glittering career. We had no hard feelings, because that fall was almost certainly more physically painful for Katie at the time than it was hard on our wallets. Incidentally, favourite Michael's Mount failed to find the frame and Tony Carroll's Havana Beat at 12-1 won the race by ten lengths, having been well behind Scheu Time before the last, so a rolling Scoop6 was the only positive.

At the end of April, Spider's long-suffering wife Anne had a pacemaker fitted. As a good husband, he endeavoured to cheer her up with a convalescent May trip to Ireland to visit some of her family members. Oh, Spider also very thoughtfully decided to take in Naas races, the National Stud, Coolmore Stud's HQ at Fethard and Castle Hyde Stud in Cork and the evening card at Tipperary. For someone recovering from a heart procedure just a week earlier, Spider had done his very best to pack a lot into the trip for her.

To be fair, it was her cousin Chris' wife Marian at Naas races who suggested they check out the National Stud. After Anne absolutely loved that visit, Spider decided to track down OTCO's old man Champs Elysees. It was all done on the hoof, and he discovered our gelding's dad was residing at Castle Hyde in Cork.

On the way, Spider decided to take Anne to a great restaurant in Cashel, Chez Hans. The plan had been to stay at Cashel Palace Hotel, but it was closed, so next stop en route to Cork was Clonmel. When they arrived at Cork the next day Ted Walsh Junior, brother to jockeys Ruby and Katie, was in place to make the introductions. Diplomatically, Spider never mentioned Scheu Time and that tumble at Aintree.

Firstly, Ted introduced the quadruple Ascot Gold Cup winner Yeats to Mr and Mrs Yates, which was a great move and they loved it. Next out was Champs Elysees, and Spider sent on a snap of OTCO's dad to the Oi The Clubb Oi's WhatsApp group for all to see where our hero had come from.

When they mentioned that they'd tried to book into Cashel Palace, Ted explained that Coolmore owner John Magnier and the boys had bought the place and were doing it up. Ted was a Cashel resident and recommended Mikey Ryan's, which Spider had thought was just a boozer, which it may have been the last time he was staying at Cashel Palace and writing a book with legendary *Coronation Street* actress Lynne Perrie, but it was now an excellent restaurant and bar.

On Ted's recommendation, they went for lunch the next day with superb steaks and fine wines all round. Very kindly, Ted had also teed up a visit to Coolmore HQ at Fethard and put them in touch with Gerry Aherne at headquarters. The next day Spider got to meet Derby winners Camelot, Australia, Ruler Of The World and Galileo with Gerry kindly showing them round.

They even got to pat Australia and Galileo; the latter apparently 600,000 euros a jump and he managed a good couple of hundred of them annually. Anne pointed out that the stud was spotlessly clean and once again loved the trip. That evening they went racing at Tipperary, which fortunately for Anne wasn't a long way from Clonmel.

With Ireland being like a village, they ended up on a table at the track with some owners who knew Coolmore's Gerry Aherne. They then very thoughtfully passed on the gem that their farrier Mr M J O'Hare was riding in the last race and had a great chance. Spider had previously highlighted the very same jockey as a great rider, and by all accounts this snippet paid for his trip when Famous Saying duly won the bumper at 8.30 beating the Willie Mullins hotpot.

The World Cup was the sporting highlight of the summer, and Spider had booked a golf trip to Belgium and France thanks to a Your Golf Travel deal that offered a full refund if your golfing destination of first choice picked up the football trophy. At the Albatross Club Christmas dinner, we had made a fair donation to the Injured Jockeys Fund by bidding for a summer speedboat trip and had booked it for the day of the World Cup final.

But before then, we were to take our first ever trip to the races as owners. For some reason, none of our fellow Albatrossers fancied Nottingham's evening meeting on July 7th. Golfer Lee had a great excuse as he was playing in the Irish Open, but the reason nobody else turned up was very likely that it coincided with England's quarter-final against Sweden.

We went to The Tunnes for a barbecue feast and a Dizzy Blonde before making the trip to Nottingham for the Genting's Casino Ladies Evening card. Finbarr and his able assistant chef Jose Ferreira produced some fine fodder, and the beer garden was rammed. A first-half goal from Harry Maguire with another in the second half from Dele Alli gave England the 2-0 passport to a semi-final with Croatia, and sent the Swedes packing. We left the boozer in buoyant mood for the trek to Nottingham, and were not very far away from the track when a great stroke of timing saved our bacon.

As we got near to the student stomping ground of Lenton, a traffic light in the near distance changed to green. Richard contemplated putting his foot down, but then felt we had plenty of time so just cruised on steadily. That split second decision was fortuitous, as at the very moment we reached the lights, a black VW Golf filled with perhaps inebriated England fans sped across in front of us, having jumped the light to our right on red. A tad faster and we'd have all been hospitalised, if not dead. We took it as a sign that we were very much in luck and placed some more bets on OTCO.

Arriving in time to organise our owners and trainers passes, we managed a pre-race pint of real ale from the excellent Castle Rock Brewery with a slice of something nice from The Cheese Shop in Nottingham. Jockey Jim Crowley was on all of the Ian Williams-trained runners that evening, and Paddy A at 7-1 got the ball rolling with a cosy length-and-a-half victory over Strictly Art in the Dick Benson Memorial Handicap at 7.10.

We then had time for a spot of dinner with our owners and trainers passes, before heading down to the pre-parade ring and a chat with lucky Jim. Fortunately, JC knew exactly how to ride OTCO, which was a real stroke of luck, as neither of us did. In the same race, our fellow Albatrosser Ken Rhatigan was running his horse Jazzy Girl from the Brendan Powell stables, so we took some pre-race pictures. Our trainer Ian suggested with an emoji that OTCO would thrash Ken's mare, so we trusted the expert. By now the 7-2 had vanished from the bookies' boards and the starting price was 3-1.

It was a seven-runner field over a mile and two furlongs, and six of the runners exploded from the gates. OTCO, on the other hand, sort of meandered out and Jim held him back at the tail of the field in seventh. OTCO was stone-cold last with half a mile to go, but in the long home straight he was brought wide and began to make progress from the three-furlong pole. OTCO was in a challenging position within a furlong and led entering the final furlong, so all was looking good as the Richard Fahey-trained 6-4 favourite Ventura Gold was trailing in his wake.

But then the David Brown-trained 8-1 shot Make Good with Pat Cosgrave in the plate just wasn't going away, so Jim got to work and drove OTCO out for a neck victory. It was a thrilling finish as the second ran on well. We were elated and had been cheering our lad home from the stands. Unfortunately, Ken's filly didn't enjoy the good to firm ground and trailed in twenty-eight lengths further back in seventh. The trainer's rep had to inform the stewards that OTCO's apparent improvement in form was due to the 'gelding appreciating the step up in trip and has also learned to settle better both at home and in races.'

This was our first trip out as owners, and our next step was back to the parade ring to collect the trophy – which consisted of a bag of cheese, an exceedingly large cheesecake and a couple of bottles of beer. For us, it was the equivalent of the Jules Rimet Trophy. Spider still has a picture of us with the swag perched on his mantelpiece.

We handed over the cheesecake for the stable staff, and the winner's cheque for £3,881.40 from the Genting Casino At The Cornerhouse Handicap went straight to Mr Williams. He was worth every penny in our humble opinion, as this whole owner gig was just great. We had won shares of millions before, yet as we toasted the victory with another of Castle Rock Brewery's finest, we contemplated how this feeling of owning the winner of the race was just something else.

Immediately after the race we sent a video debrief from Jim to our co-owners, with a couple of partly deranged 'Oi the Clubb Oi's' chanted on the WhatsApp group for good measure. We imagined that many of the other chaps were equally inebriated after the fantastic England win ahead of OTCO losing his maiden tag.

We met a young man in the parade ring with team Williams, and his dad owned Paddy The Chef - running in the last race at 8.40. When we inquired about the name, our new friend - aged around eleven, explained with very almost a nod and a wink that it was a long story - something to do with a trip to Dublin his dad had been on. Enough said, we went off to shovel a few shillings on Paddy at 7-2 and he was cooking with gas in the Genting Casino Roulette Classified Stakes for a comfortable victory.

In advance, we had told Squirrel Syndicate members we were going to the track and one crafty member, an accountant called Ian had a quid on the three Ian Williams runners that evening. A 200-1 treble, as it turned out, so very well done to him, as we managed no more than a 20-1 double and a couple of lumpy singles.

OTCO had one more run on the flat that season at Chepstow on August 23rd off bottom weight of 8st 7lbs with Luke Morris up. We were not expecting a massive run, as he'd been beginning to school over hurdles and the campaign ahead would be over jumps. The Queen owned the 6-4 favourite Natural Beauty, and Andrew Balding's charge won the race well under David Probert with OTCO staying on into third.

Before OTCO's next outing, there was Spider's golfing expedition to Belgium. He was also playing at Dunkirk. His YGT freebie hadn't materialised as the Belgians got mugged by the French in the semi-final and could only finish third. France went on to win, but the boys on the golf trip had their jaunt paid for courtesy of Albatross Ivor coming up with a winning tip for John Gosden's Wissahickon at 11-1 under Frankie Dettori in the Cambridgeshire. This was passed on, and led to a very cheery Saturday for the boys on foreign fields as their trip was paid for with a punt of around £20 each way.

The next chapter in OTCO's jumping career would entail an Albatross Sunday out at Huntingdon, where OTCO and the Nicky Henderson-trained Full Bore were both running in consecutive races on November 4th. Our second day as owners was going to be fun as well, and would end with a champagne winner although not the one we really wanted.

Team Albatross saw chairman Ross and his wife Sarah bring their new-born son Henry along; Ed Babington and his wife Francoise had young Ted in tow; Ken Rhatigan had brought his good lady, and the group was completed with Spider and Squirrel at the races. The rather catchily named Cemetery Development Services Ltd Juvenile Hurdle was the second race on the card at 1.45, worth £6,498 to the winner, which was most likely going to be Dr Richard Newland's 13-8 favourite Katpoli.

A few of the group had got small money down on OTCO overnight, but we had taken 7-2 in the morning. Despite our boy hurdling fluently under Tom O'Brien, as we suspected, he found the more experienced favourite just too good first time out. The following race saw Full Bore at 10-11 favourite run out an easy nine-length winner for the Albatross Club. We were all cheering him on from the stands, then Ross and the chaps got us in for a post-race glass of champagne, which was jolly decent of them. Ken topped his day off by landing the placepot, so it was a good day all round and the 150-mile trip home flew as we discussed future racing plans.

It was the end of November when we sponsored our first race – the Scoop6SuperClub.com Handicap Chase at Uttoxeter on Sunday November 25th. It was a Class 4 two miles four-furlong affair worth £4,613 to the winner. We had arranged this as a way to get solicitor Nick Turner along to the races with his family as guests of honour. We had hoped Nick would be watching OTCO with us, but his situation had changed since we had been on the gallops. From being in remission, Nick had suffered the blow of the cancer returning and Uttoxeter wasn't too far away from his home in Worcester. It was great to see Nick with wife Joy, and their boys Ed and Robert; though as committed Christians, they were partially horrified at the prospect of The Squirrel Syndicate corrupting their sons.

The second race on the card was won by Paul Webber's Indefatigable at 5-4 favourite, and this was marked down as a decent prospect moving forward. But our race was the penultimate of the day, and we enjoyed a fine lunch ahead of racing. Richard had brought his wife Ruth. Spider's wife Anne was along, as was Finbarr from the Tunnes with his new bride Danielle, who claimed to be not drinking due to a blood test, but was actually pregnant with baby Emily.

Plumber Martin Walker made a mouth-watering appearance with his latest blonde girlfriend while Spider cut short a golfing expedition to Abersoch and brought Squirrel Syndicate member Tommy Muirhead along with Stockport rugby club legend Mr K. It was a very jolly day out indeed.

Ahead of our race, Nick and the family were to judge the best turned out horse, and afterwards they had to present the trophy to the winner. It was a real slog on the good to soft ground, but Fact Flow under Robert Dunne triumphed for trainer Dai Burchell. In the winners' enclosure ahead of the presentation Dai had a serious look on his face, but Nick and the family were all beaming as they handed over the prize.

Sadly, Nick never got to see OTCO run at the track, but one of the pictures from that happy day emerged at his memorial service the following Spring. They do say only the good die young, so most Squirrel Syndicate members will be looking forward to a long life then. Though Nick's death did highlight the fragility of existence. Now is good, so always best to enjoy the moment. Live for today and do your best.

On the upcoming Friday November 30th, Spider was off for his annual trip to the Liverpool Press Club Christmas knees-up at the city's Adelphi Hotel before leaving ahead of pudding for the long trip to Edinburgh for his second party of the day on the eve of OTCO's next outing at Newcastle. Before getting the Liverpool train, another Albatross member Gentleman George passed on a tip for a Ben Pauling runner Bright Forecast at 50-1 in the first race at Newbury.

Just after alighting at Liverpool's Lime Street, George was about make us all smile with a 50-1 winner backed into 20-1 after Bright Forecast under Nico De Boinville flew from the clouds to get up by a neck on the line. We had met Gentleman George the December before in the Queens Arms in Lambourn after Total Recall's Newbury triumph, but recollections of the celebrations that night remain hazy. Suffice to say, both George and Newbury to this day have a special place in our hearts.

The BOOMS on the WhatsApp group were almost deafening and Lee even sent on a re-run of the race, as it was such a sensational win. The next day we couldn't make it to Newcastle, though OTCO did us all proud as ever. Running on strongly in the 11.50 he gave the Nicky Henderson hotpot 2-5 favourite Style De Vole under Barry Geraghty a real run for the £12,996 prize money, going down by just a neck. This was a tremendous effort.

We vowed not to miss his next racecourse appearance and were blessed to be able to attend only a fortnight later for another big Saturday run – this time at Doncaster. It was a pre-Christmas jaunt and our third run out as owners. We were flying the Albatross Club flag, and as we walked into the packed owners and trainers dining room, we immediately spotted trainer Ian, who had secured the best seats in the house for our lunch. We were positioned directly in-front of the big screen, and we all fancied our boy each way at 25-1 to perhaps upset another odds-on favourite in the shape of Paul Nicholls Quel Destin at 8-11.

Being a rather inclement, icy cold day, we went to the main hall to watch the race among the crowds with Ian. All three of us were cheering on OTCO as he came with his run, and third place at 16-1 beaten by just over two lengths was not too shabby. Ian confided to us that next stop would be Cheltenham, as we probably had just got a good enough mark to get in the Fred Winter.

Little did he know we were hearing news from him that was beyond our wildest dreams when we embarked on our remarkable OTCO adventure. We had now followed the equine apple of our eyes to three tracks and been present for a win, a second and a gallant third. For us, this was already the stuff of fairy tales. The Cheltenham experience is a different chapter, but it's actually the next chapter, so best keep on reading.

Chapter 19

OTCO AT THE FESTIVAL

After ten weeks of rollovers, the Scoop6 win fund was up to £1,931,710 as the first leg 1.05 at Taunton went off on Saturday January 19th. We had pulled on our betting boots big time to place two perms costing £26,712, so wanted to get a slice of the win fund.

The bonus pot hit the £1,030,922 mark, so another £3 million-plus combined Scoop6 when you took into account the £235,654 place fund. As well as Taunton, Betfred had brought two races from Navan – one from Ascot and a couple from Haydock – into the mix.

Our main perm required all six bankers, or five bankers plus a non-banker, and cost £20,232. The second perm, a 5×3×4×3×6×3 costing £6,480, had fewer selected non-bankers in legs three and four with the same bankers in the other legs.

We got off to a brilliant start with a banker one-two as Silver Quay at 7-1 beat 7-2 favourite Dollnamix with non-banker Telson Barley at 12-1 in third and Menapian at 50-1 in fourth. From 673,299 tickets in at the start, just 97,573 were now standing after the father-daughter combination of Jimmy and Bryony Frost fired in their winner.

The second leg was the 1.35 at Navan and we got another winning banker as the mother and son team of Mags and Danny Mullins got Agusta Gold at 7-1 over the line in front. The Mullins' horse beat non-bankers Chatam Street Lad at 9-2 and Jimmy Breekie at 12-1. This left 10,555 tickets in the win fund and the second had nearly twice as many tickets on. The 2.10 at Navan saw our single banker Goose Man at 7-2 favourite just prevail from gambled-on non-banker Bother Dubh 6-1, with selected non-bankers Load Up Time at 17-2 and Lady Writer at 9-1 in third and fourth. This left 3,004 tickets in the win fund.

Ascot at 3pm saw a non-banker one-two-three as selected non-banker

Cyrname at 4-1 beat Doitforthevillage at 14-1 with Happy Diva at 7-1 back in third. This left 403 tickets in the win fund, and we had eighteen of those. We now needed bankers in the final two legs. Our plan in this race was to cover the favourite and second favourite as bankers. Belami Des Pictons was made a non-runner after racing started, but we would have promoted Cyrname to banker status if we had known, so we were very disappointed to say the least.

We were smiling again after the 3.15 at Haydock with a banker one-two as Wakanda at 6-1 beat Robinsfirth at 7-1 with non-banker Ballydine at 13-2 in third. This left fifty-two tickets in the win fund, and we had three going into the final leg – the second would have been better as just thirty-two tickets were on him. The final leg provided a thrilling finish to the 4.15 at Haydock and it went to the judge for a photograph. Sadly, our banker Silva Escape at 7-2 was beaten by a nostril on the line by non-banker Closing Ceremony at 8-1 with Highland Hunter at 5-1 back in third.

There were three winning tickets paying £643,903, but if our jockey had Silva's head down on the line, we would have had around £200,000 reasons to celebrate. We had forty of the 2,077 place lines paying £113.40 per ticket, which was a small consolation.

It was extra painful as we would have had Cyrname in as a banker if the non-runner had been declared ahead of noon and that would have put us on Closing Ceremony in the last for a return of £482,927. It can be fine margins and timing really can be everything when placing a big perm like this.

One of the three winners was a Betfred customer who had placed a single £2 line. The three ticket holders got together for the bonus bid the following week, and when Paisley Park at 10-3 favourite beat West Approach at 20-1 in the 3.35 at Cheltenham, they each added £343,640 to take their overall hauls to £987,543. So someone won almost £1 million for just £2 – the absolute joy of the Scoop6! It wasn't lost on us that if we had known about that non-runner the week before, then we'd have landed a quarter of that bonus pot, so £257,730 on top of the £482,927, or a cool £740,657 in total. When we recount the tale, we can all still feel the tears running down our cheeks again. It hurt even more at the time. The pain of the fresh loss is so much harder to bear.

But the Cheltenham Festival was just around the corner, and we had reasons to be cheerful once again. For as per the plan, OTCO had got in at the foot of the weights for the Fred Winter on the Wednesday, or the Boodles Juvenile Handicap Hurdle as it had been renamed. We knew our grey OTCO was a diamond, and at 50-1 we also knew he was a bit of value.

We booked into the very posh Manor By The Lake for a couple of nights, and that set the tone for the trip. We arrived on the Tuesday and got a fantastic recommendation for an after-racing curry from Sarah our chauffeur. Before then, we had an Albatross dinner hosted by chairman Ross on the first night in the hotel, and Richard was most amused by an early introduction.

Football agent Dougie Keen, who we'd met fleetingly at the Christmas lunch, was in attendance with a glamorous lady friend. It turned out that his acquaintance Elissa had met Spider in a previous existence. When Elissa revealed she had been in the TV series *Desperate Scousewives* and that he'd interviewed her, the look on his face was absolutely priceless. Richard could see that behind The Spider's smile, his brain was vacant – he clearly had no recollection of ever meeting the lady before. To add to the moment, we were then off to dinner round the same table. Despite the fine wines and fantastic meal, Richard could tell Spider was still trying to process the when and where of this earlier encounter. It was great to see someone with a near photographic memory going so blank. The meal, followed by coffees and discussion of OTCO's chances the next day, made for a very merry start to the festival.

Up early for breakfast, *Racing Post* at the ready, it was race day for OTCO and we had to pinch ourselves at the prospect of going to the festival as owners. On the table in front of us was golfer Lee with Close House owner Graham Wylie, who hadn't had the best of starts to the meeting as his well-fancied Ballyward fell at the seventeenth fence in the National Hunt Chase on the opening day and had to be put to sleep.

Lee though was going through the form with gusto, and taking calls with information about all sorts of runners that day. Just like us, they are massive racing fans and the atmosphere in the breakfast room was still slightly subdued after the loss of a runner. Tides turn in racing and that day with OTCO running in the penultimate race, Lee placed a

£240 Super Heinz. We must admit at breakfast when we heard the word Heinz our thoughts were on the brand of baked beans, but Lee's bet was certainly set to bring home the bacon. Over breakfast it was confirmed that the ground was soft, and fellow Albatrosser Ed Babington, who had tipped up his Beat The Judge at 40-1 when winning in December at Kempton, revealed that his lad trained by Gary Moore would almost certainly be a non-runner due to the going change.

Next stop for us was the Guinness Village for a pre-racing pint to quell the nerves of these elated first-time festival owners. We also met up with Ross, Johnno, Chief, Ivor and the Albatross squad in full team colours of bright yellow tie and matching pocket handkerchief gizmo. We then took in the delights of the Racing Breaks box, where Fleetwood manager Joey Barton was entertaining his team alongside the AFC Wimbledon squad, at that point under legendary manager Neal Ardley.

In the box was Your Golf Travel co-founder Andrew Harding with fellow Albatrosser George Smyly, who was keen on December's Newbury 50-1 winner Bright Forecast outrunning his odds of 25-1 in the opener. Our punting got off to a flyer with another Albatross member Henry St George tipping up Ballymore Hurdle winner City Island at 8-1. Bright Forecast was backed into 20-1 and finished a fair third with Barry Geraghty on Champ at 9-2 in second, so we got the winner and an each-way draw.

In the next race we liked Paul Nicholls Topofthegame at 4-1. He beat Nicky Henderson's 3-1 shot Santini, with Delta Work the 15-8 favourite well back in third. Incidentally, Lee had the first two winners up in his Super Heinz, but the third race proved the world's former number one golfer was human after all, when his pick, Killultagh Vic at 16-1, finished last. Nicky Henderson claimed the Coral Hurdle prize with William Henry at 28-1 beating Willie Mullins' 28-1 shot Wicklow Brave by a short head.

Next up, the Queen Mother Champion Chase was often the race of the meeting, with the chasers flying at full pelt over the fences. We all pretty much knew that this renewal was going to be won by Hendo's star performer Altior. Lee had him in his Heinz at 4-11 favourite and he got the job done cosily from the gallant grey Politologue at 9-1. The next race was the stamina sapping Glenfarclas Cross Country, and Tiger

Roll was back to do it again at 5-4 favourite. Spider had tipped Tiger Roll for another Grand National at 20-1 when the weights came out, so wasn't going mad today, though we both felt the Tiger would roar home and he duly did.

We had all had a fair few quid on OTCO at 50-1 and the moment of truth was soon upon us. A couple of us, Richard and Spider to be precise, were now in the parade ring at Cheltenham and we felt our boy had a live chance. They took a great team picture in the ring ahead of the race and Ed with his wife Francoise, in the absence of Beat The Judge, joined us to cheer on OTCO. Expectation was heavy in the air as this was his moment, or so we all hoped, as the odds came in to 33-1.

OTCO under Tom O'Brien broke well went off with the pack and was fairly prominent. We were in the first handful at the head of the twenty-one-runner field as they set off into the country. Hopes were high as OTCO was tracking the leaders, but after the fifth flight he appeared to lose his action and started to slip back through the field. We were all naturally worried that something was amiss, and Tom sensibly pulled him up ahead of the last.

Meanwhile up front, Band Of Outlaws the 7-2 favourite gave Lee his fifth winner so far on the day in that very super, Super Heinz. We waited for a debrief from Tom and he told us he felt something had gone wrong as OTCO began lugging to the left. It transpired later, after an appointment with the vet, that OTCO had a kissing spine and perhaps the Cotswold undulations hadn't suited him that day. Trainer Ian though rallied the troops with the suggestion that he'd love to get our lad to Melbourne for the race that stops the nation, with thoughts of a trip down under to cheer on OTCO to lighten the mood. However, with the knowledge that our lad had to see the vet, both Richard and Spider didn't have the heart to stay at the track.

Like Lee, we fancied Irish raider Envoi Allen in the last. Unlike him, we hadn't got 9-2, so decided to leave the 2-1 favourite alone as he duly romped home for that sensational six-timer payout for OTCO's co-owner. We were thrilled for him and even clapped and cheered his last selection on as we left the course. It was disappointing to have had OTCO in with such a chance, only for an injury to get in the way of a shot at a winning run. But as we strolled back into town, we counted our blessings as we knew he would race another day, and Melbourne could even be on the menu. More fodder for the ever-expanding, you-couldn't-make-it-up files.

We decided an early curry might cheer us both up, and Prithvi was right by the Inn On The Park on the walk back. We were clearly in luck as we slipped into the last two available seats in this tremendous restaurant, which was a fabulous recommendation from Sarah. Richard had the rabbit starter and Spider had something equally unusual. The mains were marvellous with a venison curry among the highlights, and it was all washed down with some wonderful red wine.

Refreshed after dinner, with provisional plans in place for Melbourne 2022 chalked in the diary, we decided on a pub crawl back to the Manor. As ever, being Cheltenham, the bars were really quite busy, though that's quite an understatement. It was absolutely rammed, and by the time we reached the hotel it was, as Zebedee from the Magic Roundabout regularly said, 'Time for bed.'

The next morning, we were up bright and early to enjoy the delights of the breakfast buffet. The day before was behind us, and fresh form study was now required. Having heard on *talkSPORT* that Lee had landed £48,200 for his Super Heinz, we congratulated him on his win, and kept an ear peeled for any snippets from his table. It wasn't too hard as Barry Geraghty had two great chances in the opening contests with Defi Du Seuil and Sire Du Berlais. We had already identified Any Second Now as a great bet in the Fulke Walwyn Kim Muir Handicap that closed the card. Like the relentless winner-finding machine he was, Lee mentioned all three, so we were cheered that we'd backed the right ones. We didn't get a fourth pick for a fantastic Lucky 15, but the three actually won at starting prices of 3-1 favourite, 4-1 favourite and 6-1; although we'd got a bit better than those starting prices from the bookies in the morning.

At breakfast, Richard couldn't resist a Bloody Mary from the 'mix your own drink' section on the buffet, and Lee was also in the mood to celebrate as he tried to get the boys at Betfair to deliver a few bags to the course for him. Like most of us, he enjoys feeling the folding after a win. While the other guests went to the track, we headed North talking about the most memorable Cheltenham trip Spider had taken in his thirty years as a regular. We really couldn't believe it, and in the words of Arnold Schwarzenegger, we vowed we'd be back, but that's a whole new story and we'll come to that later.

Our next race trip was a jolly jaunt with Squirrel Syndicate members to Aintree. It was a wonderful Thursday, enjoying the hospitality in the old weighing room once again. Almost déjà vu from the year before, Spider was getting clapped on the back for tipping up the warm Grand National favourite at 20-1, so all was well with the world as we all really fancied Tiger to be on a roll. His namesake Tiger Woods actually won the Masters that year, and some real shrewdies got the winning double at odds of more than 100-1. Highlight of the Thursday at Aintree was Supasundae at 15-2 beating the 5-6 favourite Buveur D'Air in the Betway Aintree Hurdle. AP McCoy had tipped this up at our Racing Breaks Cheltenham preview a year or so earlier and we kept the faith.

It was funny as we sipped the traditional pints of Guinness, and Spider told us a strange story. A couple of years earlier he'd been on Bowling Green Barry's stag do at Aintree. It was Ladies Day, and they ran into a hen party offering to keep their seats warm.

As he chatted to bridesmaid Lisa Hennessey and bride Dominque McGahey, they revealed how a couple of clubs in the city centre had put a dampener on their big day. They had done this by banning their planned expedition out after racing, with Dominque handcuffed to a dwarf dressed as an Oompa Loompa. Spider told how he was intrigued and got some pictures taken, while SuperClub stag Barry was revelling elsewhere.

Apparently, in the bar were a couple of female correspondents for the *Daily Mail*, who revealed how they loved dwarf stories. It really was another episode from the 'you-couldn't-make-it-up files,' as Spider had Mafia Pat from Channel 4 and first-time racegoer John Kidd on his fiftieth birthday in tow. Hitman Pat knew this was just another day at the races for Spider, and all par for the course. But retired policeman John was looking on stunned, shaking his head in disbelief. We've seen things similar, if not stranger with our own eyes, so know just how we couldn't make it up.

Chapter 20

GOLDEN TICKET

That summer, the third day at Royal Ascot was looking interesting with Frankie Dettori firing in the first four winners at 5-1, 13-2, 4-1 and evens. We heard from Albatross George that Biometric at 28-1 was a bet in the fifth race on the card, the Britannia Stakes.

Frankie's mount Turgenev was hammered into 7-2 favourite, while Ralph Beckett's charge went in to 25s and back out to 28s. Two furlongs out, Frankie was in front. A furlong from home he was still there, leading the nearside group. Then our Albatross tip under Harry Bentley swooped, and Biometric won, going away in the final fifty yards.

Despite Dettori riding home the first four winners in the Scoop6, the 28-1 success of Biometric left just one ticket alive going into the finale. That was on Frankie's mount Questionnaire. But the Italian could not deliver the earlier magic of the afternoon, as Ireland's Ballydoyle brigade dominated the lucky last with a one-two-three. So, a £96,233 win fund headed into Friday, while the bonus fund had grown to £312,685.

The Frankie five-timer being foiled was a fantastic stroke of luck for the bookies, as they were all having nightmares of Dettori going through the card again, like he did at Ascot in September 1996. That was the year of his Magnificent Seven. In Las Vegas, watching the meeting from afar, there was a chap who Frankie had turned into a Yankee with his seven-timer. Managing the sports book in the Flamingo was a Brit called Pete Saxton, who used to run the Bob Johnson bookies in Poynton, Cheshire.

On the day of Frankie's seven winners, Pete had a 25p win Super Heinz on all his mounts. The Super Heinz consists of 120 bets, so that's twenty-one doubles, thirty-five trebles, thirty-five four-folds, twenty-one five-folds, seven six-folds and a seven-timer accumulator, though our golfer pal Lee Westwood would certainly know this. Pete took the early prices, and most importantly the 14-1 on the last runner Fujiyama Crest. He had originally phoned Coral asking for a 10p win bet, only to be told the minimum stake was 25p. It turned out that each extra 5p worth of bets staked was worth just under £50,000 and Pete collected £247,999 instead of £99,199. The Coral maximum payout was £250,000, so Pete was bang on the money with his perfect stake.

He took his fortune and moved to Vegas, marrying a showgirl. She went on a Viv Nicholson-style spend, spend, spend spree with him before divorcing and waltzing off with half the remaining pot. But Pete persisted and gained US citizenship a couple of decades after Frankie's Magnificent Seven. We'd met him in The Three Tunnes back in the day and Spider often saw him at the races, but seeing him at his casino home in the gambling capital of the world was cool for all Squirrel Syndicate members who visited Las Vegas.

That story reminds us of a dinner we had at Belle Vue dogs about fifteen years earlier as guests of the Tote, who had just appointed Trevor Beaumont as CEO from his previous post as managing director at Coral. He was a proper bookmaker and good company. He regaled us with a fantastic tale of fighting the fires as Frankie scorched away on that September afternoon with his Magnificent Seven.

Trevor was leading the trading team at Coral HQ and had rung round the other big boys – Ladbrokes, William Hill and probably Paddy Power – to try and get them all to batter Fujiyama Crest in the final leg. But Trevor told us how the others had all given up. He was the only one piling money on Fujiyama Crest at the track to try and bring the starting price down.

Among those to take his lumpy bets was bookie Gary Wiltshire. He also ended up working at the Tote after laying Frankie for fortunes on that fateful day had bankrupted him. Gary told in his book, *Winning It Back*, how he lost £1 million that afternoon. He had originally planned to be taking bets at Worcester, but a pile-up on the M40 at Banbury made him turn round and head to Ascot instead. A horrendous sliding doors moment for him.

About seven years after that meeting, Trevor was back running the Tote as Betfred CEO after Fred Done had splashed out £265 million for the Tote operation. If memory serves us correctly, Fred was ready to spend £365 million on the Tote a year or so before it came to market. But PM Gordon Brown embarked on a fire sale after the economic crash of 2008. Spider was on champagne at the festival in the Cotswolds at about this time, telling Betfred's communications director that a change of Government was on the cards and the Tories would most likely let the Tote go for closer to £265 million which, as it turned out was a bang-on-the-money estimate. He's still not had his cut of the £100 million saving, but lives in hope.

In 2019, Fred was considering offloading the Tote part of his betting empire, and it came to pass later in the year. We thought the new Tote owners could be good for the world's best bet, the Scoop6, and we hoped for a return to the glory days. In recent times we had ended up playing the bet just a handful of times each year. Our perception was that it no longer represented value, just like the jackpot after it started getting split between different meetings to make it more difficult in the Betfred years. It's a fine line between growing the pools and making the bet bad value. Talks this year with new Tote boss Alex Frost indicate they could be rejigging things the right way with the expansion of their global World Pool.

Fred did run the bet well in those early years, but back then he did have the terrestrial TV connection with Channel 4. ITV now have the gig, but appear too busy with their telephone lines trying to entice people in to play for £50k, when the real viewer engagement and tremendous excitement of life-changing sums can only come from exotic pool bets like the Scoop6.

In another life, Spider had a hand in the early publicity for ITV's 'Who Wants to Be a Millionaire?' A fine lunch at the Montreux TV Festival with the then director of programmes at ITV David Liddiment, a former executive producer of Coronation Street, gave the newly appointed TV Editor an old-fashioned scoop. Spider exclusively revealed how a programme with fifteen multiple choice questions to make a millionaire was being planned by the network.

He's certain that a bet that makes millionaires, which can be followed leg by leg on terrestrial TV, would be an ideal part of any true racing programme and would pile on viewers. This would be not only good for ITV, but also the Tote and racing as it could bring in a whole new raft of viewers to the sport of kings. The excitement building leg by leg, with rollovers just adding to the interest, is what made Squirrel Syndicate members play whenever we thought it was worthwhile.

That July saw the twentieth anniversary of our once favourite bet, which was launched on King George VI & Queen Elizabeth Stakes Day back in 1999. In those ensuing years the bet made twenty-seven millionaires – a lot more than ever won the prize on Chris Tarrant's and now Jeremy Clarkson's quiz show. In 1999 Frankie Dettori landed the big race aboard Daylami. He did the trick again twenty years later on John Gosden's Queen of Racing Enable, who battled to a hard-fought neck win from Michael Stoute's Crystal Ocean. Frankie and Enable next went to York for the Darley Yorkshire Oaks and landed that for a delighted owner Khalid Abdullah. But the main target for Frankie and the wonder mare was the Arc De Triomphe at Longchamp in October.

It just so happened that Arc weekend coincided with an enormous EuroMillions lottery pool after it reached five capped rollovers, and the €190 million draw on October 8th was well worth playing. Spider and Anne had seen Enable crowned Queen of the Turf in Paris twelve months earlier and were back for the return jaunt with another visit to the champagne bar at Longchamp.

They had driven over to stay with Squirrel Syndicate member Professor Graham Roberts and his wife, Bea, in Lille, before heading off to Longchamp as a group on the Sunday. Spider had encouraged Richard to pop over to place our EuroMillions perm in France, as we'd discovered that our Continental cousins get much better value for their money in these draws.

Richard was initially highly sceptical, but the recent consecutive rollovers and the current rule that any rollover of €190 million must be paid out on the fifth capped draw, did provide tremendous value on that one particular draw. Richard flew into Charles De Gaulle that evening and was planning a train ride from there to Lille.

Earlier in the day, one of the Albatross chaps named Chop had pointed out what tremendous value Waldegeist was at 20-1 against favourite Enable. Spider took a similar view about value to be found against the odds-on shot. Earlier that summer, he had been over to

Chantilly for the French Derby and was impressed by the winner of that called Sottsass. He had bumped into Frankie at Chantilly, where the Professor's teenage son Mathieu, on his first ever visit to the races, got a personal introduction to the world's greatest jockey. Bizarrely, almost simultaneously, Spider's wife, Anne, was being interviewed on French TV about Frankie's mount. Immediately after her, they had Hollywood A-lister Owen Wilson being interviewed. Not sure what either of them really knew about the day's racing, but they were certainly both enjoying it, and that's the main thing.

Back to Longchamp, Frankie and Enable failed to follow up, beaten a length and three-quarters by Chop's tip. Spider, though disappointed at not witnessing a history-making moment, did at least have the consolation of decent bets landed on the winner, the exacta and the trifecta, with Sottsass placed in third. Their next punt at the track was on the William Haggas-trained mud-lover One Master at around 7-2. That winner ensured they were booking a top five-star hotel in Paris for the evening. With the Prof driving, they headed off to one of the finer arrondissements for a slap-up spread.

Richard managed to call from the airport, just as the Prof and Bea were saying their goodbyes after the meal. Very kindly, Prof Graham offered him a lift direct to Lille and his accommodation. It was almost like winning the jackpot, as he didn't have to mess around with the rail network. The pick-up went like clockwork, and Squirrel was soon settling in chez Prof and Bea.

The next day he visited a PMU bar called Le Bras D'Hambourg. Spider had identified it as ideal for placing our Euros perm and had lined up the owner to handle our business. Richard started on the strong French lager served there, and began outlining the perm for the Tuesday night draw. The next day, after a fast train arrived from Paris, Spider and Anne were also in town to assist. The perm placement was going slowly as the squiffy Squirrel downed *demi* after *demi*. It became an all afternoon and evening team affair. The reinforcements were also partial to the fine French lager, so we had to really concentrate as slip after slip was slipped over the counter. It was a real chore, but the ales helped lighten the load.

By Tuesday morning the job was done. Richard had booked a flight out of Charleroi airport near Brussels for that evening. At draw time he would be in the air and unable to see the numbers as they came out. Mr and Mrs Spider very kindly offered to take him to the airport, as they were having a night in Belgium. Someone had to be in place to collect the 190 million, and Prof Graham had offered to keep it in his account if required.

We decided to stop off for a splendid Belgian lunch but, despite it being a Tuesday afternoon, the town we rocked up in was very quiet with hardly any bars open. After lunch it was off to the airport to deposit The Squirrel. The rest of the team headed to their hotel in La Louvière, checking in before heading out to watch the EuroMillions Draw. It wasn't anywhere near as thrilling as the Arc, and we didn't match the balls for the 190 million Euro jackpot, which oddly enough was won by someone in Blighty. We did get extra tickets on and had some small returns to collect. You have to be in it to win it, but we didn't win big this time.

Drum roll, cheesy music, this EuroMillions video was even slower than the draw on the Tuesday that was not shown live on TV. Anyhow in the clip they showed later on, the first ball appeared and it was number 44 – so we had 1,512 lines with it on. We needed the next drawn to be any one of 31 numbers from the 49 remaining, as we had cover with the 19 other high numbers plus 4, 7, 9, 10, 14, 17, 19, 20, 24, 27, 29 and 30 on the low side. But we came unstuck with ball 15 and could no longer hit all five main numbers.

We did subsequently get another high ball, so a pair of high numbers, and those combined with ball 7 and a lucky star 12 on one perm, brought us fifteen lines of 3+1 at €14.90 each and sixty lines of €8.10 each. Four other perms brought small returns, thirty-five lines of 2+1 at €8.10, then another three perms each brought in thirty-five lines of 2+0 at €4.10 each. We did turn a near 140 million to one shot of getting 5+2 stars into a 37,000-1 shot. We were actually aiming to get 5+1 which was more like 1,900-1 against. The thinking was that if nobody did get 5+2, the jackpot would instead be shared between those getting 5+1 as per the rolldown rules.

We managed to collect 714 euros in smaller prizes, but the bank card was inexplicably blocked from receiving the other half of the estimated returns. Our French friends in the various PMUs (the French bar/betting shops of the Pari-Mutuel) around Dunkirk and Calais were unable to assist us. Nevertheless, we paid out on assumed total returns of €1,423.50 plus some unused funds of £756.66, at that Tuesday afternoon rate of 1.115 euros to a pound.

Anyhow, we unearthed some interesting facts for National Lottery EuroMillions players in the UK:

Ticket price in the UK is £2.50 and in Euroland €2.50

The lowest prize (for 2 main numbers and no stars) in this particular draw, was £2.90 so a 40p win for UK players, but in Euroland it was €4.10 so a win of €1.60. The outright UK winner with five main numbers and both lucky stars landed £170,221,000 which was the capped €190,000,000 converted at the rate of €1.116 to £1. But in the case of the four ticket holders who picked the five main numbers with one lucky star, the three in Euroland received €5,227,531 each and the UK player only received £3,696,996.80 making for an effective exchange rate of 1.414 . It was looking like Brexit wasn't going to be a bad thing, as our continental cousins were having our pants down even on the EuroMillions lottery.

Our best Scoop6 result ahead of Cheltenham was not managing to get a perm on at all, thanks to the new look Tote website on February 15th, 2020. Like almost everyone else, we'd have got through to the final leg and suffered heartache, so a good result not getting on.

We liked the races the Tote had selected; it was like the old days – tough, yet winnable. Spider had gone to South Africa for some racing action at Kenilworth and The Sun Met with some chums from the International Racing Club. He flew home and then back out to Portugal on a YGT trip to the Algarve with his Waldorf Society golfing pals at the end of February, followed by a week touring from Faro with Anne afterwards. He was jetting back in March for our annual expedition to Cheltenham, with a suite booked at the Manor By The Lake. But the world was soon going to become a very different place.

We arrived at Cheltenham on the Tuesday, and Italy was already in lockdown as the planet was beginning to fall into the grips of a pandemic. Coronavirus in the shape of Covid-19 was going to kill off a lot of fun and a lot of people.

On the first day at the festival, we met a smashing chap called Richard in the Arkle Bar. He was recovering from some illness and could only manage three hours or so per day at the track. He was a Liverpool fan and had tickets to the Atlético Madrid game the next night at Anfield, but was talking about giving the match a miss to return to Cheltenham instead. We arranged to possibly meet him on the Wednesday back in the Arkle Bar, but sadly he didn't show, and we hoped he'd headed off for the footie. We saw and heard one young man coughing and sneezing outside the bar and his spittle went much more than two metres, so we did start to fear the worst about the virus being on the march.

A Tuesday night curry at Prithvi, then a pub crawl taking in the Queens and a few other venues followed, so we survived day one relatively intact. Over the meal, OTCO came up in conversation and we discovered that one of the co-owners was celebrated Hollywood movie producer George Waud. The 2006 movie *Snakes on a Plane* among others had his name on the credits. As well as films, George was into his horses, and talking of his involvement in syndicates to the *Racing Post*, he said: 'Horseracing can be an expensive hobby to have – racehorses tend to have more shoes than my wife.' We recounted his classic line on our journey back to the hotel.

Though sadly back at the Manor By The Lake, Lee wasn't booked in this year as he may well have been Stateside preparing for another crack at the Masters at Augusta; another event that was about to be canned and put back to November and just when Westy was in such golden form. The chance of earwigging a Super Heinz was now history, but for a change it looked like Lee hadn't actually backed all the winners on the first couple of days.

We bumped into Albatross administrator Tom Cates as we touched down at the track, exchanging pleasantries, and all shared knowledge. Albatross chairman Ross missed his first festival since student days, directly as a result of the havoc the pandemic was wreaking on the travel industry. We had seen Ross at another fantastic Racing Breaks Cheltenham preview evening he was hosting at the M steak restaurant on Threadneedle Street. He was fearful even then that the pandemic would cause pandemonium. Unfortunately, he wasn't wrong.

Our second day at the track yielded a couple of winners. We went back to the Arkle Bar, but no sign of Richard from the day before, though we did get the beers in for Paddy Power's Paul Binfield and William Hill's Rupert Adams, who kept dashing off to do bits of work between beverages. But the best part of the day was to happen after the last race when we met Shinners and Tree, a couple of Welsh Albatross members who loved their racing and their golf.

After champagne at the track, we headed off to a bar in town called The Retreat, but there was no surrender as we supped our body weights in ale. An interesting character in there had a minder with him, who was handing out wet wipes to all and sundry. It was a good thought, but probably didn't halt the spread of the virus through the thick, boozy atmosphere inside.

Shinners noted that The Squirrel, although appearing shambolic at first glance, did have some hidden talents, and could be ideal to play the part of the next Doctor Who. Tree regaled us with tales of Charlotte Church being a regular at his local pub in Cardiff.

On a meandering route back to our hotel, we took in the Beehive and even more beer. As ever it seemed like a good idea at the time. We were heading North the next day, so no joy of being owners at this year's festival and the shadow of Covid-19 was all around.

When we got back, we caught the later races on TV at Spider's, and decided to meet again the next day for Gold Cup action in The Three Tunnes. We reserved a table in the gastro pub and enjoyed a fine lunch watching all the races. Albatross member Roy Matterson had been in a box where Barry Geraghty gave a talk every day on his mounts and his ideas on the day's racing. Always good to have the leading jockey at the festival giving you an insight, and there was BOOM after BOOM for the King of South Africa, as Roy is affectionately known due to his SA connections.

Spider had no info but thought Indefatigable at 40-1 in the last race was the bet of the meeting. We had seen this Paul Webber horse win at Uttoxeter on the day we sponsored the Scoop6 SuperClub.com Handicap Chase, and it had gone in the notebook then. Most of us failed to back it, but it was the get-out-of-jail stakes and it did win, although the starting price was only 25-1. If he had heard anything solid from the stable or connections, he would have passed it on. But it was purely a form pick, so he decided against putting it up, though with the benefit of hindsight it might have been worth mentioning.

The Tunnes was busy on Gold Cup Day, but little did any of us know that inside a week or so, all pubs, bars and restaurants in the UK would be asked to close, as the nation headed into Lockdown. Dug the Tyre had been in Tenerife for the festival and had backed Indefatigable, so was in a good mood. Upon his return, Dug discovered that four people he knew had attended the festival in the Best Mate enclosure on different days, but all of them had been struck down with Covid-19. It also turned out that Millwall fan Roy was absolutely battered by the virus, along with fellow Albatrossers Chief, Jack Stephenson, Justin Rodley, Shinners and Richard.

Shinners was involved with a lab that offered highly accurate antibody tests, and Richard snapped his arm off at £60 for one. A couple of weeks after Cheltenham, he had felt run down. No cough, no temperature, but his legs felt heavy, and he was massively tired. His wife, Ruth, worked on the Covid wards at Manchester's Wythenshawe Hospital, so Shinners suggested she also take the test. Remarkably, Ruth tested negative while Richard tested positive. Like most Squirrel Syndicate members, Richard has always worked on getting lucky, but getting the golden ticket on a global pandemic might be one of his most remarkable wins. He'd managed to overcome the virus, only suffering mild symptoms, and now had an immune system ready to fight off any further attack with an army of immunoglobulins.

Nowadays, The Squirrel Syndicate is playing National Lottery Must Be Won Lotto Draws and multiples with Saturday Series bets on the horses. The first 21 MBW Lotto syndicates saw £151,000 staked and £111,000 in returns, so a loss so far of £40,000. The inspiration for the scheme was the *Huffington Post* story 'Jerry and Marge Go Large' about a couple from Michigan, who landed $26 million over ten years of playing Must Be Won draws in the USA and it's all about the maths. As with all Squirrel Syndicate schemes, the MBW Lotto plan is long term, and the aim is profit. As it stands, the jury is still out; but we all feel a decent win is round the corner. Watch this space... as another book might just be on the cards if we land a £20 million pot.